Buzz for *Knock 'em Dead Resumes*

"Two recruitment firms both gave me compliments on my resume. At Volt the recruiter said, 'This is the best resume regarding format that I have seen in a long time.' At Robert Half they stated the same thing, that the format was easy to read and very professional. Your Knock 'em Dead Interactive Job Search Guide, and *Knock 'em Dead Resumes & Templates* have been lifesavers for me!"

—P.K., Operations Administration, San Diego

"I was sending out hordes of resumes and hardly getting a nibble—and I have top-notch skills and experience in my field. I wasn't prepared for this tough job market. When I read your book, however, I immediately began applying some of your techniques. My few nibbles increased to so many job interviews I could hardly keep up with them!"

—C.S., Chicago, Illinois

"This book is as good as it gets. Put the time into following step by step and you will have a dramatically different view of your own skills. Plus, you'll end up with a fantastic resume."

—J.A., Boise, Idaho

"After I sent my new resume and cover letter, I got four interviews in one week and refused two interviews. I want to say thank you: Thank you for doing this for millions of professionals who work hard, and thank you for changing our lives—job seeking is life, it is for everyone who takes their life seriously."

—N.P., Chicago, Illinois

"First of all, thank you soooo much! It was YOU who helped me move from under-evaluating myself to accurately presenting who I truly am on my resume [and, thus, at interviews]. As a result, this brought my salary up by a giant leap."

—E.A. (no address given)

"I bought all three of your books: *Knock 'em Dead Resumes*, *Knock 'em Dead Cover Letters*, and *Knock 'em Dead: The Ultimate Job Search Guide*. I read each book cover to cover. I went for the interview yesterday with a mental health center. They said they would call me by the end of the week. Soon as I got home I wrote a follow-up letter; I mailed it express to get there noon next day. I got the call from the hiring manager within the hour letting me know that I have the job. I think he called me as soon as he put the letter down."

—K.G. (no address given)

"This book was wonderful! I've been in a management role for multiple years and the ideas in this book helped me determine what I should be looking for. The information in the book was spot on and spoke to the reader in volumes in just a few short pages."

—K.W., St. Louis, Missouri

"For job hunters of all ages this book is valuable. It provides a comprehensive guide to thinking about your experience, defining your personal brand, and translating it into a resume that will get attention. The text and 100 sample resumes are up-to-date and should help the majority of searchers find a style and sample text in their field."

—T.K., Carmel, Indiana

Buzz for *Knock 'em Dead Resumes*

"After reading your book, *Knock 'em Dead Resumes*, I rewrote my resume and mailed it to about eight companies. The results were beyond belief. I was employed by one of the companies that got my new resume and received offers of employment or requests for interviews from every company. The entire job search took only five weeks."

—J.V., Dayton, Ohio

"You resonated through your understanding of the realities of our current job climate and practical approaches, especially the resume Target Job Deconstruction Process. Awesome."

—M.M., Chicago, Illinois

"I re-jigged my resume exactly as you outlined in your book and one employer said, 'You can tell this person has a real love of PR from his resume.' Within three weeks I had three job offers and was able to pick and choose the perfect job for myself."

—M.W., Detroit, Michigan

"I am very grateful for your *Knock 'em Dead* series. I have read the trio and adopted the methods. In the end, I got a dream job with a salary that is almost double of my previous! By adopting your methods, I got four job offers."

—C.Y., Singapore

"Your book is simply fantastic. This one book improved my yearly income by several thousand dollars, and my future income by untold amounts. Your work has made my family and myself very happy."

—M.Z., St. Clair Shores, Michigan

"I cannot tell you what a fabulous response I have been getting due to the techniques you describe in your books. Besides giving me the tools I needed to 'get my foot in the door,' they gave me confidence. I never thought I could secure an excellent position within a month!"

—B.G., Mountain View, California

"I read and used *Knock 'em Dead Resumes* as I searched for a job. I was called for an interview and was up against ten applicants. To make a long story short, I interviewed on Monday morning and by Monday afternoon knew I had the job."

—E.H. (no address given)

"I have averaged at least an interview per day for the last couple weeks, after two months of very sporadic interview activity. Some of this might be plain good luck, but I think revising my resume and cover letters several weeks ago had a positive effect."

—L.E. (no address given)

KnOCK DEaD 'em

RESUMES

12TH EDITION

A killer resume gets MORE job interviews!

MARTIN YATE, CPC

New York Times bestseller

Avon, Massachusetts

Published by
Adams Media, a division of F+W Media, Inc.
57 Littlefield Street, Avon, MA 02322. U.S.A.
www.adamsmedia.com

ISBN 10: 1-4405-9619-0
ISBN 13: 978-1-4405-9619-3
eISBN 10: 1-5072-0157-5
eISBN 13: 978-1-5072-0157-2

Printed in the United States of America.

10 9 8 7 6 5 4 3 2 1

Cover design by Heather McKiel.

This book is available at quantity discounts for bulk purchases.
For information, please call 1-800-289-0963.

CONTENTS

Your resume is the most financially important document you will ever own. When it works, you work, and when it doesn't work, you don't.

How to create a template for the story your resume needs to tell in order to be successful.

Fifty percent of the success of any project depends on the preparation. Taking the time to gather the right information for your resume makes the difference between interviews and no interviews.

In any job search you are selling a product: You are a bundle of skills and capabilities suited to a particular set of challenges. Like any product you will do better when you give a distinct identity to what you are taking to market.

A resume's format can help emphasize or de-emphasize aspects of your professional background.

The most effective way to get a premium, powerful resume for a professional job in the shortest time with the least hassle.

CHAPTER 7 How to Give Your Resume Punch . . . 123

First impressions are important. Editing polishes your content and helps it deliver a greater punch.

CHAPTER 8 Resume Customization, Alternative Resumes, and Formats Needed for an Effective Job Search . . . 133

With the job search the way it is today, you may need to repackage your background into three or more different delivery vehicles.

CHAPTER 9 Ready to Launch . . . 159

Everyone hates reading resumes, so here are some powerful strategies to make your resume data dense and visually accessible to distracted readers.

CHAPTER 10 The Resumes . . . 165

One hundred-plus killer resumes that got real jobs for real people.

ACKNOWLEDGMENTS

Knock 'em Dead books have been in print here in America and in many languages around the world for twenty-five-plus years, and owe their success to constant updating and the millions of satisfied professionals whose careers are helped by them. This is only possible because *Knock 'em Dead* books work; they help you change the trajectory of your professional life.

There is a very small group who helps me write such books, and constantly update classics like *Knock 'em Dead Resumes*: Peter Archer, my managing editor of so many years he is now a grandfather; my editor Will Yate, who's consistent, conscientious, and persnickety in the best of ways; and Angela Yate, who takes care of our business and allows me the time to do good work; she also acts as the first sounding board on the many issues that can make the difference between a good book and a perennial classic.

INTRODUCTION

The Facts of Life

On the list of things you want to do in life, fixing your resume is right up there with hitting yourself in the head with a hammer. Yet owning a killer resume is the foundation of every successful job search; show me a stalled job search and I'll show you a flawed resume. What you learn in these pages will give you the best resume you have ever owned, and if you pay close attention, you will learn how to change the trajectory of your career.

Your resume is the most financially important document you will ever own: When your resume works, you work; when it doesn't, you don't. It's the primary branding tool to introduce yourself to your professional world, and properly fashioned, it ensures that prospective employers and future colleagues see you as you want to be seen. Slack off on your resume and you can say goodbye to that new job and career success.

No one likes writing a resume, but it's an essential part of defining a commodity that your professional world is eager to embrace. When it comes to a job search, you are a commodity, and your resume is the styling and packaging that sells the product. This is critical in a world where your resume all too often disappears into resume databases with millions of others. When recruiters do find it, your resume will get a scan lasting five to forty-five seconds, and if a clearly defined and relevant brand doesn't jump out, they'll move on to the next one.

Knock 'em Dead Resumes will give you control over these issues, delivering a resume that will consistently get pulled from the resume databases and will resonate with recruiters on that first scan and also on deeper, more careful readings.

Remember: Managers hate to interview; they just want to find and hire someone who *gets* the job, so they can get back to work. *Knock 'em Dead Resumes* shows you how to convince hiring managers that you are a competent professional who *gets* the job. It will prepare you to talk about the job's big issues and answer the tough questions in ways you never thought possible . . . and it's all based on a commonsense approach you'll be able to grasp and apply to your future.

CHAPTER 1

YOUR RESUME—THE MOST FINANCIALLY IMPORTANT DOCUMENT YOU'LL EVER OWN

> *Read this book with a highlighter—*
> *it will save time as you refer back to important passages.*

YOUR RESUME IS the most financially significant document you will ever own. When it works, the doors of opportunity open for you. When it doesn't work, they won't.

No one enjoys writing a resume, but it has such a major impact on the money you earn during your work life, and consequently on the quality of your life outside of work, that you know it needs to be done right.

You didn't come to this book for a good read. You came because you are facing serious challenges in your professional life. The way the professional world works has changed dramatically in the past few years, and nothing has changed as much as corporate recruitment. When hiring practices have changed beyond recognition, your approach to getting hired needs to be re-evaluated from top to bottom.

In these pages, you are going to learn very quickly how to build a resume that works. But you're going to learn something more. Since my approach to resumes is part of a larger strategy for achieving long-term career and personal success, everything I teach you about developing a kick-ass resume will apply to the broader challenges of the job search, interviewing, and career management.

In other words, not only will you leave this book with a killer resume, you'll leave it with critical job search and interview strategies, and even some amazing insights into winning raises and promotions.

Self-Awareness: The Key to Professional Survival and Success

Understanding what employers want and need from a specific job title, and how they express and prioritize those needs, will tell you what it takes to win and succeed in that job. It will also give you some hints about the story your resume needs to tell in order to get your foot in the door.

Employers Just Want to Make a Buck

Employees only get added to the payroll to help make a buck, to enhance profitability in some way. Think about this: If you owned a company, there just isn't any other reason you would add workers to your payroll. So it is implicit in any employment contract that *your job contributes to profitability in some way.*

Depending on your job, you can help an employer make a buck by:

- Making money for the company
- Saving money for the company
- Saving time/increasing productivity

No matter what your job, no matter how impressive your title, at its very core, your position exists to help an employer maintain and increase profitability by:

- The *identification* of problems within your area of responsibility
- The *prevention* of problems within your area of responsibility
- The *solution* to problems within your area of responsibility

No resume gets read, no one gets interviewed, and no one gets hired unless someone somewhere is trying to solve a problem. That problem may be finding a quicker way to manufacture silicon chips, speed up the accounts receivable process, leverage social networking for brand management, or any one of a million other profit challenges.

The only reason your job exists is because your employer needed someone to identify, prevent, and solve the problems that regularly occur in this area of professional expertise; it exists because not having someone like you is costing the company money.

Problem solving—the application of *critical thinking* to the challenges within your area of expertise—is what you are paid to do. It is why every job opening exists, and why every job gets filled with the person who seems to have the firmest grip on how to identify, prevent, and solve the problems that make up the everyday activities of that job.

Why No One Wants to Read Your Resume

You may think that resume writing is a tough job, but only if you've never had to *read* them. Go to the resume samples section at the end of the book and try to read and understand six resumes in a row. Your brain will first go numb, then start to melt, and by the sixth you'll understand why no one is really that anxious to read your resume.

No one reads resumes unless they have to, so when your resume does get read, it means that a job exists: a job that has been carefully defined, budgeted, and titled, with a salary range that has been authorized and for which funds have been released. *Whenever a recruiter searches a resume database or reads a resume, she is doing it with a specific job and the language and priorities of that job description in mind.*

Why a Hiring Manager May Never Get the Chance to Read Your Resume

The ongoing impact of technology on our world of work causes the nature of all jobs to change almost as rapidly as the pages on a calendar. Resumes today rarely go straight to a recruiter's or manager's desk (though I'll show you how to make this happen); more often they go to a resume database.

This means that before anyone actually looks at your resume, it must first have been pulled from that database *by a recruiter with a specific job and the language and priorities of that job description in mind*. Keep in mind that some of those databases contain more than 35 million resumes.

With this in mind, you can see that if your resume's just a jumble of everything you've ever done, or of everything that *you* happen to think is important (without reference to what your customers are actually buying), it is never going to work.

Understand Your Customer

"The customer is always right," "the customer comes first," and "understand your customer" are phrases that underlie all successful business stories. In the same way that corporations tailor products to be appealing to *their* customers, you need to create a resume tailored to *your* customers' needs.

Your resume works when it matches your skills and experiences to the responsibilities and deliverables of a specific target job. This requires that your resume focus on how employers—your customers—think about, prioritize, and describe the job's deliverables: those things you are expected to deliver as you execute your assigned responsibilities.

A resume focused on a specific target job and built from the ground up with the customers' needs in mind will perform better in the recruiters' resume database searches, and it will resonate far more with human eyes already glazed from the tedium of resume reading.

This Is Not Your Last Job Change

In a world without job security, when job and even career changes are happening ever more frequently, being able to write a productive resume is one of life's critical survival skills.

This is probably not your first, and almost certainly won't be your last, job change. You are somewhere in the middle of a half-century work life, a span during which you are likely to have three or more distinct careers and are statistically likely to change jobs about every four years; where economic recessions come around every seven to ten years and age discrimination can begin to kick in around age fifty.

Enlightened Self-Interest

When I started to talk about these issues of personal survival twenty-five years ago, I was called a communist and asked how I could suggest that Americans be disloyal to their employers. History has shown that it is the corporations that broke the employment contract, yet today we still hear of companies demanding unblinking loyalty from their employees. If you accept this double standard, your life and the lives of your loved ones will suffer.

Wake up! Times have changed. You need a tougher, more pragmatic approach to your professional life. You still need to do your best for your employer and your team, but you also need put yourself first, because you need to survive and, hopefully, prosper in life. To do that, you need to find a more sophisticated approach to managing your professional life and guiding your destiny.

Start to think of yourself as a corporation: Me, Inc., a financial entity that must always plan and act to ensure its economic survival. Like any corporation, Me, Inc. constantly has new products and services in development. These are the ever-evolving skill bundles that define the *professional you*. Again, just like any corporation, these products and services are branded and sold to your targeted customer base: employers who hire people like you.

The success of Me, Inc. depends on how well you run your company, and like every successful company, you'll need initiatives for Research and Development, Strategic Planning, Marketing, Public Relations, and Sales:

- *Research and Development:* Every company is continually involved in the identification and development of products and services that will appeal to their customers. You must have similar ongoing initiatives. This translates into skill building in response to market trends, which you do by connecting to your profession and by monitoring the changing market demands for your job on an ongoing basis.
- *Strategic Planning:* The development of career management strategies. You'll begin to think of your career over the long term, of where you want to be and how you are going to get there. How you will stay on top of skill development, and how you will develop and maintain a desirable *professional brand*.
- *Marketing and PR:* The effective branding of Me, Inc. as a desirable product requires establishing credibility for the services you deliver and positioning these services so that the *professional you* becomes visible to an ever-widening circle. You want to make yourself known within a company, to encourage professional growth, and within your profession, to encourage your employability elsewhere.
- *Sales:* Me, Inc. needs a state-of-the-art sales program to market your products and services.

Your new resume is the primary sales tool for Me, Inc., the company you embody. It is the most financially important document you will ever own, and you can learn how to do it right, starting right now.

CHAPTER 2

Your Customer Knows What He Wants— How to Get Inside His Head

"THE CUSTOMER IS always right" is probably the first business lesson we ever learn. The customer has the money to buy the product you want to sell and that customer knows exactly what he wants; when you accurately tailor your product to your customer's needs, you'll experience a much shorter and more successful sales cycle. This chapter is about how to effectively customize your resume to your customers' needs.

Your resume is the primary marketing device for every job and career change (probably between twelve and twenty changes) throughout your career. In addition, it plays a role in subsequent internal promotions. In short, it is absolutely vital in determining your professional success. Yet when it comes to creating a resume, the most financially valuable document any of us will ever own, no one ever seems to think about what the customer wants to buy! Instead, we just want to get it done as quickly as possible and with as little thought and effort as possible.

Your current resume is probably a simple recitation of all you have done: It lists everything that you *think* is important. I bet this resume just isn't working. That's because a simple recitation of all your accomplishments and activities results in a hodgepodge of what you think is important, *not what your customers **know** is important*. When you build a resume that tries to be all things to all people, you are creating the equivalent of a Swiss Army knife. Have you ever looked at a Swiss Army knife? It's got knife blades, bottle openers, screwdrivers . . . it does practically everything. But companies aren't hiring human Swiss Army knives; they are hiring human lasers, with exceptional skills focused in a specific area. *You need a resume that speaks to the priorities of your customers,* because they won't make the time to struggle through an unfocused resume to see if you might have what they want. Why should they, when enough people have taken the time to learn what's needed?

Settle on a Target Job Title

With just a few years' experience in the professional world, most people reach a point where they have experience that qualifies them for more than one job; still, this is not an argument for having a general resume as your primary marketing document. Right now, there are probably two or more jobs you can do, but with the way recruitment works today, you have no choice but to go with a resume that focuses on a single target job. So your first task is to look at all the jobs you can do (they are all probably closely related in some way) and choose which one will represent the prime thrust of your job search.

After your primary resume is completed, it is fairly easy to create a resume for any additional job you want to pursue. I'll explain exactly how you do this later in the book, but to set your mind at ease, that second job-targeted resume will have a number of things in common with the job you described in your primary resume. This means that you'll already have a template to start with, plus the dates, layout, chronology, contact information, and possibly even the list of employers you're going to contact. I'll show you a methodology that helps you quickly refashion and edit your primary resume into a resume for that second or third target job.

But you don't get any of those good things until you build a primary resume, so before going further, you need to think through your options and decide on the job title that your *primary resume* will target.

You can make this decision on many unique criteria, but assuming your main goal is to get back to work, or out of the hellhole you work in today, your best bet is to go with the job you can nail. This is the job that you can make the most convincing case for on paper, the strongest argument for in person, and the job where, when you hit the ground running, you won't trip over your shoelaces. Once you've decided, you build a primary resume around this target job.

To Really Understand Your Target Job, Deconstruct It

The most productive resumes start with a clear focus on the target job and its responsibilities, from the point of view of the recruitment process and the selection committee. In other words, the customer comes first, so let's get inside the customer's head.

There's a practical and easy way to get inside the employer's head. It's called a Target Job Deconstruction (TJD). It's a way to get a tight focus on what your customers are buying and what will sell before you even start writing your resume. Take half a day to do a TJD and your investment will yield:

- A template for the story your resume *must* tell to be successful
- An objective standard against which you can measure your resume's likely performance
- A complete understanding of where the focus will be during interviews
- A very good idea of the interview questions that will be heading your way and why
- Relevant examples with which to illustrate your answers
- A behavioral profile for getting hired and promoted, and therefore . . . greater professional success throughout your career
- A behavioral profile for *not* getting hired and for ongoing professional failure

Target Job Deconstruction: The Way Into Your Customer's Head

Step #1: Collect Postings

Collect 6–10 job postings of *a single job* you can do and would enjoy. Save the postings in a folder and also print them out. If you are interested in more than one job, you must prioritize them. The most productive resumes focus on a single job. I'll show you a very fast and effective editing technique a little later in the chapter to develop a custom resume for each job (and also a place to use that Swiss Army knife resume that currently isn't working).

Not sure where to start? Try these job aggregators (or spiders, robots, or bots) that run around thousands of job sites looking for jobs with your chosen keywords:

www.indeed.com
www.simplyhired.com
www.jobbankusa.com
www.sourcetool.com
www.jobster.com

Step #2: Create a Document

Create a new document and title it "TJD for (your chosen target job title)."

Step #3: Identify Target Job Titles

Start by inserting in your document the subhead: "Target job titles." Then copy and paste in all the variations from your collection of job descriptions. Looking at the result you can say, "When employers are hiring people like this, they tend to describe the job title with these words." From this, you can come up with a suitably generic target job title for your resume, which you will type after your name and contact information. This will help your resume's database performance and also act as a headline, giving the reader's eyes an immediate focus.

Step #4: Identify Skills and Responsibilities

Add a second subhead titled "Skills/Responsibilities/Requirements/Deliverables/etc." Look through the job postings—it might be easier to spread the printouts across your desk. You are looking for a requirement that is common to all of your job postings. Take the most complete description and copy and paste it (with a 6 beside it, signifying it is common to all six of your samples) into your document. Underneath this, add additional words and phrases from the other job postings used to describe this same requirement. Repeat this exercise for any other requirements common to all six of your job postings.

The greater the number of keywords in your resume that are directly relevant to your target job, the higher the ranking your resume will achieve in recruiters' database searches. *And the higher your ranking, the greater the likelihood that your resume will be rescued from the avalanche and passed along to human eyes for further screening.* This database search has led directly to the denser resumes that are more common today and the increasing prevalence of Core Competency sections that capture all relevant keywords in one place. (More about Core Competency sections later.)

Repeat the exercise for requirements common to five of the jobs, then four, and so on, all the way down to those requirements mentioned in only one job posting.

Step #5: Identify Problems to Solve

At their most elemental level, all jobs are the same—all jobs focus on problem identification, prevention, and solution in that particular area of expertise; this is what we all get paid for, no matter what we do for a living.

Go back to your TJD and start with the first requirement. Think about the problems you will typically need to identify, solve, and/or prevent in the course of a normal workday as you deliver on this requirement of the job. List specific examples, big and small, of your successful identification, prevention, and/or solution to the problems. Quantify your results when possible.

Repeat this with each of the TJD's other requirements by identifying the problems inherent in that particular responsibility. Some examples may appear in your resume as significant professional achievements, while others will provide you with the ammunition to answer all those interview questions. Interviewers are concerned with your practical problem identification and solution abilities, and they want to see them in action. That's why some questions at job interviews begin, "Tell me about a time when . . ." So at the same time that you're working on your resume, you're also beginning to collect the illustrations you will use in response to those interview questions.

Step #6: Identify the Behavioral Profile of Success

Think of the *best* person you have ever known doing this job and what made her stand out. Describe her performance, professional behavior, interaction with others, and appearance: "That would be Carole Jenkins, superior communication skills, a fine analytical mind, great professional appearance, and a nice person to work with." Do this for each and every requirement listed on your TJD, and you are describing the person all employers want to hire. *This is your behavioral profile for professional success.* Apply what you learn from this exercise to your professional life. It will increase your job security by opening doors to the inner circles that exist in every department and company, and by leading to the plum assignments, raises, and promotions that over time add up to professional success.

Step #7: Identify the Behavioral Profile of Failure

Now think of the *worst* person you have ever known doing this job and what made that person stand out in such a negative way. Describe his performance, professional behaviors, interaction with others, and appearance: "That would be Jack Hartzenberger, morose, critical, passive-aggressive, always looked like he slept in his suit, and smelled like it too." You are describing the person that all employers want to avoid and, incidentally, a behavioral profile for professional suicide.

Now You Know Your Customers' Needs

Once you complete and review your TJD, you will have a clear idea of exactly the way employers think about, prioritize, and express their needs when they hire someone for the job you want.

Now you know the story your resume needs to tell to be maximally productive in the resume databases, in order to get it retrieved for human review. You now have the proper focus for a killer resume.

When doing the TJD, you'll come across some skills that you possess or even excel at: "Wow, all six of these job postings require competency in Microsoft Excel, and I'm the office Excel guru!" But there will be other skills that you don't have, or that need polishing: "Wow, everyone's looking for six sigma and lean management skills and I don't even know what those words mean." As a rule of thumb (the separate issues of changing careers aside), you need about 70 percent of a job's requirements to pursue that job with reasonable hope of landing interviews, especially in a down economy, when competition is more fierce. If you complete the TJD process and realize you don't make the grade, you have probably saved yourself a good deal of frustration pursuing a job you had no real chance of landing. What you need to do in this instance is pull your title goals back one level. Use this TJD and the missing skills it identifies as a professional development tool: To warrant that next promotion, you'll need to develop these abilities.

Here is an example of what the first page of a TJD might look like. I've taken this from the work of a resume client and it is used with permission:

TJD (TARGET JOB DECONSTRUCTION) FOR SOLUTIONS CONSULTANT

Different job titles for the same Target Job:

- Pre-Sales Consultant
- Pre-Sales Specialist
- Sales Engineer
- Solution Consultant
- Solutions Consultant
- Solutions Engineer

Skills/Responsibilities/Requirement/Deliverables/Etc. common to 6 Job Descriptions

- No responsibilities common to six

Common to 5 Job Descriptions

- **Prepare and deliver value-based sales presentations and software demonstrations to prospective customer audiences.**
- Configure and deliver software demonstrations.
- Conducts and participates in sales calls and demonstrates the value of solution and product.
- Prepare and conduct demos along with Sales team.
- Deliver simple, appealing, and compelling product demonstrations.
- Demonstrate solutions that address customer requirements and provide business value.
- Participate in demo design and planning.

Common to 4 Job Descriptions

- **Discover customer needs and requirements.**
- Determine customer problem areas.
- Understand customer's unique needs.
- Assess customer requirements.
- Identify business drivers and solution requirements.
- Discovery conversations.
- Discover customer needs and requirements, determine customer problem area, and articulate recommended solution/product.
- Assess customer requirements and translate them into a vision with a specific outcome that the customer can understand.
- Translate a customer's needs into a solution-oriented vision.
- **Collaborates with partners to plan and execute biz dev strategies.**
- Provide partner training to build sales expertise of partners.
- Communicates product advantages and value to partners.
- Works closely with the sales team and partners.
- Technical evangelist to community of partners and customers.
- **Work closely with sales teams.**
- Act as a technical resource & liaison between sales force and customer.
- Collaborates with sales team to document sales and solution strategies.
- Works closely with the sales team and partners.
- Member of the account team.
- Assist sales team in qualifying, developing, and managing sales opportunities.
- Collaborate with others on the sales team.

The TJD continues for another page and a half but this is enough to give you the idea.

Here is a simple before-and-after example that will illustrate how powerful this process can be. The resume is for a young graduate with a computer science degree looking for her first position in the professional world. When we first spoke, she had been out of school for nearly three months and had had a couple of telephone interviews and one face-to-face interview. Her search was complicated by the fact that she is a foreign national and needed to find a company that would sponsor her. This is not easy at the best of times, but in today's tough job environment, it is a significant additional challenge. The first resume is the one she was using; the second she created after completing the Target Job Deconstruction process.

JYATITI MOKUBE

10611 ABERCORN STREET, APT 85
SAVANNAH, GA 31419
SOFTWAREGAL@GMAIL.COM
(401) 241-3703

Education

- Armstrong Atlantic State University, Savannah, GA
- MSc. Computer Science (3.5 GPA), December 2007
- University of Technology, Kingston, Jamaica
- BSc. Computing & Information Technology, November 2005
- Graduated Magna Cum Laude (3.7 GPA)

Key Skills

- Programming
- Programming Languages: C, C++, Java, VB.Net
- Database Programming: SQL
- Website Design
- Design Languages/Tools: HTML, CSS, JavaScript, Dreamweaver.
- Problem Solving and Leadership
- Honed an analytical, logical, and determined approach to problem solving and applied this as group leader for my final year (undergraduate) research project.
- Team Player
- Demonstrated the ability to work effectively within a team while developing a Point-of-Sale system over the course of three semesters.
- Communication
- Demonstrated excellent written and oral communication skills through reports and presentations while pursuing my degrees, and as Public Relations Officer for the University of Technology's Association of Student Computer Engineers (UTASCE).

Work Experience

January 2006–December 2007
- Armstrong Atlantic State University, Savannah, GA
- Graduate Research Assistant, School of Computing
- Developed a haptic application to demonstrate human-computer interaction using Python and H3D API.
- Developed an application to organize text documents using the Self-Organizing Map algorithm and MATLAB.

July–November 2005
- Cable & Wireless Jamaica Ltd, Kingston, Jamaica
- Internet Helpdesk Analyst
- Assisted customers with installing and troubleshooting modems and Internet service-related issues via telephone.

July–August 2003
- National Commercial Bank Ja. Ltd, Kingston, Jamaica
- Change Management Team Member
- Generated process diagrams and documentation for systems under development using MS Visio, MS Word, and MS Excel.

Awards/Honors

- President's Pin for graduating with a GPA above 3.75 — November 2005
- Latchman Foundation Award for Academic Excellence & Outstanding Character — March 2005
- Nominated School of Computing student of the year — March 2005
- Recognized by Jamaica Gleaner as top student in School of Computing & IT — February 2005
- Nominated for Derrick Dunn (community service) Award — March 2004
- Honor roll/Dean's List — 2002–2005

Languages

- French (fluent), Italian (basic)

Extracurricular Activities

- Singing, acting, chess, reading
- Member of Association for Computing Machinery, AASU student chapter

References

- Available upon request.

JYATITI MOKUBE

10611 Abercorn Street, Apt 85
Savannah, GA 31419
softwaregal@gmail.com, (401) 241-3703

Talented, analytical, and dedicated Software Engineer with strong academic background in object-oriented analysis and design, comfort with a variety of technologies, and interest in learning new ones.

SUMMARY OF QUALIFICATIONS

- Excellent academic record. Achieved 3.55 GPA (Master's) and 3.77 GPA (Bachelor's, Dean's List for all eight semesters).
- Familiarity with the software development lifecycle, from identifying requirements to design, implementation, integration, and testing.
- Familiarity with agile software development processes.
- Strong technical skills in Java development and Object-Oriented Analysis and Design (OOA/D).
- Strong understanding of multiple programming languages, including C, C++, JavaScript, Visual Basic, and HTML.
- Familiar with CVS version control software.
- Excellent communications skills with an aptitude for building strong working relationships with teammates.
- Proven background leading teams in stressful, deadline-oriented environments.

TECHNICAL SKILLS

Languages:	Java, JavaScript, C, C++, Visual Basic, HTML, SQL, VB.Net, ASP.Net, CSS
Software:	Eclipse, NetBeans, JBuilder, Microsoft Visual Studio, Microsoft Office Suite (Word, PowerPoint, Excel, Access), MATLAB
Databases:	MySQL, Oracle
Operating Systems:	Windows (NT/2000/XP Professional)
Servers:	Apache Server

EDUCATION

MS in Computer Science, Armstrong Atlantic State University, Savannah GA, December 2007
- Completed a thesis in the area of Computer Security (Digital Forensics: Forensic Analysis of an iPod Shuffle)

BS in Computing & IT, University of Technology, Kingston, Jamaica, November 2005

LANGUAGES

Fluent in English, French, and Italian

PROFESSIONAL EXPERIENCE

Armstrong Atlantic State University, Savannah, GA   01/2006–12/2007

Graduate Research Assistant, School of Computing
- Developed a haptic application to demonstrate human-computer interaction using Python and H3D API.
- Developed an application to organize text documents using the Self-Organizing Map algorithm and MATLAB.

Cable & Wireless Jamaica Ltd, Kingston, Jamaica   07/2005–11/2005

Internet Helpdesk Analyst
- Assisted customers with installing and troubleshooting modems and Internet service-related issues via telephone.

National Commercial Bank Ja. Ltd, Kingston, Jamaica   07/2003–08/2003

Change Management Team Member
- Generated process diagrams and documentation for systems under development using MS Visio, MS Word, and MS Excel.

AWARDS/HONORS

- President's Pin for graduating with a GPA above 3.75   11/2005
- Latchman Foundation Award for Academic Excellence & Outstanding Character 03/2005
- Nominated School of Computing student of the year   03/2005
- Recognized by Jamaica Gleaner as top student in School of Computing & IT   02/2005
- Nominated for Derrick Dunn (community service) Award   03/2004

PROFESSIONAL AFFILIATIONS

Association for Computing Machinery (ACM)

REFERENCES

Available upon request.

Without the research that defines exactly what your customers want to buy, you cannot hope to develop an effective resume that will be discoverable in recruiters' database searches, and your lack of insight into what the customer wants and what you can offer in response will also hinder your interview performance. I have taken professionals from entry level through C-suite executives in *Fortune* 25 companies through this process. They all say a couple of things: It was a pain but it was also a logical, sensible, and valuable exercise that pays back your time and effort in many ways and situations, as you will see.

Now, what was the result of this resume revamping? She started using the new resume and almost immediately got an invitation to interview. She subsequently relocated out of state and started work for that company on April 14; she has been promoted and is still with the company today.

The target-job-focused resume opened doors, positioned her professionally, told her what the employer would want to talk about, and was a powerful spokesperson after she left the interview. The end result was a great start to a new career. It all came about because she took the time to understand how her customer—the employer—was thinking about and expressing the job she wanted to do!

Here is another example, starting with an original resume. Then, the person conducted a Target Job Deconstruction, and you'll see her third resume draft followed by her final, eighth version of the resume. The final version generated eight interviews and a couple of weeks later I got an email that said in part, "*Two offers, twice what I was expecting, and that is without the signing bonus or the stock options. Amazing!!*" This is a senior PR professional with a substantial track record, coming back to the workplace after four years largely spent raising children and doing a little PR work when time allowed. The resume process took about three weeks parallel with organizing a job search plan of attack.

Look at each of these three versions of an evolving resume to see how a really stellar resume comes together. The first resume is a best effort without having done a Target Job Deconstruction. The second document is the third version of her resume and begins to reflect the focus that the TJD made possible. Finally, you will see the eighth and final version of the resume, and you already know what that achieved after being coupled with a good job search plan of attack.

Nancy Wright

123 Main Street
Anywhere, VA 22652

(555) 555-5555
example@yahoo.com

Public Relations Experience

Nancy Wright has more than thirteen years of public relations experience, primarily focused on high-tech and start-up companies. An Olympic gold medalist in swimming, Wright also spent twelve years serving as a free-lance color commentator for sports/news outlets including NBC and ESPN.

Wright & Company Public Relations, *Founder and Principal* **2003 – present**

Provide the professional work of a large public relations agency along with the personal service available from a smaller company. Develop and execute PR campaigns that meet the specialized needs of each client. Programs and services include corporate and product positioning, ongoing PR strategy and tactics, leadership branding, media training, speaker placement, and ongoing media contact. Clients have included: *AirPlay Networks, ReligiousSite.com, PanJet Aviation.*

Three Boys Public Relations, *Co-Founder and Principal* **2001 – 2003**

Established a Silicon Valley PR firm that helped high-tech companies accomplish objectives by managing leadership positioning, strategic branding, and publicity. Clients included:
- *ABC Systems* – Project work included managing all annual Sales Conference communications for Charles Smith, Group Vice President, U.S. Service Provider group. Helped launch Smith's new fiscal year strategy, objectives, and goals to his 1,000+ employees.
- *NextLink Technologies* – Successfully positioned the start-up as an industry leader by leveraging the market's widespread use of NextLink's industry-standard GreatD networking software. Rapidly expanded the company's leadership position by garnering positive coverage in all targeted publications.

ABC Systems, *Marketing Manager* **2000 – 2001**

Directed internal marketing activities for the iProduct after ABC acquired InfoGame and its technology. Shortly after the acquisition, ABC reorganized InfoGame and later licensed the iProduct trademark to Apple.

InfoGame Technology Corporation, *Public Relations Manager* **1998 – 2000**

Designed and executed all company and product strategy. Placed hundreds of stories with news and feature media including the Today Show, Regis & Kathie Lee, ABC's Y2K special hosted by Peter Jennings, The Wall Street Journal, The New York Times and Fast Company. Within eighteen months of launching InfoGame's PR, the company was acquired by ABC Systems.

XYZ Public Relations, *Account Manager; Senior Account Executive; Account Executive* **1996 – 1998**

Designed and managed all PR strategy and activities for start-up and unknown software, Internet, and networking companies. Managed teams of up to 10 PR professionals. Promoted annually for delivering results for the following clients:
- *InfoGame Technology Corporation* – Repositioned InfoGame from fledgling company to a leader in the Internet appliance space. Introduced the new management team, the iProduct and the back-end software. Garnered positive coverage in hundreds of media outlets including The Wall Street Journal, The New York Times, and USA Today. InfoGame was acquired by ABC Systems within 18 months of PR campaign.
- *Triiliux Digital Systems* – Accelerated Triiliux and its CEO out of obscurity and into a position of undisputed leadership. Successfully positioned CEO as an industry expert with ongoing speaker placement and quotes in all of Triiliux's top publications. Placed CEO on the magazine cover of the company's topmost publication. Triiliux was acquired by Intel after the two year PR campaign.
- *LinkExchange* – Transformed unknown company into a "player" in the Internet advertising arena. Placed hundreds of stories in both business and industry media including the The Wall Street Journal, CNNfn, and AdWeek. LinkExchange was acquired by Microsoft after an eighteen month PR campaign.

- *The Internet Mall* – Launched this obscure company to the press, landing continual coverage in all top Internet and business publications including The New York Times and Internet World. Within a year of the campaign, the company was acquired by TechWave, now Network commerce.

Other Relevant Experience

Motivational Speaker/Guest Celebrity   **1989 – present**
Coach audiences at corporations, business forums, schools, and functions how to effectively set and achieve goals, using the road to the Olympics as a model. Travel the country making guest appearances at events, functions, and parades. Past or present clients include: IBM, Hardees, Speedo America, Busch Gardens, Alamo Rent-A-Car, and others.

Television Color Commentator   **1988 – 2000**
- Provided expert commentary for swimming events, including the Olympics for NBC.
- Provided half-time interviews and feature packages for the Miami Heat.
- Work included NBC, ESPN, FoxSports, SportsChannel, Turner Sports, SportSouth, and others.

The College Conference, Associate Commissioner   **1991 – 1993**
- Managed all aspects of Conference television and marketing packages.
- Increased marketing revenue by 33% in the first year.

International Swimming Hall of Fame, Assistant Director   **1989 – 1991**
- Helped drive fundraising efforts for new building.
- Served as one of three spokespeople for the Hall of Fame, delivering speeches at community events.
- Successfully managed and completed all fundraising aspects for the NCAA Wall of Fame.
- Developed community affairs programs.

Awards and Honors
- Two Olympic gold medals (1984 Los Angeles, USA), and a silver and bronze (1988 Seoul, Korea).
- Two-time NCAA Champion.
- 26-time NCAA All-American.
- Hall of Fame Inductee: International Swimming Hall of Fame, University of Florida Athletic HOF, Region Swimming HOF, Anywhere High School HOF.

Education
University of Florida, Bachelor of Science, Journalism   **1989**

Nancy Wright, Account Supervisor

123 Spring Mountain Way, Fort Hood, VA 12345 • example@yahoo.com • Tel: 540.555.1234 Cell: 540.555.2345

Performance Profile/Performance Summary

High tech public relations professional with 11 years' experience – including seven in Silicon Valley – in a variety of sectors including software, Internet, networking, and consumer electronics. Substantial experience in PR campaigns that lead to company acquisitions. Expertise in all aspects of strategic and tactical communications, from developing and managing PR campaigns, multiple accounts, and results-oriented teams, to writing materials and placing stories. Twenty years' experience as a motivational speaker and twelve as a free-lance TV color commentator. Two-time Olympic gold medalist.

Core Competencies

High Tech Public Relations • Strategic Communications • Counsel Executives • Manage Teams • Manage Budgets • Multiple Accounts • Multiple Projects • Leadership Positioning • PR Messaging • Client Satisfaction • Media Training • Media Relations • Pitch Media • Craft Stories • Place Stories • PR Tactics • Press Releases • Collateral Materials • Research • Edit • Manage Budgets • Manage Teams • Mentor • Strong Writing Skills • Detail Oriented • Organizational Skills • Motivated • Team Player • New Business

Strategic Public Relations Leadership

Position companies as both industry leaders and sound investments. The following four companies were acquired within two years of commencing the PR campaigns: InfoGear Technologies (acquired by Cisco), Trillium Digital Systems (acquired by Intel), LinkExchange (acquired by Microsoft), and The Internet Mall (acquired by TechWave, now Network Commerce).

Executive Communications Manager

Develop executive communications. Created positioning for ****, Group VP, and launched it to his 1,000+ employees at the ABC Sales Conference. Refined ****'s public speaking delivery and style.

Media Coverage

Proactively place stories. Samplings of past placements include: ABC World News Tonight, CNN, The Today Show, Associated Press, Baltimore Sun, Boston Globe, Business Week, Fast Company, Financial Times, Forbes, Fortune Magazine, Inc., MSNBC.com, New York Times, Parade, San Jose Mercury News, SJ Business Journal, SF Chronicle, USA Today, Wired, Wall Street Journal, AdWeek, CommsDesign, Computer Reseller News, Computer Retail Week, Computer Shopper, Computer World, CRN, CNET, EE Times, Embedded.com, Internet.com, InformationWeek, Internet.com, Internet Telephony Magazine, Light Reading, Network World, Phone+, PC Magazine, Red Herring, TMCnet, VoIP News, VON and ZDNet, Dataquest, Forrester Research, Frost and Sullivan, Jupiter Communications and Yankee Group.

PROFESSIONAL EXPERIENCE

Wright & Associates Public Relations, Anywhere, VA   **2006-present**

Develop and deliver strategic communications that meet the specific needs of each client. Drive all PR strategy and tactics, messaging, media training, media relations, budget management, story creation and placement. Sampling of past or present clients include AirTight Networks (also a former InfoGear, Cisco, NextHop client), JesusCentral. com (eHealthInsurance.com founder), and ProJet Aviation.

Co-Founder and Principal, **Three Boys Public Relations**, Redwood City, CA   **2001-2003**

Silicon Valley PR firm that partnered with high tech clients to meet their corporate objectives. In charge of developing and managing all strategic and tactical aspects of public relations including thought leadership, leadership branding, press materials, stories, media relations, and publicity.

- Cisco Systems – Acting Executive Communications Manager to Carlos Dominguez, VP.
- NextHop Technologies – Company's first PR counsel. Repositioned obscure company, impaired by trademark dilution, into an industry leader. (Acquired by U4EA Technologies in 2008.)

Marketing Manager, ABC Network Systems, San Jose, CA   **2000-2001**

Directed internal, cross-functional marketing activities for the iProduct® after Cisco acquired InfoGear and its technology. Shortly after the acquisition, Cisco dissolved the InfoGear/Managed Appliances Business Unit (MASBU) and later licensed the iProduct trademark to Apple.

Public Relations Manager, InfoGame Technology Corporation, Redwood City, CA   **1998-2000**

Company's first PR counsel. Advised CEO and VP of marketing on all aspects of PR. Developed and implemented ongoing PR campaign, strategies, and tactics.
- Established "iProduct Reviews" program, garnering hundreds of additional positive stories.
- Managed and inspired cross-functional teams of marketing, operations, and customer service.

Account Supervisor, Senior Account Executive, Account Executive, XYZ Advertising & Public Relations (Acquired by FLEISHMAN-HILLARD in 2000), Mountain View, CA   **1996-1998**

Promoted annually for successful track record of positioning unknown start-up companies into industry leaders. Designed and managed all PR strategy and activities for start-up, software, Internet, and networking companies. Managed teams of up to ten PR professionals.
- Accelerated Triiliux and its CEO out of obscurity and into undisputed leadership. Continually landed top speaking placements and media coverage.
- Transformed the unknown LinkExchange into a highly publicized leader in the Internet advertising arena. Placed hundreds of stories in both business and industry media.
- Designed and managed InfoGear Technology's repositioning from fledgling company to a leader in the Internet appliance space.
- Launched newcomer The Internet Mall, landing continual coverage in all top Internet and business publications.

OTHER RELEVANT EXPERIENCE

Motivational Speaker/Guest Celebrity

Representative clients: IBM, Hardees, Speedo America, Busch Gardens, Alamo Rent-A-Car   **1989-present**
- Coach audiences on how to use the Olympic model to set and achieve goals, and succeed in business and life.

Television Sports Commentator

Swimming analyst for NBC, ESPN, FoxSports, SportsChannel, Turner Sports, and others   **1988-2000**
- Covered the Barcelona Olympics. Half-time reporter for Miami Heat and Southern Conference games.

AWARDS & ACHIEVEMENTS

Four Olympic swimming medals: two gold, one silver, one bronze
- Southland Corporation's Olympia Award for academic and athletic leadership.
- Southeastern Conference, NCAA, and USA Swimming Champion.
- Hall of Fame Inductee: International Swimming Hall of Fame, University of Florida, Pacific Northwest Swimming, Washington State Swimming Coaches Assoc., Mercer Island H.S.

EDUCATION

University of Florida, Gainesville, FL
- Bachelor of Science in Journalism.
- Minor in Speech.

123 Main Street
Anywhere, VA 22222

Nancy Wright

Home (555) 555-5555
Mobile (555) 333-5555
example@yahoo.com

Group Manager • Account Director • PR Manager

Performance Profile/Performance Summary

High-tech public relations professional with 13 years' experience, including nine in Silicon Valley, in the software, Internet, networking, consumer electronics, and wireless industries. Substantial experience in PR and strategic communications campaigns that lead to company acquisitions. Experienced in all aspects of strategic and tactical communications from developing and managing multiple campaigns, accounts, and results-oriented teams to developing and placing stories. Seasoned motivational speaker and freelance TV color commentator. Two-time Olympic gold medalist.

Core Competencies

High-Tech Public Relations	Craft & Place Stories	Budget Management	Client Satisfaction
Strategic Communications	Strong Writing Skills	Account Management	Organizational Skills
Executive Communications	Media Training	Project Management	Thought Leadership
PR Messaging & Tactics	Multiple Projects	Detail Oriented	PR Counsel
Story Telling	Story Placement	Acquisition Positioning	Social Media
Collateral Materials	Counsel Executives	Pitch Media	
Leadership Branding	Strong Editing Skills	Market Research	
Analyst Relations	New Business Development	Build & Lead Teams	
Media Relations	Team Management	Mentor	

Strategic Public Relations Leadership

Orchestrated PR campaigns that positioned companies as both industry leaders and sound investments. Developed and directed PR campaigns for four companies that were subsequently acquired within two years of the campaigns: *InfoGame Technologies* (creator of the first iProduct®, acquired by *ABC Network*), *Triiliux Digital Systems* (acquired by *Intel*), *LinkExchange* (acquired by *Microsoft*), and *The Internet Mall* (acquired by *TechWave*). Proven client satisfaction demonstrated in repeat business and account growth: over a span of ten years, contracted by former *InfoGame* execs to serve as communications counsel for *NextLink Technologies*, *ABC Network Systems*, and *AirPlay Networks*.

Executive Communications Management

Executive Communications Manager for iconic executive and public speaker, ****, *Group VP, Service Provider Sales, ABC Network Systems* (currently *senior VP* and *technology evangelist* for *ABC Network*). Developed communication messaging, strategy and platform skills for VP, Group VP, and C-level executives.

Media Coverage

ABC World News Tonight, CNN, The Today Show, Associated Press, Baltimore Sun, Boston Globe, Business Times, Business Week, CNN.com, Fast Company, Financial Times, Forbes, Fortune Magazine, Inc., MSNBC.com, New York Times, Parade, San Jose Mercury News, SF Chronicle, USA Today, Wired, Wall Street Journal, AdWeek, CommsDesign, Computer Reseller News, Computer Retail Week, Computer Shopper, Computer World, CRN, CNET, EE Times, Embedded Systems Design, Internet.com, InfoWorld, InformationWeek, Internet.com, Internet Telephony, LightReading, Network World, Phone+, PC Magazine, Red Herring, TMCnet, VoIP News, VON and ZDNet, Dataquest, Forrester Research, Frost and Sullivan, Jupiter Communications, Yankee Group.

—— **Professional Experience** ——

Principal   **2003 to Present**

Wright & Associates Public Relations, Anywhere, VA

Develop and deliver strategic communications. Drive all PR strategy and tactics, messaging, media training, media relations, budget management, story creation and placement for technology clients.

- Representative clients include *AirPlay Networks* (former *InfoGame* and *NextLink client*), *ReligiousSite.com* (founded by *eCompany.com* founder), and *PanJet Aviation*.

Principal   **2001 to 2003**
Three Boys Public Relations, Redwood City, CA
Developed and implemented all strategic and tactical aspects of public relations for Silicon Valley clients, including thought leadership, leadership branding, story creation and telling, media materials, stories, media relations, and publicity.
- *ABC Network Systems*—Executive Communications Manager to ****, Group VP at *ABC Network*, a highly pursued public speaker.
- *NextLink Technologies*—Company's first PR counsel. Repositioned obscure company, impaired by trademark dilution, into an industry leader by leveraging market's widespread knowledge and use of *NextLink's* industry-standard *GreatD* networking software.

Marketing Manager   **2000 to 2001**
ABC Network Systems, San Jose, CA
Directed internal, cross-functional marketing for iProduct, following ABC Network acquisition of *InfoGame* and its technology.
- Shortly after acquisition, ABC Network dissolved *InfoGame/Managed Appliances Business Unit (MASBU)*.

Public Relations Manager   **1998 to 2000**
InfoGame Technology Corporation, Redwood City, CA
Advised CEO and VP of marketing on all aspects of PR. Developed and implemented all strategies, tactics, and stories.
- Revamped the start-up's teetering image, which was ruining *iProduct* sales. After two press tours, garnered hundreds of additional stories in all top trade and consumer media with the *iProduct Reviews* program. Catapulted company into a leadership position in the Internet appliance industry, setting it up for acquisition. *iProduct* is now a household name.
- Managed and inspired cross-functional teams of marketing, operations and customer service to work outside their job responsibilities to deliver excellent service to hundreds of editors beta-testing the *iProduct 2.0*.

Account Supervisor; Senior Account Executive; Account Executive **1996 to 1998**
XYZ Advertising & Public Relations (Acquired by FLEISHMAN-HILLARD in 2000), Mountain View, CA
Promoted annually for successful track record of positioning unknown companies as both industry leaders and solid investments/acquisitions. Designed and managed all PR strategy and activities for start-up, software, Internet, and networking companies. Managed teams of up to ten PR professionals.
- Repositioned, rebranded, relaunched, and reintroduced *InfoGame*, the *iProduct 1.0* and *2.0*, positioning them collectively as leading the nascent Internet appliance space.
- Accelerated *Triiliux* and its CEO out of obscurity and into undisputed leadership through media placement and top speaking engagements.
- Transformed unknown *LinkExchange* into a highly publicized leader in the Internet advertising arena. Placed hundreds of stories in both business and industry media.
- Launched *The Internet Mall*, landing continual coverage in all top Internet and business publications.

—— **Complementary Experience** ——

Motivational Speaker/Guest Celebrity   **1989 to Present**
Coach audiences on how to use the Olympic model to set and achieve goals and succeed in business and life. Representative clients: IBM, Hardees, Speedo America, Busch Gardens, Alamo Rent-A-Car.

Television Sports Commentator   **1987 to 2000**
Swimming analyst for NBC, ESPN, FoxSports, SportsChannel, Turner Sports, and others. Covered the Olympics. Half-time reporter for Miami Heat and The College Conference.

Awards & Achievements

Winner—Two Olympic swimming gold medals plus one silver and one bronze.
Recipient Southland Corporation's Olympia Award for academic and athletic leadership.
NCAA, USA, Southeastern Conference swimming champion, and 26-time NCAA All American.
Hall of Fame Inductee: International Swimming Hall of Fame, University of Florida, Pacific Northwest Swimming, Washington State Swimming Coaches Association, Mercer Island High School.

EDUCATION—University of Florida, Gainesville, FL; B.S. in Journalism, Minor in Speech.

CHAPTER 3

YOUR RESUME IS A GARBAGE IN/ GARBAGE OUT PROPOSITION

HOW WELL THE most financially important document you are ever going to own comes out depends on what goes in. So if you don't want a garbage resume, you need a logical way to gather the right information to tell that story.

When you got inside your customer's head in the previous chapter, you gained a clear understanding of the story your resume needs to tell. Now, with the requirements and deliverables of your Target Job Deconstruction (TJD) document in front of you for focus, it's time to work through your professional life, methodically pulling out the skills and experiences that will help your resume tell the most effective story of someone who can nail this target job.

The Right Way to Look Into Your Work History

Your resume is a document that tells a story about your collective professional work experiences. For the most powerful resume, you should examine your work history through the lens of your TJD, because it succinctly defines exactly what your customer, the employer, wants to find. This gives you guidelines for the most effective ways to define the *professional you*. The information you gather will be customized to your customers' needs, giving you the raw materials for a killer resume. The more information you gather, the better. Even if some of it doesn't make it into your resume, it will still have immense value preparing you for the interviews, because this information-gathering exercise will continue to increase the insights you gain into the real *professional you* as a commodity and a brand. (More on this later.)

Fifty Percent of the Success of Any Project Is in the Preparation

Here's the link *www.my.knockemdead.com/resume-services* for the *Knock 'em Dead* professional resume-writing service. On this page, you'll find further links to the information-gathering questionnaire I use for my resume-writing service clients. It will help you gather all the resume-relevant information about your professional life in one place. To help you get the most out of this not-very-exciting task, you'll find a lot of "how to and why to" advice as you work through it.

It's obviously best to do this kind of work on your computer: You never run out of space and all the information will be collected and saved in a Microsoft Word document, ready to be molded into a finished resume. You can get the resume and competitive difference questionnaires at *www .knockemdead.com* on the "Downloads" page. Half the success of any project rests on the preparation. The work you do here in carefully analyzing where you are and what you have done goes a long way toward determining your next step and what you bring to the table to make that next step; it can also help you determine your own professional skill development program. Writing a resume means you are at a time of change in your life, it is a time of introspection and planning, so bite the bullet and make the time to invest yourself in professional success and personal fulfillment. The prep work you do today and this week is going to have a real impact on your career and life going forward.

Resume Questionnaire

Please Note: An electronic document is expandable, so if you need additional space, don't limit yourself to the lines/pages provided.

Your first step is to complete the critical Target Job Deconstruction exercise. This will create a composite job description and bring focus to the story your resume needs to tell.

Name (exactly as wanted on resume): _____

Address: _____

City: _____ State:_____ Zip: _____

Home Phone: _____ Mobile Phone: _____

Email: _____

Are you willing to relocate?   Yes ( ) No ( )

Are you willing to travel?   Yes ( ) No ( )

Please answer the following questions as completely and accurately as possible. Not all questions may apply to you. If they do not apply, mark them "N/A."

Position/Career Objective: List top three job title choices in order of preference.

If the titles are for related positions (*e.g., 1–Sales; 2–Marketing; 3–Business Development*) your resume will be developed to reflect the cross-functional target(s). If the goals are not related (*e.g., 1–Rocket Scientist; 2–Pastry Chef; 3–Landscape Designer*), the resume will be written to fit your first selection. (We will discuss creating additional versions of your resume later.)

1. _____

2. _____

3. _____

Desired Industry Segment _____

Is this a career change for you? Yes ( ) No ( )

Purpose of Resume (e.g., job change, career change, promotion, business development/marketing tool) _____

Summarize your experience in this field in a couple of sentences. Do not provide details of positions here: We only want to get the big picture; just a sentence or two about your background. *For example: I have been in the accounting field for twelve years and received three promotions to my current position, which I've held for two years.*

_____

_____

_____

_____

_____

What are some terms (keywords) specific to your line of work? *(You found these during the TJD process.)*

_____

_____

_____

_____

_____

What are the key strengths that you want to highlight on your resume? What makes you stand out from your competitors? Drill down to the essence of what differentiates your candidacy.

_____

_____

_____

_____

_____

Current Salary: _____   **Expected Salary:** _____

Education

List all degrees, certificates, diplomas received, dates received, school or college, and location of school or college. Begin with the most recent and work backward.

Name of College/Univ: _____

City/State: _____

Degree Obtained (i.e., BS, BA, MBA, AA): _____   Year Completed: _____

Major: _____   Minor: _____

Overall GPA: _____   GPA in Major: _____

Honors (include scholarships):

_____

_____

_____

Extracurricular Activities (include leadership, sports, study abroad, etc.):

_____

_____

_____

_____

_____

Name of College/Univ: _____

City/State: _____

Degree Obtained (i.e., BS, BA, MBA, AA): _____ Year Completed: _____

Major: _____ Minor: _____

Overall GPA: _____ GPA in Major: _____

Honors (include scholarships):

_____

_____

_____

_____

Extracurricular Activities (include leadership, sports, study abroad, etc.):

_____

_____

_____

_____

_____

High School (only if no college)

Name: _____ City/State: _____ Year: _____

Professional Development (training courses/seminars/workshops, etc.)

Ongoing professional education signals commitment to success. If you attended numerous courses, list the most recent and/or relevant to your career and indicate that additional course information is available. Ignore those courses that have been rendered obsolete by technology and the passage of time.

Course Name: _____

Completion Date: _____ Duration: _____

Certification Obtained: _____ Location of Training: _____

Sponsoring Organization: _____

Course Name: _____

Completion Date: _____ Duration: _____

Certification Obtained: _____ Location of Training: _____

Sponsoring Organization: _____

Course Name: _____

Completion Date: _____ Duration: _____

Certification Obtained: _____ Location of Training: _____

Sponsoring Organization: _____

Professional Certifications

_____

_____

Professional Licenses

_____

_____

Military (include branch of service, locations, position, rank achieved, years of service, honorable discharge, key accomplishments, special recognition, awards, etc.)

_____

_____

_____

Professional Organizations/Affiliations

Active membership in a professional association is a key tool for career resiliency and success.

Name of Organization (include city/state or chapter): _____

_____

Leadership Roles Held: _____

Name of Organization (include city/state or chapter): _____

_____

Leadership Roles Held: _____

Name of Organization (include city/state or chapter): _____

_____

Leadership Roles Held: _____

Name of Organization (include city/state or chapter): _____

_____

Leadership Roles Held: _____

Name of Organization (include city/state or chapter): _____

_____

Leadership Roles Held: _____

Name of Organization (include city/state or chapter): _____

_____

Leadership Roles Held: _____

Publications/Presentations

_____

_____

_____

_____

_____

_____

_____

Patents and Copyrights

You can also include here your work on projects that resulted in copyrights and patents, so long as you make clear your real contribution.

_____

_____

_____

_____

_____

_____

_____

Computer Skills (include hardware, operating systems, software, Internet, email, etc.)

Maybe it's just Microsoft Word and Excel or maybe it runs to languages and protocols. Nobody today gets ahead without technological adeptness. Capture your fluency here and update regularly; that alphabet soup of technology just might help your resume in database searches.

Hardware:

_____
_____
_____
_____

Operating Systems:

_____
_____
_____
_____

Software Applications:

_____
_____
_____
_____

Other if relevant:

_____
_____
_____
_____

Foreign Languages (indicate level of fluency and if verbal/written)

_____
_____
_____
_____

Global Experience/Cultural Diversity Awareness

In our global economy any exposure here is relevant, and it doesn't have to be professional in nature. If you've traveled extensively or you were an Army brat and grew up in ten different countries, that can be a big plus. Just name the countries, not the circumstances.

Corporate Awards/Recognition (indicate where and when received):

_____

_____

_____

_____

Community/Volunteer Activities (name of organization, years involved, positions held):

_____

_____

_____

_____

Hobbies/Interests/Avocations

Include activities with which you fill your out-of-work hours. Your resume may include those activities that say something positive about the professional you. For example, in sales and marketing just about all group activities show a desirable mindset. Bridge might argue strong analytical skills, and the senior exec who still plays competitive lacrosse and runs marathons is crazy not to let the world know.

_____

_____

_____

_____

Action Verbs

In describing your work experience at each position you have held, it might be helpful to select from the following list the action verbs that best characterize your daily work, duties, responsibilities, and level of authority. Select from the following list or use other "action verbs" when completing the sections stating: Briefly describe your routine duties, responsibilities, and level of authority.

Do not provide the information here; instead, use it as a guide in completing the information for each position you've held.

These are just suggestions. Please don't limit yourself to the use of these verbs only.

accepted	conceptualized	evaluated	interviewed
accomplished	conducted	examined	introduced
achieved	consolidated	executed	invented
acted	contained	expanded	launched
adapted	contracted	expedited	lectured
addressed	contributed	explained	led
administered	controlled	extracted	maintained
advanced	coordinated	fabricated	managed
advised	corresponded	facilitated	marketed
allocated	counseled	familiarized	mediated
analyzed	created	fashioned	moderated
appraised	critiqued	focused	monitored
approved	cut	forecast	motivated
arranged	decreased	formulated	negotiated
assembled	defined	founded	operated
assigned	delegated	generated	organized
assisted	demonstrated	guided	originated
attained	designed	headed up	overhauled
audited	developed	identified	oversaw
authored	devised	illustrated	performed
automated	diagnosed	implemented	persuaded
balanced	directed	improved	planned
budgeted	dispatched	increased	prepared
built	distinguished	indoctrinated	presented
calculated	diversified	influenced	prioritized
cataloged	drafted	informed	processed
chaired	edited	initiated	produced
clarified	educated	innovated	programmed
classified	eliminated	inspected	projected
coached	emended	installed	promoted
collected	enabled	instigated	proposed
compiled	encouraged	instituted	provided
completed	engineered	instructed	publicized
composed	enlisted	integrated	published
computed	established	interpreted	purchased

recommended	researched	set	systemized
reconciled	resolved	shaped	tabulated
recorded	restored	solidified	taught
recruited	restructured	solved	trained
reduced	retrieved	specified	translated
referred	revamped	stimulated	traveled
regulated	revitalized	streamlined	trimmed
rehabilitated	saved	strengthened	upgraded
remodeled	scheduled	summarized	validated
repaired	schooled	supervised	worked
represented	screened	surveyed	wrote

Accomplishments/Achievements/Successes

Employers look to past performance as an indication of the value you offer. When completing the next few pages of the questionnaire, refer to the following questions to refresh your memory regarding accomplishments and achievements for each position.

1. Did you increase sales/productivity/volume? Provide percentage or amount.
2. Did you generate new business or increase client base? How? What were the circumstances?
3. Did you forge affiliations, partnerships, or strategic alliances that increased company success? With whom, and what were the results?
4. Did you save your company money? If so, how and by how much?
5. Did you design and/or institute any new systems and procedures? If so, what were the results?
6. Did you meet an impossible deadline through extra effort? If so, what difference did this make to your company?
7. Did you bring a major project in under budget? If so, how did you make this happen? What was the budget? What were you responsible for saving in terms of time and/or money?
8. Did you suggest and/or help launch a new product or program? If so, did you take the lead or provide support? How successful was the effort? What were the results?
9. Did you assume new responsibilities that weren't part of your job? Were they assigned or did you do so proactively? Why were you selected?
10. Did you improve communication in your firm? If so, with whom, and what was the outcome?
11. How did your company benefit from your performance?
12. Did you complete any special projects? What were they and what was the result?

When describing your accomplishments/achievements, use the following three-step CAR format:

C = Challenge (think of a challenge you faced or problem you had to resolve)

A = Action (what action did you take?)

R = Results (what was the result of the action you took? What was the value to the company?)

Don't provide answers to all these questions here, but with each job you have held consider the 4–6 strongest contributions you made in that job. Above all, ask yourself how your current employer is better off now than when the company hired you.

Professional Experience

All right, now you're ready to assemble information about your work history and experience. Begin with your present employer/project. Include self-employment, contract, and volunteer or unpaid work if it applies to your career target.

Be sure to list different positions at the same company as separate jobs. Repeat the section below as many times as you need to in order to encompass all the professional positions you've held.

Name of company: _____

City/State: _____ Dates of employment: _____

Your actual job title: _____

Your functional/working job title if different from actual title: _____

Title of person you report to: _____

Number of people you supervise: _____

Their titles or functions: _____

Briefly describe the size of the organization (volume produced; revenues; number of employees; local, national, or international, etc.): _____

_____

What do they do, make, or sell? _____

_____

Where do they rank in their industry in terms of their competitors? _____

_____

_____

_____

What were you hired to do?

Briefly describe your routine duties, responsibilities, and level of authority. Use numbers (size) and percentages, quantify budgets, state with whom you interacted, etc. Provide two to three brief sentences about your major overall area of responsibility and list them in order of importance. Refer back to the list of action verbs to help you brainstorm.

Example

Selected to re-engineer and revitalize this $65 million business unit with accountability for thirty-two direct reports in four cities across the United States. Established strategic vision and developed operational infrastructure. Managed Supply Chain, Logistics/Distribution, Forecasting, System Integration, Project Management, Contracts Administration, and Third-Party Site Operations.

Or more simply: Drove production for world's largest wallboard plant, with 258 employees working in multiple shifts.

1. _____
_____
_____
_____

2. _____
_____
_____
_____

3. _____
_____
_____
_____

Briefly describe 3–5 of your accomplishments in this position. Use the most significant achievements or contributions that best support your career target and describe them in a brief statement, referring to the accomplishments guidelines. Use numbers wherever possible. Give facts and figures. Please note: Distill the accomplishments into their essence. How did your accomplishment contribute to bottom-line performance/ROI?

1. _____
_____
_____
_____

2. _____
_____
_____
_____

3. _____
_____
_____
_____

4. _____
_____
_____
_____

5. _____
_____
_____
_____

When Achievements Are Hard to Define

Employers look to your past performance and what you achieved as an indication of your potential value to the team. If you are in Sales, for example, identifying achievements is a no-brainer, but for many jobs the case isn't so clear-cut.

There are two types of workers in every department: those who get things done and those who watch things being done; those who make a difference with their presence and those whose goal is to squeak by until the end of the working day. Recognizing how you try to make a difference with your presence everyday can help define your potential value.

Ask yourself how the department, company, or customer is better off because of your efforts, both in general and specific terms. Think about accomplishments of which you are proud, tough projects that turned out well, disasters that were averted. Think of days you left work feeling proud and why?

Use the following questions to jog your memory about accomplishments and achievements:

- Did you increase sales/productivity/volume? Please provide percentage or amount.
- Did you generate new business or increase client base? How? What were the circumstances?
- Did you forge affiliations, partnerships, or strategic alliances that impacted success of you/department/company? What were the results?
- Did you save your company money? If so, how and how much?

- Did you design and/or institute any new system or process? If so, what were the results?
- Did you meet an impossible deadline through extra effort? If so, what difference did this make to your company?
- Did you bring a major project in under budget? If so, how did you make this happen? What was the budget? What were you responsible for saving in terms of time and/or money?
- Did you help or save a troubled customer?
- Did the quality of your work decrease typical problems or cause comment for other reasons?
- For what have you been praised on that job?
- Why do people like to work with you?
- Did you conceive, design, or (help) launch a new product or program? If so, did you take the lead or provide support? How successful was the effort? What were the results?
- Did you assume new responsibilities that weren't part of your job? Were they assigned or did you do so proactively? Why were you selected?
- Did you introduce any new or more effective systems, processes, or techniques for increasing productivity? What was the result?
- Did you improve communications in some way? If so, with whom and what was the outcome?
- Did you complete any special projects? What were they and what was the result?
- What budgets were you responsible for?

Take Your Time: You're Laying the Foundation for Career Success

Be sure to take the time to do this exercise right. It may be tempting to rush through it or look for shortcuts, but remember that you're assembling the information that's going to be the brick and mortar of your resume, the most financially important document you are ever going to own. You need it to be as complete and well thought out as possible.

CHAPTER 4

HOW TO DEFINE AND BUILD A DESIRABLE PROFESSIONAL BRAND

A RESUME IS the primary tool that all professionals use to define and disseminate their *professional brand* to an ever-expanding world of contacts. Long-term success—rewarding work without layoffs, and professional growth that fits your goals—is much easier to achieve when you are credible and visible within your profession. Creating and nurturing a *professional brand* as part of your overall career management strategy will help you achieve credibility and visibility throughout your profession, because an identifiable brand gives *you* focus and *motivation*, and *others* a way to differentiate you.

Establishing a desirable *professional brand* takes time; after all, you have to brand something that is worth branding, something your customers will resonate with. A worthwhile brand doesn't spring into being overnight, it evolves over years; but you need to start somewhere, and you need to start now.

The greater the effort you put into working toward credibility and visibility—which over time translates into a steadily widening professional reputation in your area of expertise—the quicker you enter the inner circles in your department, your company, and ultimately your profession. And it is in these inner circles that job security, plum assignments, raises, promotions, and professional marketability all dwell.

Think of your brand as the formal announcement to the professional community of how you want to be seen in your professional world. Your resume, and the social networking profiles that grow from it, are the primary tools you will use to introduce and maintain a consistent message of your brand: how you want to be seen as a professional in your field. It's the narrative of your resume that tells this story in a very particular way: It captures your experience, skills, capabilities, and professional behavioral profile *as they relate to what your customers want to buy.*

Components of a Desirable Professional Brand

A viable *professional brand* must be built on firm foundations. This means you must understand what employers look for when they hire (and subsequently promote) someone in your profession, at your level, and with your job title. Understanding how your employers think is critical for the success of this job search and for your career going forward; it's why you spent Chapter 2 learning how employers deconstruct your job into its component parts, and how they then order and prioritize those parts and, most important, the words they use to express these judgments . . . and by extension how they will reward those who give them what they want.

In this chapter, we'll examine a couple of additional and equally important dimensions of the *professional you*, ones that will play into your resume, your interviews, and your success in that next job on your career path. Specifically, we'll look at a sequence of *transferable skills and professional values* that underlie all professional success, no matter what you do. I'll also explain a process to help you identify and give voice to the unique combination of attributes that make up the *professional you*.

Over the years, I've read a lot of books about finding jobs, winning promotions, and managing your career. A few were insightful and many were innocuous, but one theme that runs through them all is the absurd and harmful advice to "Just be yourself."

"Who you are is just fine. Be yourself and you'll do fine." Wrong. Remember that first day on your first job, when you went to get your first cup of coffee? You found the coffee machine, and there, stuck on the wall behind it, was a handwritten sign reading:

YOUR MOTHER DOESN'T WORK HERE
PICK UP AFTER YOURSELF

You thought, "Pick up after myself? Gee, that means I can't behave like I do at home and get away with it." And so you started to observe and emulate the more successful professionals around you. You behaved in a way that was appropriate to the environment, and in doing so demonstrated *emotional intelligence*. Over time you developed many new ways of conducting yourself at work in order to be accepted as a professional in your field. You weren't born this way. You developed a behavioral profile, a *professional persona* that enabled you to survive in the professional world.

Some people are just better than the average bear at everything they do, and they become more successful as a result. It doesn't happen by accident; there is a specific set of *transferable skills and professional values* that underlies professional success: skills and values that employers all over the world in every industry and profession are anxious to find in candidates from the entry level to the boardroom. Why this isn't taught in schools and in the university programs that cost a small fortune is unfathomable, because these skills and values are the foundation of every successful career. They break down into these groups:

1. *The Technical Skills of Your Current Profession.* These are the technical competencies that give you the *ability* to do your job. The skills needed to complete a task and the know-how to use them productively and efficiently. These *technical skills* are mandatory if you want to land a job within your profession. *Technical skills,* while transferable, vary from profession to profession, so many of your current *technical skills* will only be transferable within your current profession.
2. *Transferable Skills That Apply in All Professions.* The set of skills that underlies your ability to execute the *technical skills* of your job effectively, whatever your job might be. They are the foundation of all the professional success you will experience in this and any other career (including dream and entrepreneurial careers) that you may pursue over the years.
3. *Professional Values.* This set of skills is complemented by an equally important set of *professional values* that is highly prized by employers. *Professional values* are an interconnected set of core beliefs that enable professionals to determine the right judgment call for any given situation.

The importance of the whole series of *transferable skills and professional values* led to an entirely new approach to interviewing and the science of employee selection: behavioral interviewing. These behavioral interviewing techniques (discussed in detail in *Knock 'em Dead 2017* and *Knock 'em Dead: Secrets & Strategies for Success in an Uncertain World*) now predominate in the selection process because of their ability to determine whether you possess those *transferable skills and professional values*.

A Review of Transferable Skills and Professional Values

As you read through the following breakdown of each *transferable skill and professional value* you may, for example, read about *communication*, and think, "Yes, I can see how communication skills are important in all jobs and at all levels of the promotional ladder, and, hallelujah, I have good communication skills." Take time to recall examples of your *communication skills* and the role they play in the success of your work.

You might also read about *multitasking skills* and realize that you need to improve in that area. Whenever you identify a *transferable skill* that needs work, you have found a *professional development project:* improving that skill. Your attention to those areas will repay you for the rest of your working life, no matter how you make a living.

Here are the *transferable skills and professional values* that will speed the conclusion of this job search and your long-term professional success. You'll find that you already have some of them to a greater or lesser degree, and if you are committed to making a success of your life, you'll commit to further development of all of them.

Transferable Skills

Technical
Critical Thinking
Communication
Multitasking
Teamwork
Leadership
Creativity

Professional Values

Motivation and Energy
Commitment and Reliability
Determination
Pride and Integrity
Productivity
Systems and Procedures

Transferable Skills

Technical Skills

The *technical skills* of your job are the foundation of success within your current profession; without them you won't even land a job, much less keep it for long or win a promotion. They speak to your *ability* to do the job, those skills necessary for the day-to-day execution of your duties. These *technical skills* vary from job to job and profession to profession.

A recruitment metrics company said in a recent study that by 2015, 60 percent of the jobs available will require skills held by 20 percent of the population. Technology constantly changes the nature of our jobs and the ways in which they are executed. As a result, if you want to stay employable, you need to stay current with the skills most prized in your professional world.

In addition to the technical skills that are specific to your job alone, and which you take from position to position within your current profession, there is also a body of skills that are as desirable in other jobs and other professions, just as much as they are in yours. Possession of these *transferable skills* will not only enhance your employability in your current profession, it is also likely to ease your transition should you ever change your career; something that the statistics say you will do three or more times over the span of your work life.

Any employer would welcome an employee who, as well as the must-haves of the job, possesses the *written communication skills* to create a PR piece or a training manual; who knows how to structure and format a proposal; who is able to stand up and make presentations; or who knows how to research, analyze, and assimilate hard-to-access data.

Some of the *transferable technical skills* sought across a wide spectrum of jobs include:

- Selling skills—even in nonsales jobs, the art of persuasive *communication* is always appreciated, because no matter what the job . . . you are always selling something to someone.
- Project management skills
- Six Sigma skills
- Lean management skills
- Quantitative analysis skills
- Theory development and conceptual thinking skills
- Counseling and mentoring skills
- Writing skills for PR, technical, or training needs
- Customer Resource Management (CRM) skills
- Research skills
- Social networking skills

While the *technical skills* of your job are not necessarily technological in nature, it is a given that one of the *technical skills* essential to almost every job is technological competence. You must be proficient in all the technology and Internet-based applications relevant to your work. Even when you are not working in a technology field, strong *technology skills* will enhance your stability and help you leverage professional growth.

Some of your *technology skills* will only be relevant within your current profession, while others (Word, Excel, PowerPoint, to name the obvious) will be transferable across all industry and professional lines. Staying current with the essential *technical* and *technology skills* of your chosen career path is keystone foundation for your professional stability and growth.

There are also *technology skills* that have application within all professions in our technology-driven world. It is pretty much a given that you need to be computer literate to hold down any job today. Just about every job expects competency with Microsoft Word, email, Excel, Power-Point, and a host of other communication tools.

Any employer is going to welcome a staff member who knows his or her way around spreadsheets and databases, who can update a webpage, or who is knowledgeable in CRM. Some of the *technology skills* that enhance employability on nontechnology jobs include:

- Database management
- Spreadsheet creation
- Word processing
- Building and designing of presentations
- Email and social media communication

Eventually, more and more of these skills will become specific requirements of the jobs of the future, but the fact that you possess these *transferable technical skills* now adds a special sauce to your candidacy for any job.

Critical Thinking Skills

As I noted earlier, your job, whatever it is, exists to solve problems and to prevent problems from arising within your area of expertise. *Critical thinking, analytical,* or *problem-solving* skills represent a systematic approach to dealing with the challenges presented by your work. *Critical thinking skills* allow you to think through a problem, define the challenge and its possible solutions, and then evaluate and implement the best solution from all available options.

Fifty percent of the success of any project is in the preparation; *critical thinking* is at the heart of that preparation. In addition, using *critical thinking* to properly define a problem always leads to a better solution.

Communication Skills

As George Bernard Shaw said: "The greatest problem in communication is the illusion that it has been accomplished." Every professional job today demands good *communication skills*, but what are they?

When the professional world talks about *communication skills*, it is referring not just to *listening* and speaking but to four primary skills and four supportive skills.

The primary *communication skills* are:

- Verbal skills—what you say and how you say it.
- Listening skills—listening to understand, rather than just waiting your turn to talk.
- Writing skills—clear written communication creates a lasting impression of who you are and is essential for success in any professional career.
- Technological communication skills—your ability to evaluate the protocols, strengths, and weaknesses of alternative communication media, and then to choose the medium appropriate to your audience and message.

The four supportive *communication skills* are:

- Grooming and dress—these tell others who you are and how you feel about yourself.
- Social graces—how you behave toward others in all situations; this defines your professionalism.
- Body language—this displays how you're feeling deep inside, a form of communication that precedes your speech. For truly effective communication, what your mouth says must be in harmony with what your body says.
- Emotional IQ—your emotional self-awareness, your maturity in dealing with others in the full range of human interaction.

All the *transferable skills* are interconnected—for example, good *verbal skills* require both *listening* and *critical thinking skills* to accurately process incoming information and enable you to present your outgoing verbal messaging persuasively in light of the interests and sophistication of your audience so that it is understood and accepted. Develop effective skills in all eight of the subsets that together comprise *communication skills* and you'll gain enormous control over what you can achieve, how you are perceived, and what happens in your life.

Multitasking

This is one of the most desirable skills of the new era. According to numerous studies, however, the *multitasking* demands of modern professional life are causing massive frustration and meltdowns for professionals everywhere. The problem is NOT *multitasking*, the problem is the assumption that *multitasking* means being reactive to *all* incoming stimuli and therefore jumping around from one task to another as the emergency of the moment dictates. Such a definition of *multitasking* would of course leave you feeling that wild horses are attached to your extremities and tearing you limb from limb.

Few people understand what *multitasking* abilities are really built on: sound *time management* and *organizational skills*. Here are the basics:

ESTABLISH PRIORITIES

Multitasking is based on three things:

1. Being organized
2. Establishing priorities
3. Managing your time

THE PLAN, DO, REVIEW CYCLE

At the end of every day, review your day:

- What happened: A.M. and P.M.?
- What went well? Do more of it.
- What went wrong? How do I fix it?
- What projects do I need to move forward tomorrow?
- Rank each project. A= Must be completed tomorrow. B= Good to be completed tomorrow. C= If there is spare time from A and B priorities.
- Make a prioritized To Do list.
- Stick to it.

Doing this at the end of the day keeps you informed about what you have achieved, and lets you know that you have invested your time in the most important activities today and will do so again tomorrow. That peace of mind helps you feel better, sleep better, and come in tomorrow focused and ready to rock.

Teamwork

Companies depend on teams because the professional world revolves around the complex challenges of making money, and such complexities require teams of people to provide ongoing solutions. This means that you must work efficiently and respectfully with other people who have totally different responsibilities, backgrounds, objectives, and areas of expertise. It's true that individual initiative is important, but as a professional, much of the really important work you do is done as a member of a group. Your long-term stability and success require that you learn the arts of cooperation, team-based decision making, and team *communication*.

Teamwork demands that a *commitment* to the team and its success comes first. This means you take on a task because it needs to be done, not because it makes you look good.

As a *team player* you:

- Always cooperate.
- Always make decisions based on team goals.
- Always keep team members informed.
- Always keep commitments.
- Always share credit, never blame.

If you become a successful leader in your professional life, it's a given that you were first a reliable *team player*, because a leader must understand the dynamics of *teamwork* before she can leverage them. When *teamwork* is coupled with the other *transferable skills and professional values, it results in greater responsibility and promotions.*

Leadership Skills

Leadership is the most complex of all the *transferable skills* and combines all the others. As you develop *teamwork skills*, notice how you are willing to follow true leaders, but don't like falling in line with people who don't respect you and who don't have your best interests at heart. When others believe in your competence, and believe you have everyone's success as your goal, they will follow you. When your actions inspire others to think more, learn more, do more, and become more, you are becoming a leader. This will ultimately be recognized and rewarded with promotion into and up the ranks of management.

- Your job as a leader is to help your team succeed, and your *teamwork skills* give you the smarts to pull a team together as a cohesive unit.
- Your *technical* expertise, *critical thinking*, and *creativity skills* help you correctly define the challenges your team faces and give you the wisdom to guide them toward solutions.
- Your *communication skills* enable your team to *buy into* your directives and goals. There's nothing more demoralizing than a leader who can't clearly articulate why you're doing what you're doing.
- Your *creativity* (discussed next) comes from the wide frame of reference you have for your work and the profession and industry in which you work, enabling you to come up with solutions that others might not have seen.
- Your *multitasking skills*, based on sound *time management* and *organizational* abilities, enable you to create a practical blueprint for success. They also allow your team to take ownership of the task and deliver the expected results on time.

Leadership is a combination and outgrowth of all the *transferable skills* plus the clear presence of all the *professional values* we are about to discuss. Leaders aren't born; they are self-made. And just like anything else, it takes hard work.

Creativity

Your *creativity* comes from the frame of reference you have for your work, profession, and industry. This wide frame of reference enables you to see the *patterns* that lie behind challenges, and so connect the dots and come up with solutions that others might not have seen. Others might be too closely focused on the specifics of the issue—thus, they don't have that holistic frame of reference that enables them to step back and view the issue in its larger context.

There's a big difference between *creativity* and just having ideas. Ideas are like headaches: We all get them once in a while, and like headaches, they disappear as mysteriously as they arrived. *Creativity*, on the other hand, is the ability to develop those ideas with the strategic and tactical know-how that brings them to life. Someone is seen as creative when his ideas produce tangible results. *Creativity* also demands that you harness other *transferable skills* to bring those ideas to life. *Creativity* springs from:

- Your *critical thinking skills*, applied within an area of *technical expertise* (the area where your *technical skills* give you a frame of reference for what works and what doesn't).
- Your *multitasking skills*, which in combination with your *critical thinking* and *technical skills* allow you to break your challenge down into specific steps and determine which approach is best.
- Your *communication skills*, which allow you to explain your approach and its building blocks persuasively to your target audience.
- Your *teamwork* and *leadership skills*, which enable you to enlist others and bring the idea to fruition.

Creative approaches to challenges can take time or can come fully formed in a flash, but the longer you work on developing the supporting skills that bring *creativity* to life, the more often they *will* come fully formed and in a flash. Here are five rules for building *creativity skills* in your professional life:

1. **Whatever you do in life, engage in it fully.** Commit to developing competence in everything you do, because the wider your frame of reference for the world around you, the more you will see the patterns and connectivity in your professional world, delivering the higher-octane fuel you need to propel your ideas to acceptance and reality.

2. **Learn something new every day.** Treat the pursuit of knowledge as a way of life. Absorb as much as you can about everything. Information exercises your brain, filling your mind and contributing to that ever-widening frame of reference that allows you to see those patterns behind a specific challenge. The result is that you will make connections others won't and develop solutions that are seen as magically creative.

3. **Catch ideas as they occur.** Note them in your smartphone or on a scrap of paper. Anything will do, as long as you capture the idea.

4. **Welcome restrictions in your world.** They make you think, they test the limits of your skills and the depth of your frame of reference; they truly encourage *creativity*. Ask any successful business leader, entrepreneur, writer, artist, or musician.

5. **Don't spend your life glued to YouTube or the TV.** You need to live life, not watch it go by out of the corner of your eye. If you do watch television, try to learn something or motivate yourself with science, history, or biography programming. If you surf the Internet, do it with purpose.

Building *creativity skills* enables you to bring your ideas to life; and the development of each of these seven interconnected *transferable skills* will help you bring your dreams to life.

Professional Values

Professional values are an interconnected set of core beliefs that enable professionals to determine the right judgment call for any given situation. Highly prized by employers, this value system also complements and is integral to the *transferable skills*.

Motivation and Energy

Motivation and *energy* express themselves in your engagement with and enthusiasm for your work and profession. They involve an eagerness to learn and grow professionally, and a willingness to take the rough with the smooth in pursuit of meaningful goals. *Motivation* is invariably expressed by the *energy* you demonstrate in your work. You always give that extra effort to get the job done right.

Commitment and Reliability

This means dedication to your profession, and the empowerment that comes from knowing how your part contributes to the whole. Your *commitment* expresses itself in your *reliability*. The *committed* professional is willing to do whatever it takes to get a job done, whenever and for however long it takes to get the job done. Doing so might include duties that might not appear in a job description and that might be perceived by less enlightened colleagues as "beneath them."

Determination

The *determination* you display with the travails of your work speaks of a resilient professional who does not back off when a problem or situation gets tough. It's a *professional value* that marks you as someone who chooses to be part of the solution.

The *determined* professional has decided to make a difference with her presence every day, because it is the *right* thing to do.

She is willing to do whatever it takes to get a job done, and she will demonstrate that determination on behalf of colleagues who share the same values.

Pride and Integrity

If a job's worth doing, it's worth doing right. That's what *pride* in your work really means: attention to detail and a *commitment* to doing your very best. *Integrity* applies to all your dealings, whether with coworkers, management, customers, or vendors. Honesty really *is* the best policy.

Productivity

Always work toward *productivity* in your areas of responsibility, through efficiencies of time, resources, money, and effort.

Economy

Remember the word "frugal"? It doesn't mean poverty or shortages. It means making the most of what you've got, using everything with the greatest efficiency. Companies that know how to be frugal with their resources will prosper in good times and in bad, and if you know how to be frugal, you'll do the same.

Systems and Procedures

This is a natural outgrowth of all the other *transferable skills and professional values*. Your *commitment* to your profession in all these ways gives you an appreciation of the need for *systems and procedures* and their implementation only after careful thought. You understand and always follow the chain of command. You don't implement your own "improved" procedures or encourage others to do so. If ways of doing things don't make sense or are interfering with efficiency and profitability, you work through the system to get them changed.

Development of *transferable skills and professional values* supports your enlightened self-interest, because it will be repaid with better job security and improved professional horizons. The more you are engaged in your career, the more likely you are to join the inner circles that exist in every department and company, and that's where the plum assignments, raises, and promotions live.

Transferable Skills, Professional Values, and the Secret Language of Job Postings

There are six keywords and phrases that you see in almost every job posting: *communication skills, multitasking, teamwork, creativity, problem solving*, and *leadership*. They are so commonly used that they are often dismissed as meaningless.

Far from being meaningless, they represent a secret language that few job hunters understand. The ones who do "get it" are also the ones who get the job offers. Understanding the secret language of job postings can supercharge your resume and your cover letters and will help you turn job interviews into job offers. That is because these six key phrases represent the very skills that power success; they represent the specific *transferable skills* that enable you to do your job well, whatever your job may be. You know them as *transferable skills* because no matter what the job, the profession, or the elevation of that job, your possession of these skills can make the difference between success and failure.

Decoding Made Easy

For example, when problem-solving skills are mentioned in a job posting, it means the employer is looking for someone who knows his or her area of responsibility well enough to identify, prevent where possible, and solve the problems that the job generates on a daily basis. The employer wants someone who has thought through and can discuss the challenges that lie at the heart of that job and who has developed intelligent strategies and tactics in response.

Think about how a job-posting requirement for "teamwork" applies to your job. Consider which deliverables of your work require you to interact with other people and other departments to get your work done. For example, an accountant working in Accounts Receivable will think about problem accounts and how such accounts can require working with sales and the nonpaying customer, as well as working laterally and upward within the Accounting Department.

Teamwork also embraces other *transferable skills*—for instance, the *communication skills* you need to work effectively with others. You understand that talk of *communication* always refers to verbal, written, and *listening skills*, and you also know that, to an employer, it also refers to the supporting *communication skills* of:

1. Digital communication literacy
2. Dress
3. Body language
4. Social graces
5. Emotional maturity

Together, these five components of effective *communication* impact the power and persuasiveness of all your interactions with others.

When you relate each of the *transferable skills* to each of your professional responsibilities, you'll discover the secrets to success in your profession. When you express your possession of them in your resume and cover letters, you can dramatically increase interviews. When you understand how these skills impact every action you take with every responsibility you hold, and you can explain to interviewers how you integrate these skills into all you do, you become a more desirable employee and colleague.

In Your Resume

You might decide to highlight special achievements with a *Performance Highlights* or a *Career Highlights* section. This is usually a short sequence of bulleted statements, each addressing one of the company's stated requirements and thereby emphasizing the fit between employer needs and your capabilities. Illustrate with an example if you can do so succinctly:

Performance Highlights

35% increase in on-time delivery + 20% reduction in client complaints

Effective Operations Management demands understanding every department's unique problems and timelines. Building these considerations into daily activities helped:

- Finance & Supply Chain, saved $55,000 in last three quarters
- Increased productivity, with a 35% increase in on-time delivery

These on-time delivery increases were achieved with improved communications, connecting Purchasing, Supply Chain, Customers, and Customer Service:

- Delivered 20% reduction in client complaints

In a Cover Letter

Where there is more space, these same achievements might appear with the company's requirement above:

"Problem-solving skills"
- Thorough knowledge of the problems that impact productivity in Operations enabled a 35% increase in on-time delivery.

"Work closely with others"
- Improvements in on-time delivery made possible by improved communications with Purchasing, Supply Chain, Customers, and Customer Service. This delivered a 20% reduction in client complaints.

"Multitasking"
- Effective Operations Management demands understanding of every department's critical functions and timelines. Building these considerations into daily activities helped Finance & Supply Chain save $55,000 in last three quarters.

In Your Life

Every time you see a job posting that mentions any of the *transferable skills or professional values*, think how *that skill or value is applied in each aspect of your work*. Then recall examples that illustrate how you used that skill in the identification, prevention, and solution of the daily problems that get in the way of the smooth functioning of your job.

Understanding the secret language of job postings will do more than help you land that next job; it can change your destiny. When you apply that understanding to your professional life, you will be known and respected as a consummate professional, the kind of man or woman that everyone wants to work with.

Understanding the *transferable skills and professional values* you possess and how they differentiate you from others is an important step in defining your *professional brand*. The examples of your application of these skills or the impact of these values on your work can be used in your resume, in your cover letters, and as illustrative answers to questions in interviews. But most important, if you want to be successful, these skills need to become a part of your life.

Now I'm going to take you through a process—Identifying Your Competitive Difference— that helps you identify your professional strengths and, ultimately, your competitive difference. Having a firm grip on your unique blend of competencies will help set you apart in your resume and in your interview performance.

Identifying Your Competitive Difference

The people who will hire you need to differentiate you from other candidates. The following questionnaire will help you identify all the factors that help make you unique. Each of these is a component of your *professional brand*.

Over the years you have developed certain skills, behaviors, and values that define the way others see you. Each of these is a component of your *professional brand*, but you probably can't identify all the differentiators that help make you unique; we need to change that.

There is a series of *transferable skills and professional values* that are admired by employers the world over that can be applied in any job and at any level; they describe the habits and priorities that are at the heart of all professional success.

Transferable Skills and Professional Values

Understanding the *transferable skills and professional values* that help people become successful in the professional world, will help in three distinct ways:

- When you identify one of these *transferable skills or professional values* as something you possess, you will integrate it into your personal brand. It will appear in your resume and become a conscious part of everything you do in your professional life, including how you answer questions at job interviews.
- When you identify one of these *transferable skills or professional values* as something that you do not possess or that needs development, it can support your pursuit of success by immediately becoming part of your professional development program.

- These skills and values form the foundations of long-term survival and career success; developing them is going to set you apart from your competitors in this job transition.

Although they can be developed in school or in almost any activity to which you are dedicated to doing well, the *transferable skills and professional values* that are most desirable to employers are largely developed as a result of your experiences in the workplace.

Some people are just better than average at everything they do, and they become more successful as a result. It doesn't happen by accident—they build and apply the *transferable skills and professional values* to everything they do in their work. They break down into these groups:

1. *The technical skills of your current profession.* These are the technical competencies that give you the ability to do your job. Those skills needed for a task and the know-how to use them productively and efficiently.

   These technical skills are mandatory if you want to land a job within your profession. Technical skills, while transferable, vary from profession to profession, so many of your current technical skills will only be transferable within your current profession.

2. *Transferable skills that apply in all professions.* The set of skills that underlies your ability to execute the technical skills of your job effectively, whatever that job might be. They are the foundation of all the professional success you will experience in this and any other career (including dream and entrepreneurial careers) that you may pursue over the years.

3. *Professional values.* A set of beliefs that enable all professionals to make the many judgment calls required during the working day to ensure that the best interests of the department and the employer are always promoted. They complement the transferable skills and together form a firm foundation for a successful professional life. You'll have noticed that you already have most of them to a greater or lesser degree, and if you are committed to making a success of your life, you'll commit to further development of all of them:

Transferable Skills	Professional Values
Technical	Motivation and Energy
Critical Thinking	Commitment and Reliability
Communication	Determination
Multitasking	Pride and Integrity
Teamwork	Productivity and Economy
Leadership	Systems and Procedures
Creativity	

A New Breed of Transferable Technical Skills

The *technical skills* of your profession are the foundation of all success; without them you won't even land a job, much less succeed in your career. *Technical skills* speak to your ability to do the job, those essentials necessary for success in the day-to-day execution of your duties. It means you know which skills and tools are needed for a particular task and possess the know-how to use them productively and efficiently. These *technical skills* vary from profession to profession and do not necessarily refer to anything technical per se; nor do they refer to *technology skills*.

However, it is a given that one of the *technical skills* essential to every job is technology integration. You must be proficient in all computer and Internet-based applications relevant to your work. Even when you are not working in a technology field, strong *technology skills* will enhance stability and help you leverage professional growth.

When people are referred to as "professionals," it means they possess the appropriate *technical* and *technology skills* necessary for success in their profession, and have interwoven them with the other major *transferable skills*. Staying current with the essential *technical* and *technology skills* of your chosen career path through ongoing professional education is going to be an integral part of your growth and stability. That's why the education section toward the end of your resume can be an important tool in developing your *professional brand*: It speaks to your technical competence and your *commitment*, exemplified by your continuing pursuit of professional skills.

Technology constantly changes the nature of our jobs and the ways in which they are executed. As a result, if you want to stay employable, you need stay current with the skills most prized in your professional world.

In addition to the *technical skills* that are specific to your job or profession, there is a body of skills that transcend industry lines. These skills will not only enhance your employability in your current profession, but ease your transition should you ever change your career—something that the statistics say you will do three or more times over the span of your work life.

Employers are always on the lookout for employees who, in addition to the must-haves of the job, possess the *written communication skills* to write a PR piece or a training manual, who know how to structure and format a proposal, who are able to stand up and make presentations, or who know how to research, analyze, and assimilate hard-to-access data.

Some of the *transferable technical skills* sought across a wide spectrum of jobs include:

- Selling skills: Even in nonsales jobs the art of persuasive communication is always appreciated, because no matter what the job, you are always selling something to someone.
- Project management skills
- Six Sigma skills
- Lean management skills
- Quantitative analysis skills

- Theory development and conceptual thinking skills
- Counseling and mentoring skills
- Customer Resource Management (CRM) skills
- Research skills
- Social networking skills

There are also skills that have application within all professions in our technology-driven world. It is pretty much a given that you need to be computer literate to hold down any job today, as just about every job expects competency with MS Word and email. Similarly, Excel and PowerPoint are becoming skills it is risky not to possess. Any employer is going to welcome a staff member who knows his way around spreadsheets and databases, who can update a webpage or is knowledgeable in CRM.

Some of the *technology skills* that enhance employability on nontechnological jobs include:

- Database management
- Spreadsheet management
- Documents
- Presentations
- Communications

Eventually more and more of these skills will become specific requirements of the jobs of the future, but until then, possession of these skills will add a special sauce to your candidacy for any job.

When you identify one of these *transferable skills*, learned behaviors, and core values as something you possess, it can become part of your brand signature. Ongoing development and consistent application of *transferable skills*/learned behaviors become an integral part of the *professional you*.

They can and should appear in your resume.

They will inform the way you approach your work everyday.

They will inform the substance of your answers to questions at job interviews.

They become part of you and in return will make you more successful.

When you identify a *transferable skill* / learned behavior that you do not possess, it should immediately become part of your professional development program, because these attributes go way beyond the branding concept; they underlie your long-term survival and success.

The Competitive Difference Questionnaire

The following questionnaire will help you identify all the differentiators that help make you unique. Each of these is a component of your *professional brand*. You aren't going to discover anything earth shattering here, just a continuum of behaviors and beliefs you've always had but the value of which you've perhaps never understood. It'll be a series of those, "Of course, I knew that" moments. It will then be logical and natural to integrate them into your resume and in your answers to questions at interviews, giving you "ownership" of your brand; it will feel right, it will fit.

> You can find an MSWord version of the Competitive Difference Questionnaire (CDQ) at *www.knockemdead.com* on the Downloads page.

The Competitive Difference Questionnaire

List and prioritize the transferable skills, behaviors, and values that best capture the essence of the professional you.

_____

_____

_____

_____

Which of the transferable skills, behaviors, and values have you identified for further professional development? What are you going to do about it?

_____

_____

_____

_____

What skills/behaviors/values or other characteristics do you share with top performers in your department/profession?

_____

_____

_____

_____

What have you achieved with these qualities?

_____

_____

_____

_____

What makes you different from others with whom you have worked?

_____

_____

_____

_____

What do you see as your four most defining transferable skills and professional values and how does each help your performance?

_____

_____

How do your most defining professional traits help you contribute to the team?

1. _____
2. _____
3. _____
4. _____

How do your most defining professional traits help you contribute to your departmental goals and/or help you support your boss?

1. _____
2. _____
3. _____
4. _____

Why do you stand out in your job/profession?

_____

_____

_____

If you realize you don't stand out and you want to, explain in a few sentences why the people you admire stand out. What plans do you have for change?

_____

_____

_____

In what ways are you better than others at your workplace who hold the same title?

_____

_____

_____

What excites you most about your professional responsibilities?

_____

_____

_____

What are your biggest achievements in these areas?

_____

_____

_____

What do your peers say about you?

_____

_____

_____

What does management say about you?

_____

_____

_____

What do your reports say about you?

_____

_____

_____

What are your top four professional skills?

Skill #1: _____

Quantifiable achievements with this skill: _____

Skill #2: _____

Quantifiable achievements with this skill: _____

Skill #3: _____

Quantifiable achievements with this skill: _____

Skill #4: _____

Quantifiable achievements with this skill: _____

What are your top four leadership skills?

Skill #1: _____

Quantifiable achievements with this skill: _____

Skill #2: _____

Quantifiable achievements with this skill: _____

Skill #3: _____

Quantifiable achievements with this skill: _____

Skill #4: _____

Quantifiable achievements with this skill: _____

What do you believe are the three key deliverables of your job?

_____

_____

_____

What gives you greatest satisfaction in the work you do?

_____

_____

_____

What **value** does this combination of transferable skills, professional values, and achievements enable you to bring to your targeted employers?

_____

_____

_____

_____

Now compile endorsements. Looking at each of your major areas of responsibility throughout your work history, write down any positive verbal or written commentary others have made on your performance.

_____

_____

_____

_____

After rereading your answers, make three one-sentence statements that capture the essence of the professional you and your competitive difference.

_____

_____

_____

_____

Take these three statements and rework them into one sentence. This is your competitive difference.

_____

Once you have completed the Competitive Difference Questionnaire and identified what your competitive differences are, you'll feel a new awareness of the *professional you*. You can integrate this new awareness and your competitive differences into your resume, and, in the process, give form to your brand. But before we do that, let's cover some final *professional brand* considerations.

A True and Truthful Brand

You have to be able to deliver on the brand you create. It must be based on your possession of the *technical skills* of your profession, those *transferable skills* that you take with you from job to job, and the *professional values* that imprint your approach to professional life.

It is all too easy to overpromise, and while an employer might be initially attracted by the pizzazz of your resume, whether or not you live up to its value proposition decides the length and quality of the relationship.

If a box of cereal doesn't live up to the brand's hype, you simply don't buy it again; but sell yourself into the wrong job with exaggerations or outright lies and it is likely to cost you that job, plus the possibility of collateral career damage that can follow you for years.

Benefits of a Defined Professional Brand

Understanding the skills and attributes that make for professional success might be your most immediately recognizable benefit. But your *professional brand* is also extremely valuable for your long-term survival and success. The fact that you know who you are, what you offer, and how you want to be perceived will differentiate you from others. And because you understand yourself and can communicate this understanding, you will have a professional presence.

Your Professional Brand and the Long Haul

Globalization has made your job less secure than ever, yet you are a financial entity that must survive over what will be at least a half century of work life. You'll recall our earlier discussions about change being a constant in the modern career. So while you develop an initial *professional brand* as part of your job search strategy, you don't want to shelve it once you've landed a new job.

In this new, insecure world of work, it makes sense to maintain visibility within your profession. It is nothing more than intelligent market positioning for Me, Inc. The professional identity/brand built into your new resume will become part of the profile you keep posted on LinkedIn and your other professional networking sites. This increases your credibility and visibility within your profession as well as with the recruitment industry, making you more desirable as an employee and increasing your options.

CHAPTER 5

RESUME FORMATS

FIRST IMPRESSIONS ARE important. You have the right and the obligation to package your professional experience to its greatest benefit.

Everyone has different work experience: You may have worked for just one employer throughout your career, or you may have worked for five companies in ten years. You may have changed careers entirely, or you may have maintained a predictable career path, changing jobs but staying within one profession or industry.

The look of your resume—the format you choose—depends on what your unique background brings to the target job. There are three broadly defined resume formats, but their goals are the same:

1. To maximize your performance in the resume databases
2. To demonstrate your complete grasp of the job's deliverables
3. To create a professional brand for someone who lives and breathes this work
4. To showcase relevant achievements, attributes, and accumulation of expertise to the best advantage
5. To minimize any possible weaknesses

Resume experts acknowledge three major styles for presenting your credentials to a potential employer: Chronological, Functional, and Combination. Your particular circumstances will determine the right format for you.

The Chronological Resume

The chronological resume is the most widely accepted format. It's what most of us think of when we think of resumes—a chronological listing of job titles and responsibilities. It starts with the current or most recent employment, then works backward to your first job.

This format is good for demonstrating your growth in a single profession. It is suitable for anyone with practical work experience who hasn't suffered prolonged periods of unemployment. It is not always the best choice if you are just out of school or if you are changing careers, where it might draw attention to a lack of specific, relevant experience.

The distinguishing characteristic of the chronological resume is the way it ties your job responsibilities and achievements to specific employers, job titles, and dates.

This is the simplest resume to create:

The Chronological Resume (page 1)

PARAG GUPTA

104 W. Real Drive • Beaverton, OR 97006 • (503) 123-4286 • parag.gupta@technical.com

SYSTEMS ENGINEER: Motivated and driven IT Professional offering 9+ years of hands-on experience in designing, implementing, and enhancing systems to automate business operations. Demonstrated ability to develop high-performance systems, applications, databases, and interfaces.

- Part of TL9000 CND audit interviews that helped Technical get TL9000 certified, which is significant in Telecom industry. Skilled trainer and proven ability to lead many successful projects, like TSS, EMX, and TOL.
- Strategically manage time and expediently resolve problems for optimal productivity, improvement, and profitability; able to direct multiple tasks effectively.
- Strong technical background with a solid history of delivering outstanding customer service.
- Highly effective liaison and communication skills proven by effective interaction with management, users, team members, and vendors.

Technical Skills

Operating Systems:	Unix, Windows (2000, XP, 7), DOS
Languages:	C, C++, Java, Pascal, Assembly Languages (Z8000, 808x, DSP)
Methodologies:	TL9000, Digital Six Sigma
Software:	MS Office, Adobe FrameMaker, MATLAB
RDBMS:	DOORS, Oracle 7.x
Protocols:	TCP/IP, SS7 ISUP, A1, ANSI, TL1, SNMP
Tools:	Teamplay, ClearCase, ClearQuest, M-Gate keeper, Exceed, Visio, DocExpress, Compass
Other:	CDMA Telecom Standards – 3GPP2 (Including TIA/EIA-2001, TIA/EIA-41, TIA/EIA-664), ITU-T, AMPS

Professional Experience

Technical, Main Network Division, Hillsboro, OR   Jan 1999–Present

Principal Staff Engineer • Products Systems Engineering • Nov 2004–Present

- Known as "go-to" person for CDMA call processing and billing functional areas.
- Created customer requirements documents for Technical SoftSwitch (TSS) and SMS Gateway products. All deliverables done on/ahead schedule with high quality.
- Solely accountable for authoring and allocation, customer reviews, supporting fellow system engineers, development and test, and customer documentation teams.
- Support Product Management in RFPs, customer feature prioritization, impact statements, and budgetary estimates.
- Mentored junior engineers and 1 innovation disclosure patent submitted in 2007.
- Resolved deployed customer/internal requirements issues and contributed to Virtual Zero Defect quality goal.
- TOL process champion and part of CND focus group that contributed to reducing CRUD backlog (NPR) by 25% and cycle time (FRT) by 40%.
- Recognized as the TL9000 expert. Triage representative for switching and messaging products.
- Achieved "CND Quality Award" for contribution to quality improvement, May 2007.

Senior Staff Engineer • MSS Systems Engineering • May 2002–Oct 2004

- Led a team of 12 engineers for 3 major software releases of TSS product included around 80 features/enhancements to create T-Gate SE deliverables.

The Chronological Resume (page 2)

- Mentored newer engineers to get up to speed on TSS product.
- Created requirements for TSS product, 30 features/enhancements contributing to 5 major software releases. Recognized as overall product expert with specific focus on call processing and billing.
- Played integral role in successfully implementing proprietary commercial TSS billing system.
- Supported PdM organization by creating ROMs, technical support for RFPs (Vivo, Sprint, TELUS, TM, Tata, Inquam, Alaska, Reliance, Pakistan, PBTL, Mauritius, Telefonica, Brasicel, and Angola).
- Proactively identified functional areas of improvement for requirements coverage, contributed to resolving several faults, improved customer documentation, and provided reference for future releases as well as other customers.
- Received "Above and Beyond Performance Award" Oct 2003

Senior Software Engineer • EMX Development • Aug 2000–Apr 2002

- Successfully led and coordinated the cross-functional development teams, 30 engineers, to meet the scheduled design, code, and test completion dates ensuring Feature T-Gates are met.
- Feature Technical Lead for Concurrent Voice/Data Services feature, the largest revenue-generating feature for KDDI customer.
- Feature Lead for Paging Channel SMS feature. Created requirements and design; led implementation phase of five engineers' team; supported product, network, and release testing; and created customer reference documentation.
- Performed the role of functional area lead for Trunk Manager and A1 interface functional areas. Provided 2-day Technical Workshops for internal/customer knowledge sharing and functional area transition from Caltel.
- Provided customer site testing and FOA (First Office Application) support for major EMX releases and off-hours CNRC (Customer Networks Resolution Center) support.
- Received "Bravo Award" May 2001, Sep 2001, Jan 2002

Software Engineer • EMX Development • Jan 1999–Jul 2000

- Developed design and code for SMS feature as a Trunk Manager functional area lead for the largest FA impacted by the feature. Supported product, network, and release testing.
- Contributed to customer release documentation. Supported feature-level SMS testing at various internal labs and customer sites resulting in successful deployment at customer sites.
- Designed and coded phases for wiretap and virtual circuits feature development, initial assessment of internal and customer EMX PRs (problem reports) to route/classify issues and providing problem assessments for many of these PRs.
- Created an implementation process to serve as reference for new hires.
- Provided CNRC support during the Y2K transition.
- Received "Above and Beyond Performance Award" Jan 2000, Dec 2000 and "Certificate of Outstanding Achievement" Jun 1999

Education: Master of Science in Computer Engineering • University of Portland, Portland, OR • 1998
Bachelors of Engineering in Electronics • Technology and Science Institute, India •1996

Significant Trainings Include
- Open Source Software • WiMAX • Agile Management for Software Engineering
- WSG Requirements Process • Product Security

The Functional Resume

The functional resume format focuses on the professional skills you bring to a specific target job, rather than when, where, or how you acquired them. It also de-emphasizes employers and employment dates by their placement on the second page, which typically gets less attention than your lead page. Because the focus is on the skill rather than the context or time of its acquisition, job titles and employers can likewise play a lesser part in this format.

The functional format is still used. Although it is thought less effective than other formats, this may in part be attributable to the more challenging sells it is chosen for:

- Mature professionals with a storehouse of expertise and jobs pursuing encore careers
- Entry-level professionals whose skimpy experience might not justify a chronological resume
- For those in career transition who want to focus on skills rather than locus of the experience, because that experience was developed in a different professional context
- People returning to the workplace after a long absence

Though functional resumes are more freeform than chronological ones, they should share certain structural features:

Target Job Title

For any resume to be effective, it must be conceived with a specific target job in mind, and this is especially true for a functional resume. Because it focuses so strongly on skills and the ability to contribute in a particular direction, rather than on a directly relevant work history, you really must have an employment objective clearly in mind.

A Performance Profile or Career Summary

Your target job should be followed by a short paragraph that captures your professional capabilities as they address the major requirements of the target job as you defined them in the TJD exercises.

Core Competencies

A core competencies section in your functional resume will help its performance in databases, and the use of critical keywords early on shows that you have the essential skills for the job.

Performance Highlights

Based on your target job, this is where you identify the skills, behaviors, and accomplishments that best position you for the job. Notice how clearly these demonstrate competence in the example that follows.

Dates

If your employment history lacks continuity, a functional resume allows you to de-emphasize dates somewhat by their placement, but an absence of employment dates altogether will just draw attention to a potential problem. See Chapter 6 for more about how to handle employment dates.

Everything else related to functional resumes follows the rules outlined in Chapter 6.

A Functional Resume That Works

Functional resumes are not as popular as they once were, but in some circumstances, they really are the best choice. Below is a functional resume of someone applying for a job as an art gallery or museum curator whose only prior experience was as an art teacher. Read the first page and then ask yourself if you know what a good gallery director or museum curator needs to know. I'll give you a few more interesting insights after the example.

A couple of interesting observations about this resume:

- It is more informal in tone than many examples you will see in the book, but as it reflected someone in a profession where personality is a significant part of the job, there is nothing wrong with that. Given these considerations, I decided to give the resume a personal flavor, and the very first words of the performance profile immediately draw the reader into a conversation with a passionate and committed professional: "My professional life is focused on art in all it embraces."
- There are professions where a less formal tone is more generally acceptable, usually education, the arts, and the caring professions.
- It is quite clear this person really understands the work of a curator. The first time it was used, this resume resulted in an interview within seventy-two hours, and a job offer was extended at the end of the first hour.
- Now for the kicker: The fact that this person had only been the arts department chair of a private elementary through middle school was never an issue, because he so clearly understood the demands of the target job. That was possible because his TJD research allowed the resume to be properly focused and prepared him for exactly the topics that would come up at the interview.

Charles Chalmers

Manhattan NY 11658 • (212) 555-2578 • fineartist@earthlink.net

Senior Curator

Performance Profile/Performance Summary

My professional life is focused on art in all it embraces: drawing, painting, sculpture, photography, cinema, video, audio, performance and digital art, art history, and criticism; my personal life is similarly committed. Recently relocated to Manhattan, I intend to make a contribution to the New York arts community that harnesses my knowledge, enthusiasm, and sensibilities.

Core Competencies

Photographer ~ editor ~ drawing ~ painting ~ sculpture ~ photography ~ cinema ~ video ~ audio ~ performance and digital art ~ art history and criticism ~ global artist networks ~ alumni groups ~ first-rank private collectors ~ social networking-themed, resourced, sequenced shows ~ campus & community involvement ~ education & outreach ~ installation-hang, light, and label-media kits ~ artist materials ~ Photoshop-art-staff management ~ curriculum development ~ art handlers-maintenance ~ printers ~ catering ~ graphics ~ portfolio prep-int/ext shows ~ theatre sets ~ streamed video gallery tours

Performance Highlights

ART HISTORY

Thorough knowledge of art history from caves of Lascaux through current artists such as Bruce Nauman, Jessica Stockholder, and Luc Tuymans. Film history from Lumiere Brothers to Almodovar. Current with key critical art and film theory. Ongoing workshops and lectures with the likes of Matthew Barney, Louise Bourgeois, and Andy Goldsworthy.

RESEARCH NEW ARTISTS

Connected to cutting-edge art and artists through involvement with the art communities and galleries of New York and Boston and the faculty, student, and alumni networks of RISD, Columbia, Boston Museum School, New England School of Art & Design, and now Mass Art. Twenty years of Manhattan gallery openings and networking with artists at MOMA, PS1, Guggenheim, Whitney, Metropolitan, Film Forum, International Center for Photography workshops and lectures.

SOURCING ART WORK

Through local artists, regional and global artist networks, intercultural artist exchanges, alumni groups, first-rank private collectors, personal and family networks, and Internet calls for submissions.

ART AND THE COMMUNITY

Conception and launch of themed, resourced, and sequenced shows that invigorate campus and community involvement. Reconfigure existing art spaces to create dynamic dialogue with visitors. Education and outreach programs.

The Functional Resume (page 2)

ART INSTALLATION

Maintain fluidity of gallery space in preparing exhibitions with recognition of size/time considerations for the art, to insure a sympathetic environment for the presented works. Hang, light, and label shows in sequences that create dialogue between the works.

PUBLIC RELATIONS MATERIALS

Energizing invitations, comprehensive press kits, illustrated press releases, and artist binder materials. Sensitive to placing art in historical/cultural context. Photoshop.

Management experience

Fourteen years art-staff management experience, including curriculum development. Responsible for art instructors, art handlers, maintenance crews, and working with printers, catering, and graphic arts staff.

Professional experience

1994–2005 Chair of Visual Arts, The Green Briar School

Duties: Curriculum development, portfolio preparation, internal and external monthly shows, theatre sets, monthly video news show, taught art history and all the studio arts, managed staff of three.

1989–2004 President Art Workshops

Duties: Private art studio and art history curriculums, staff of four. Private groups to Manhattan museums and gallery tours.

1980–1989 Freelance artist, photographer, and editor

Highlights from the sublime to the ridiculous include: Taught photography at Trinity School, Manhattan; photographer for the Ramones; editor of *Pioneer*, insurance industry trade magazine; assistant to Claudia Weill, documentary filmmaker, director of *Girlfriends*.

Education

MFA. Magna cum laude. Columbia University, 1983
Awards: ****** ***** Prize for film criticism
Taught undergraduate Intro to Film, under ****** ***** and ****** ******.

Subscriptions

Art in America, Art News, Artforum, New York Times, Parkett, Sight & Sound, Film Comment, Modern Painters.

Memberships

MOMA/PS1, Whitney Museum of American Art, Guggenheim, Metropolitan Museum of Art, DIA.

Recent exhibitions

2004. Corcoran Center Gallery, Southampton, NY
2005. Corsair Gallery, 37 West 33rd St. NY
2006. Fuller Museum, Brockton MA
2002. 2007. Zeitgeist Gallery, Cambridge MA

- The second time this resume was used, a core competencies section was added to increase database visibility. In the middle of the 2008–10 recession, he was called by an executive recruiter, had two interviews, and was hired at a 50 percent increase in salary to run one of the nation's blue-chip galleries.

This functional resume was successful because the writer took the time to go through the TJD process and was then able to tell a captivating and believable story, demonstrating that he had exactly the credentials needed.

The Combination Resume

This format has become the resume of choice for performance in a database-dominated world. This format has all the flexibility and strength that comes from combining both the chronological and functional formats:

- It allows you maximum flexibility to demonstrate your thorough grasp of the job and its deliverables
- It encourages greater data density and detail of information, which improves database retrieval performance
- It offers more flexibility and scope for establishing a professional brand:

Target Job Title
(Here's the job I'm after.)

Performance Profile
(This is a snapshot of what I can do.)

Core Competencies
(Here are the key professional skills that help me do my job well.)

Technology Competencies
(Optional: Here are the technical skills that help me do my job well.)

Performance Highlights
(Optional: outstanding achievements)

Professional Experience
(Where and when everything happened)

This format takes more effort to create, but it is the most productive format in database performance, resonates most powerfully with human eyes, and gives the greatest scope for creating a strong *professional brand*, which we covered in Chapter 4.

Choose a Template

If you haven't already, now is a good time to start choosing a resume template. Go to the resume section, Chapter 10, to find examples suitable to your needs. You can get more than 100 resume templates in *Knock 'em Dead Resumes & Templates* at *www.knockemdead.com*.

It is common to look for resume templates that reflect someone in your profession. This is *isn't necessary*! Resume templates are designed to showcase a particular work history; they have never been designed with particular professions or jobs in mind. There is no magically ordained format for resumes by profession. You should look for a layout you find appealing and fits your needs regardless of the job title and work history shown in that example.

Choose your template based on its ability to accommodate your story in a visually appealing way. You will find examples of all these styles in the sample section later in the book, and ready-to-use resume templates in Microsoft Word in the eBook section at the *www.knockemdead.com*.

John William Wisher, MBA
1234 Bainbridge Blvd.
West Chicago, IL 60185

example@email.net

630.555.1234 630.555.2345

Expert leadership in cost effective supply chain, vendor, and project management within *Fortune* organizations.

EXECUTIVE PROFILE

A visionary, forward-thinking SUPPLY CHAIN AND LOGISTICS LEADER offering 20+ years of progressive growth and outstanding success streamlining operations across a wide range of industries. Excellent negotiation and relationship management skills with ability to inspire teams to outperform expectations. Proven record of delivering a synchronized supply chain approach through strategic models closely mirroring business plan to dramatically optimize ROI and manage risk.

Supply Chain Strategy:—Successfully led over 500 supply chain management initiatives across a wide spectrum of businesses, negotiating agreements from $5K to $27M. Implemented technology solutions and streamlined processes to reduce redundancies and staffing hours, improving both efficiency and productivity. Industries include: automotive and industrial manufacturing, consumer goods, government and defense, health care, high tech, and retail.

Industry Knowledge:—Extensive knowledge base developed from hands-on industry experience. Began career in dock operations with experience in Hub and Package Operations, multi-site retail operations management, to custom supply chain strategy development over twenty-one-year career with UPS.

Supply Chain Process Costing:—Built several information packets on total cost of ownership (TCO) and facilitated several C-level negotiations to identify and confirm opportunities. Worked to increase awareness among stakeholders on efficiencies and cost-saving measures ROI. Delivered $3.75M total cost savings to client base over three-year period.

Operations Reorganization:—Designed and implemented new sales force alignment and reporting structure; increased daily sales calls by 20%, reduced travel mileage 23%, and head count by nine; total annual cost savings of $920K.

Logistics:—Experienced across all modes of transportation: ocean, air freight, LTL, TL, mail services, and small package. Performs complex analysis to develop strategy based on cost and delivery requirements.

Project Management:—Implemented complete $1.2M redesign of 11 new UPS Customer Centers. Managed vendor and lease negotiations, developed budgets, training, and sales structure. All 11 centers up and operational on time and on budget.

Cost & Process Improvements

- Implemented complete warehouse redesign for a large optical distributor. Optimized warehouse operations through engineering a new warehouse design, integrating and automating technology, and synchronization of goods movement through ocean, air, ground, and mail services. Reduced transportation expense by 15%, increased production levels by 25%, reduced inventory by 15% and staffing by 20%.

- Built custom supply chain for a nationally recognized golf club manufacturer. Improved service levels by 30%, reduced damage by 45%, and integrated technology to support shipping process automation, reducing billing function staffing hours 50%.

Trust-Based Leadership

Vendor/Client Negotiations

Cross-Functional Collaboration

Supply Chain Mapping

Financial Logistics Analysis

Contingency Planning

Risk Management

Competitive Analysis

Haz Mat Compliance

Inventory Planning, Control, & Distribution

Recruiting/Training/Development

Project Management

Organizational Change Management

Distributive Computing

Budget Management

Labor Relations

The Combination Resume (page 2)

PROFESSIONAL BACKGROUND

United Parcel Service (UPS), Addison, IL   1986 to Present
World's largest package-delivery company and global leader in supply chain services, offering an extensive range of options for synchronizing the movement of goods, information, and funds. Serves more than 200 countries and territories worldwide and operates the largest franchise shipping chain, the UPS Store.

DIRECTOR/AREA MANAGER—SUPPLY CHAIN SALES, 2005–Present

Promoted to lead and develop a cross-functional sales force of 18 in consultative supply chain management services to Chicago-area businesses. Directs development of integrated supply chain management solutions across all modes of transportation, closely mirroring client business plans. Mentors team in Demand Responsive Model, a proven methodology to quickly align internal and external resources with changing market demands, situational requirements, and mission critical conditions. Manages $100M P&L.

Accomplishments:
- Implements over 100 multimillion-dollar supply chain integrations per year with 14% annual growth on 8% plan.
- Develops future organizational leaders; four staff members promoted through effective mentoring and development.
- Choreographed a supply chain movement from the Pacific Rim for a global fast-food chain to deliver 300k cartons to 15k locations all on the same day. Utilized modes of ocean, TL, air, and ground services, allowing for a national release synchronized to all locations on the same release date.
- Designed and implemented an automated reverse logistics program for a nationally recognized health food/supplement distributor. Automated returns process to reduce touches and costly staffing hours. Eliminated front-end phone contact using technology and web automation.

MARKETING MANAGER   2004 to 2005

Fast-tracked to streamline sales processes, increasing performance. Performed analysis of sales territory, historical data, operations alignment, reporting structure, and sales trends to devise solutions. Managed and coached area managers in business-plan development and execution of sales strategies. Delivered staff development in cost-reduction strategies and compliance requirements. Accountable for $500M P&L.

Accomplishments:
- Drove $500M+ in local market sales. Grew revenues 2004/2005 revenues 12% and 7% respectively.

RETAIL CHANNEL/OPERATIONS MANAGER   2002 to 2004

Charged with turning around this underperforming business unit. Managed development and implementation of new retail strategy across northern Illinois. Rebranded UPS Customer Centers and the UPS Store. Performed vendor negotiations and collaborated with nine regions to support additional implementations.

Accomplishments:
- Developed key revenue-generating initiatives across multiple channels. Attained 65% growth in discretionary sales. Several strategies adopted across the national organization.
- Re-engineered inventory for over 1,000 dropoff locations, reduced lease expenses by 45% and inventory levels by 40% through weekly measurement, inventory level development by SKU, order process automation, and order consolidation.
- Implemented new retail sales associate structure in 1,100 locations; scored highest national service levels by mystery shoppers.
- Selected as Corporate team member on Mail Boxes Etc. acquisition integration.

PROJECT MANAGER   2001 to 2002

Selected to support several underperforming business areas. Managed key segments of district business initiatives and compliance measures for 1,000 dropoff locations. Reported on status to corporate management. Supervised office staff of 16. Negotiated vendor and lease agreements.

Accomplishments:
- Rolled out and managed ongoing Haz Mat compliance program for all locations.
- Generated $6M in sales through cross-functional lead program and increased participation from 20% to 100%.
- Attained union workforce sponsorship of support-growth program through careful negotiations and persuasion.

SENIOR ACCOUNT MANAGER   1999 to 2001

Delivered $2.8M in growth on $1.1M plan, rated 3rd of 53 managers in revenue generation

ACCOUNT MANAGER   1997 to 1998

Top producer out of 53; $1.3M sales on $500K plan.

The Combination Resume (page 3)

John William Wisher, MBA

SERVICE PROVIDER   1994 to 1996
Top producer out of 53; $1.3M sales on $500K plan.

SUPERVISOR OF PACKAGE OPERATIONS   1994
Managed 65 full-time service providers. Performed post-routine analysis, operating strategy development, compliance, payroll, service failure recovery, and new technology implementation. Met 100% DOT and Haz Mat compliance. Reduced post-delivery staffing time by 50% and missed pickups by 65%.

SUPERVISOR OF HUB OPERATIONS   1988 to 1994
Managed up to 100 union employees and staff processing 75K pieces per day involving 40+ outbound bays. Performed complex staff scheduling and maintained low turnover rates. Designed new management reporting format, reducing administrative time by 20% and improved load quality by 30%.

OPERATIONS DOCK WORKER AND TRAINING LEAD   1986 to 1987

EDUCATION
MBA
National Louis University, Wheaton, IL, *4.0 GPA*

BA, Business, Supply Chain Management

Elmhurst College, Elmhurst, IL, *3.84 GPA, Magna cum laude*

Additional Specialized Courses:
- Supply Chain Mapping, 20 Hours
- Financial Logistics Analysis (FLOGAT), 10 Hours
- Hazardous Materials, 20 Hours
- Labor Relations, 30 Hours
- Managers Leadership School, 100 Hours
- Hazardous Materials, 20 Hours
- Managing from the Heart, 30 Hours

The Simplest, Smartest, Fastest Way to Write Your Resume— Keep It Simple, Stupid

THE MOST EFFECTIVE way to get a premium, powerful resume for a professional job in the shortest time with the least amount of hassle.

No one likes writing a resume, but you have to trust me when I tell you that there is no easier way than the way I am showing you. That shortcut you're thinking of? It won't work. If it did, I'd be telling you about it. This is the most streamlined way I know to give you a premium, powerful resume in the shortest time with the least amount of hassle.

Five Steps to a Great Resume

Your resume is a concise sales document that captures a snapshot of your professional life in a couple of short pages. A great finished product usually takes five steps:

1. A first draft to capture all the essentials on a basic resume template.
2. Two, three, five, or more gradually improving versions built over a week or more, as you tweak words and phrases; add and subtract; and cut, move, and paste until you cannot possibly improve it further.

   During this week or so, you should work on your resume for a couple of hours every day as you simultaneously organize, or reorganize, your job search. If you are smart enough to recognize that you need to rethink your resume to perform in the new world of work, common sense also whispers that you probably need to retool your entire approach to job search.
3. A third draft to integrate your defined professional brand throughout the resume.
4. A fourth draft, where you paste your work so far into different templates and choose the one(s) best for you. As you do this, it is quite likely that you will still be tweaking a word here and there.
5. A final draft of your formatted resume where you do a grammatical edit and complete the polishing process.

Putting Together Your First Draft

With your completed TJD and Resume and Competitive Difference Questionnaires in hand, you know both *what the customer wants* and what you have to offer. Now you need to start assembling the pieces in a way that tells your story effectively.

To help you do this most efficiently, I've created a resume *Layout Template* for you. You use this to capture graphically and review the components your resume will contain. It is *not* intended as a template for your finished resume; it's just a gathering place for all the components of a cutting-edge resume. By using it, you'll become familiar with all the resume building blocks, and when the time comes to decide on a layout and template, everything will be ready to cut and paste.

Name

Address   Telephone   Email address

Target Job Title

A target job title, perhaps followed by an *optional* brand statement, as in the following example, helps database visibility and gives focus to the reader. The brief optional brand statement delivers value proposition you bring to the job, example:

Pharmaceutical Sales

Poised to outperform in pharmaceutical software sales repeating records of achievement with major pharmaceutical companies

Performance Profile/Performance Summary

What goes here? Take the most common requirements from your TJD and rewrite as a performance profile/performance summary. Helps database visibility and creates immediate resonance with reader's eyes. A maximum five lines of text can be followed by a second paragraph or list of bullets.

Core Competencies

A list of all the skills you identified in your TJD. Repeat each skill listed here in context of the jobs where it was applied. This increases database visibility and gives reader immediate focus, "Oh s/he can talk about all of these things . . ." Example:

4-Handed Dentistry	Infection Control	Preventative Care
Oral Surgery/Extraction	Casts/Impressions	Emergency Treatment
Root Canals	Diagnostic X-Rays	Instrument Sterilization
Prosthetics/Restorations	Teeth Whitening	Radiology

Technical Competencies

An optional category depending on professional relevance.

Performance Highlights

An optional category depending on your experience.

Professional Experience

Employer's name	Dates
The company's focus	
Job Title	

If you are going to bold/caps anything, draw attention to what is most important: your job title.

Contact information at the top of each page. Keep your resume tightly edited but do not worry about page count. Reason: Jobs are more complex than they used to be, the additional info increases database performance, and readers won't mind as long as the resume is telling a relevant story.

Employer's name	Dates
The company's focus	
Job title	

Repeat employment history as necessary.

Education
May come earlier if these are critical professional credentials (as in medicine, law, etc.) that are especially relevant to job requirements, or highlight an important strength.

Licenses/Professional Accreditations
May come earlier if these credentials are critical credentials, especially relevant, or highlight an important strength.

Ongoing Professional Education

Professional Organizations/Affiliations

Publications, Patents, Speaking

Languages
Add them to the end of performance profile/performance summary and repeat them here.

Military Service

Extracurricular Interests
Add them here, if they relate to the job. Sports demonstrate fitness; chess, etc., denotes analytical skills; they can all be relevant.

(Closing brand statement)
Optional. If you use one, do *not* give it a heading,
as in the above parentheses. Example:
"I believe that leadership by example and conscientious performance management underlies my department's consistent customer satisfaction ratings."

(References)

Never list references on your resume. Employers *assume* that your references are available, but it certainly doesn't hurt to end with a bold statement (but only if you have empty space at the end of the page and nothing else to add):

References Available on Request
Or
Excellent references available on request.
Or
My references will verify everything in this resume.

Why can't you choose a template right now? Because you select a template based on its layout and suitability to tell a particular story. This means you first have to determine all the components that will be in your story, and you don't know that till you've collected all the relevant information in one place. It's too soon to choose final templates at this point.

The layout template is *not* intended as a final resume template, but as a tool to help you learn the component parts your resume needs to be maximally productive and to give you a sense of progress in the resume-development process.

You'll find more than 100 resume templates on *www.knockemdead.com* in the eBook *Knock 'em Dead Resume Templates.*

How to Build Your Resume

Name

Give your first and last name only because that is the way you introduce yourself to someone in person. It isn't necessary to include your middle name(s), and unless you are known by your initials, don't use them on your resume.

It is not necessary to place Mr., Ms., Miss, or Mrs. before your name, unless yours is a unisex name like Jamie, Carroll, or Leslie; if you feel it necessary, it is acceptable to write Mr. Jamie Jones or Ms. Jamie Jackson. If you always add Jr. or III when you sign your name and that is the way you are addressed to avoid confusion, go ahead and use it.

Address

If you abbreviate—such as with *St.* or *Apt.*—be consistent. The state of your residence, however, is always abbreviated, for example: MN, WV, LA. The accepted format for laying out your address looks like this:

Maxwell Krieger
9 Central Avenue, Apartment 38
New York, NY 23456

Many people feel that, from a personal privacy perspective, street addresses are no longer necessary on a resume, so this is equally acceptable:

Maxwell Krieger
New York, NY 23456

But with a resume, if space is an issue, you can put your contact information on a single line:

Maxwell Krieger, New York, NY 23456

It is no longer thought necessary to include your exact physical address; city and state is considered adequate.

If you are employed and pursuing a confidential job search, it is acceptable to omit both your name and address. Your name would be replaced by a target job title and followed by email and telephone contact information.

Telephone Number

Always include your area code and never use a work telephone number. If you still have a landline, most telephone companies now have a master-ring feature, allowing you, at no extra charge, to have two or three different numbers on your phone line, each with a distinctive ring. It might not be a bad idea to use one of these available alternate numbers as your permanent career-management number. Then whenever it rings, you can be sure to finish crunching the potato chips before answering the call.

You should include your cell number, and if you don't have a master-ring system through your telephone provider, you might decide to use the cell number as your primary contact. Because we tend to answer our cell phones at all times, if a job call comes at a bad time, you should be prepared to say that you'd like to talk but will need to call back.

Email As a Marketing Tool

In an Internet-based job search, your email address is a powerful marketing tool, but for most job hunters it's a lost opportunity. Since it's the first thing any recruiter or potential employer sees, it's a perfect opportunity for immediately positioning your credentials.

This might be a good time to retire those addresses like binkypoo@yahoo.com, bigboy@ hotmail.com, or DDdoll@live.com, or at least restrict them to exclusively nonprofessional activities where they won't detract from your professional reputation.

Most email hosts allow you to register a number of different email addresses, so simply add an email account devoted exclusively to your job search and career-management affairs.

Create an account name that reveals something about your professional profile, such as *SystemAnalyst@hotmail.com* or *TopAccountant@yahoo.com*.

This type of email address acts as a headline to tell the reader who is writing, and to give some idea of what the *communication* is about. When names like *TopAccountant@yahoo.com* are already taken, you will be encouraged to accept something like *topaccountant1367@yahoo.com*.

Before you accept this, try adding your area code (*TopAccountant516@yahoo.com*) or your zip code (*TopAccountant11579@yahoo.com*), both of which add information useful to an employer in your local target market but which usually won't mean much to someone outside of that market.

Using a profession-oriented email address does double duty: It succinctly introduces the *professional you*, and it protects your identity. In a competitive job search, the little things can make a big difference; the way you introduce yourself is one of them. Finally, your email address is an integral part of your contact information, and should always be hyperlinked on your resume so that a simple click will launch an email so the reader can respond easily. It's another of those little things your competitors forget.

> *The contact information on your resume can also include a link to your LinkedIn profile. You can hyperlink your customized LI or add a LinkedIn badge that contains your LI URL.*

We are just entering the world where a link on your resume to a social media profile is becoming a standard requirement for creating a powerful resume and to date, as a profession, we have been adding the link immediately under the email address.

Just as we go to press with this edition, at *www.knockemdead.com* professional resume-writing services we are testing a variation of this where we put the LI badge at the end of the resume. Our thinking has been that a reader won't click on a social media address unless the candidate represented is of interest, so we are testing having that badge at the very end of the resume; if a recruiter is interested this is where and when he or she would logically click on the link to learn more.

I cannot yet tell you if it works or not, but I suggest you might try our testing approach. We are creating separate versions of the resume for our clients that have the badge at the front end and back end of the resume and suggesting they send out twenty of each to see which performs better for them. At this time I can only suggest the same and ask you to let me know the results.

Target Job Title

Eighty percent of resumes lack a target job title, and this makes a resume less accessible to a harried recruiter who might spend as little as five seconds reviewing it before moving on to another candidate's resume where the writer has better focus and *communication skills*.

Recruiters use a target job title in database searches, so using one at the start of your resume helps it get pulled from a resume database for review by a recruiter. Additionally, once it is in front of human eyes, having a target job title gives both a recruiter and hiring manager immediate visual focus.

A target job title comes immediately after your contact information, at the top of your resume, and is most often centered on the page, is in a larger font than body copy, and is often in bold. It acts in the same way as a movie, TV show, and book or blog title: It draws the reader in by giving him a focus for what he is about to read.

The first thing any resume reader looks for is focus. A target job title explains what the resume is about. Decide on a target job title by taking all the title variations you collected in the TJD process. You should choose a common or generic target job title, something to widen your appeal. Here are some examples taken from finished resumes:

- **Certified Occupational Health Nurse Specialist**
- **Global Operations Executive**
- **Campaign Field Director**
- **Marketing Management**
- **Operations/Human Resources/Labor Relations/Staff Development**
- **Career Services Professional**
- **Operations Management**
- **Healthcare Review—Clinical Consultant**
- **Agricultural/Environmental Manager**
- **Horticultural Buying—International Experience**

Integrating a Professional Brand Into Your Resume

Your *professional brand* is communicated throughout your resume, but never more so than with your opening (and sometimes closing) brand statements. The first place you begin to establish a *professional brand* is with your target job title, where you consciously decide on the job that best allows you to package your skill sets and create a *professional brand*.

A target job title followed by a considered brand statement gives the reader a fast focus on the resume's purpose and the type of person it represents. Your opening brand statement is a short phrase following the target job title that defines what you will bring to the job. It says, "These are the benefits my presence on your payroll will bring to your team and your company."

Opening Brand Statement

Notice how the following brand statements focus on the benefits brought to the job, but do not take up space identifying the specifics of how this was done. *Professional brand* statements often start with an action verb such as "Poised to," "Delivering," "Dedicated to," " Bringing," "Positioned to," or "Constructing":

Pharmaceutical Sales Management Professional

Poised to outperform in pharmaceutical software sales, repeating records of achievement with major pharmaceutical companies.

Senior Operations/Plant Management Professional

Dedicated to continuous improvement ~ Lean Six Sigma ~ Startup & turnaround operations ~ Mergers & change management ~ Process & productivity optimization ~ Logistics & supply chain

Bank Collections Management

Equipped to continue excelling in loss mitigation/collections/recovery management.

Mechanical/Design/Structural Engineer

Delivering high volume of complex structural and design projects for global companies in Manufacturing / Construction / Power Generation.

Account Management/Client Communications Manager

Reliably achieving performance improvement and compliance within Financial Services Industry.

Marketing Communications

Consistently delivering successful strategic marketing, media relations, & special events.

Administrative/Office Support Professional

Ready, willing, and competent; detail-oriented problem solver; consistently forges effective working relationships with all publics.

Senior Engineering Executive

Bringing sound technical skills, strong business acumen, and real management skills to technical projects and personnel in a fast-paced environment.

Use Headlines to Guide the Reader

Headlines act like signposts, guiding a jaded and distracted reader through your resume. Your resume's job is to open as many doors for you as it can. It does this by making the information as accessible as possible to the target customer. Using headlines in your resume is both a visual and textual aid to comprehension, helping that tired-eyed, distracted reader absorb your message. Here are the headlines you will most likely use and the way they guide and make life easy for the reader:

Target Job Title
(Here's the job I'm after)

Performance Profile or **Performance/Career/Executive Summary**
(This is what I can do for you)

Core/Professional Competencies
(Here are all the key professional skills that help me do my job well)

Technology Competencies
(Here are the *technology skills* that help me do my job well)

Performance Highlights
(Here are some examples of my performance using the expertise you are interested in)

Professional Experience
(Where and when everything happened)

In little more than half a page, these headlines help the reader gain a quick grip on what you can bring to the table. Once you have a recruiter's attention, she will read your whole resume with serious attention.

Consistent Brand Messaging

Integrate your professional strengths, the building blocks of your brand, into the resume as you write it. As you revise and polish your resume, monitor and tweak your work to ensure that all the messaging supports the central concepts of your brand, especially in these sections of your resume:

- Performance Profile
- Professional Competencies
- Performance/Career Highlights
- Professional Experience
- Closing Brand Statement

Performance Profile

After your target job title and opening brand statement comes the performance profile. The essence of every manager's (read: hiring authority's) job is performance management, and they spend a portion of every year thinking about and giving performance reviews. For that reason, this new and powerful headline will resonate with every manager. It speaks to your grasp of the job and your goal orientation. It also encourages you to stay with the issues you know to be important to your target readers.

Take the major requirements from your TJD and turn them into 3–5 sentences, or no more than five lines without a paragraph break. The Performance Profile should clearly convey your understanding of the customer's priorities.

You can use headlines like Career/Professional/Executive Summary, but be aware that these traditional headlines encourage you to think about everything *you've* done rather than focus on customer needs.

Never Use Job Objective

Stay away from Job Objective (or Career Objective) if you can, for these reasons:

1. At this stage, no one cares what you want. The only issue is whether you can do the job.
2. Job Objective as a headline will not help your performance in database searches or resonate with recruiters' eyes, so you are wasting valuable selling space.

If you must use a Job Objective because you are at the start of your career and have no experience, that's okay—your competitors are in the same boat. Tilt the game in your favor by starting your objective with "The opportunity to" and then, referring to your TJD exercise, rewrite the target job's major priorities as your job objective. This will make a big difference in your resume's *productivity*.

Of the three traditional options for this important section of your resume—Career Summary, Job Objective, and Performance Profile—you will find the "Performance Profile" headline most productive. Recruiters and managers respond because it succinctly captures what you bring to the job.

How to Create a Performance Profile

The Performance Profile or Performance Summary section of your resume comes right after the Target Job Title. Its intent is to capture your skills as they relate to the job's most dominant requirements; this gets the critical skills of the job and its most relevant keywords right at the front of the resume. This gives the document focus for the reader and helps make the resume more discoverable in database searches. To create a powerful Performance Profile:

1. Take the 3–6 most important/common requirements identified in your TJD exercise and write 3–6 bulleted statements that capture your skills as they relate to the priorities identified in your TJD.
2. Combine all this information into just 3–5 short sentences. Together they will clearly show what you bring to the target job.
3. Check against your TJD to see that, wherever possible, you use the same words employers are using.
4. Dense blocks of text are hard on the eyes. If you have more than five lines, break the text into two paragraphs.

Your goal with a performance profile is to demonstrate that you possess exactly the kinds of skills employers seek when hiring this type of person. It's a powerful way to open your resume both for its impact with the resume search engines and because it gives the readers the information they need: You're explaining what you bring to the table, based on their own prioritization of needs.

The finished product will be a performance profile that captures the *professional you* in words most likely to be used in database searches and have a familiar ring to hiring managers' ears.

Using Keywords in a Performance Profile

The words that employers use in job postings will be used by recruiters as search terms when they are searching the resume databases; so *using the same words in your resume as employers do in their job postings—words you know are important—will help get your resume pulled from the resume databases into which you load it.* Use them immediately, because search engine algorithms give weight to placement of words nearer the top of a document. Use as many keywords as you reasonably can in your performance profile.

Here's a performance profile for a Corporate Communications Management professional:

PERFORMANCE PROFILE

9 years' strategic communications experience, developing high-impact and cost-efficient media outreach plans for consumer and business audiences in media, entertainment, and technology practice areas. Experienced in managing corporate and personal crisis communications. Goal and deadline oriented, with five years' experience managing internal and external communications. Adept at working with multiple teams and stakeholders.

Professional Competencies

A Professional/Core Competencies section is designed to capture all the skills you bring to your work in a succinct and easily accessible format, usually single words or short phrases in three or four columns. *Think of your core competencies section as an electronic business card that allows you to network with computers.* The positioning of likely keywords at the top of a document is favored by the search engines, and will help your resume's ranking in database searches; each one acts as an interest generator for the recruiter or hiring manager.

Recruiters and hiring managers appreciate a Professional Competencies section as a summary of the resume's focus. Each keyword or phrase acts as an affirmation of a skill area and possible topic of conversation. Confirming lots of topics to talk about so early in the resume is a big bonus for your candidacy. It acts as a preface to the body copy, in effect saying, "Hey, here are all the headlines. The stories behind them are immediately below," so the reader will pay closer attention.

There's no need to use articles or conjunctions. Just list the word, starting with a capital—"Forecasting," for example—or a phrase, such as "Financial Modeling."

Here's an example of a Competencies section for a PR professional:

Professional Competencies

High-Tech Public Relations	Project Management
Strategic Communications	Detail Oriented
Executive Communications	Acquisition
PR Messaging & Media Relations	Positioning
Craft and Place Stories	Pitch Media
Strong Writing Skills	Market Research
Media Training	Build & Lead Teams
Multiple Projects	Mentor
Story Placement	Client Satisfaction
Counsel Executives	Organizational Skills
Tactics	Thought Leadership
Strong Editing Skills	PR Counsel
Collateral Materials	Social Media
New Business	Leadership Branding
Team Management	Story Telling
Budget Management	Analyst Relations
Account Management	

And an example from a Hospitality Management resume:

Core Competencies

- Revenue Optimization
- Staff Development
- Spanish
- Customer Service
- Brand Integrity
- P&L
- Payroll
- Food Cost Reduction
- Training Manuals
- Cost Containment
- Team Building
- Time Management
- Productivity Growth
- Client Relations
- Turnover Reduction
- 250 Covers Daily
- 300 Pre-Theater
- Purchasing
- POS Systems
- Recruitment & Selection
- Operations Management
- Policy & Procedures
- Accounting/POS Support
- Inventory Control
- Problem Solving
- Liquor Inventory
- Cash Reconciliation
- Administration
- Marketing/Advertising

If you work in technology, or you have developed an extensive slate of technology competencies, you might choose to add a Technology Competencies section. It breaks up the page and it is easier to absorb when they are separated.

Here's an example of a separate Technology Competencies section:

Technology Competencies

Operating Systems:	Unix, Windows (2000, XP, 7), DOS
Languages:	C, C++, Java, Pascal, Assembly Languages (Z8000, 808x, DSP)
Methodologies:	TL9000, Digital Six Sigma
Software:	MS Office, Adobe FrameMaker, Matlab
RDBMS:	DOORS, Oracle 7.x
Protocols:	TCP/IP, SS7ISUP, A1, ANSI, TL1, SNMP
Tools:	Teamplay, ClearCase, ClearQuest, M-Gatekeeper, Exceed, Visio, DocExpress, Compass
Other:	CDMA Telecom Standards – 3GPP2 (Including TIA/EIA-2001, TIA-EIA-41, TIA/EIA-664), ITU-T, AMPS

Adding to Professional Competencies

Your resume is a living document, and its content may well change as your job search progresses. Whenever you come across keywords in job postings that reflect your capabilities, but which are not in your resume, it is time to add them. If nowhere else, at least put them in the Professional Competencies section.

Use Keywords Often

1. Give the most important of your professional competencies first in the Performance Profile section of your resume.
2. Include a complete list of your skills in the Professional Competencies section. It is the perfect spot to list the technical acronyms and professional jargon that speak to the range of your professional skills, especially if they won't fit into the Professional Experience section of your resume.
3. A Professional Competencies section should remind you to use as many of the keywords as you can in the Professional Experience part of your resume, where usage will show the context in which those skills were developed and applied.

This strategy will make your resume data dense for improved database performance, while also demonstrating that you have the relevant skills and putting them in context for the recruiter in a **visually accessible** manner. Yes, it will make your resume longer (we'll discuss this issue shortly); just know it has a much better chance of being pulled from the resume databases, and because its content is completely relevant to the needs of the job and readily accessible to the recruiter, you will get an improved response rate.

Make Room for Supporting Skills on Your Resume

If you want your resume pulled from the databases and read with serious attention, you know it needs to focus on the skills you bring to a single target job. However, employers still want to know about your supporting skills.

For example, a colleague and hiring manager in the IT world says, "I don't just want to see evidence that someone is a hotshot in, say, the .NET Framework; I also want to see that he/she can get around with other languages, so that I know (a) that the candidate understands programming as distinct from just .NET, and (b) that if my company introduces a new programming language/development environment in the future, I have someone who will be able to handle that."

You can still get this important information about *supporting skills* into your resume, without taking up too much room, by adding them to your Professional Competencies section.

You'll start the section with those skills most important to your target job, but you can then add all those skills that support your all-around professionalism.

The appearance of these *supporting skills* in the Professional Competencies section can help your resume's performance in database searches, and it helps put your primary skills in the larger context of your complete professional abilities. And because they are supporting skills, it doesn't matter that you don't include them in the context of the jobs you've held.

Skills Prioritization

Your professional skills are most readily accessible when they appear in three or four columns. This section contains a list of your important professional skills and so needs to be near the top of your resume, for these reasons:

1. Coming after a Target Job Title and a Performance Summary that focuses on the skills you bring to the target job, skills reflect employer priorities. You are helping both the discoverability of your resume when it sits in resume databases and its impact upon knowledgeable readers.

2. The Applicant Tracking System (ATS) programs that recruiters use to search resume databases in turn use algorithms that reward relevant words near the front of a document as a means of judging that document's relevance to the recruiters' search terms. So your professional skills need to be relevant to the target job and come near the top of your resume—just as we have been suggesting for years. (This, perhaps, is because I have been using ATS systems since 1987 when they first came to the fore and have an understanding of how they work.)

3. A recent study showed that once a resume has been pulled from a resume database, recruiters spend an average of six seconds on a first-time scan of that resume. This means your qualifications have to jump out. You make them do so by using a Target Job Title, followed by a Performance Summary that reflects employer priorities as you determined in your TJD work, and followed in turn by a Professional Skills section that supports all the above claims of professional competency with a list of your relevant skills. This gives a recruiter plenty of time to see your abilities in that first six-second scan.

However there is another issue at play when it comes to the Professional Skills section of your resume. Ultimately it will be read by someone who really knows this job, who is aware of what's a "must-have" and what's a "nice to have."

The easiest way to explain this is with an example: A couple of years back we prepared a resume for a dental assistant, and she gave us a list of all the important *technical skills* of her job. We put these into three columns for visual accessibility, and something terrible jumped out at me: Her list started with "Teeth whitening" and ended with "Four-handed dentistry." What was so terrible about this? All the skills were there.

Yes they were, but in the West we read from left to right and top to bottom, so common sense says that the most important skills for a job should come before the less important skills. We immediately switched these phrases so that "Four-handed dentistry" (a highly marketable skill) came first and "Teeth whitening" (a more routine skill) came last.

Bear this story in mind when you are creating your own Professional Skills section: By prioritizing the skills you are subtly telling the man or woman who will ultimately hire you that you have a firm grasp of the relative importance of all the necessary *professional skills* of your work. That point adds to the clear focus and power of the opening first half page of your resume. If you follow these directions, the opening sections of your resume will show that:

- You can do the job
- Your skills list backs up your statements of ability
- You understand the relative importance of the component parts of your job.

The result is that in the first half page of your resume, and well within the framework of a six-second scan, you have gone a long way toward making the short list of candidates who will be brought in for interview.

Grids and Tables in Resume Formatting

A moment ago, I mentioned Applicant Tracking Systems. These came into being almost thirty years ago to help recruiters find resumes in their growing databases. In the early days, the ATS programs had problems dealing with italics, lines, boxes, bolding, some kinds of bullets, the tables that give resume layout a precise snappy look, and some fonts; they also had difficulties reading a lot of various layouts.

We have come a long way in twenty-seven years. Just as you are not using the software you used in the mid 1980s (if you were alive and working then), neither are companies.

The colleagues whom I trust on these matters don't think these formatting issues are nearly of the importance they used to be. Personally, I don't think that the precise formatting that comes with the use of grids and tables matters at all.

For example, you can usually count on Europe and elsewhere to be behind the United States when it comes to technology (yes, I know there are exceptions but let's stick to the lesson point being made here). Last year we wrote a resume for a European Medicines Agency marketing guy living in Vienna, Austria. His resume was built with grids and tables; he uploaded it into fifteen then ultimately twenty-five databases and got interviews with all seven of his top target companies within two weeks. The formatting had no negative impact whatsoever. Common sense tells me that while corporations tend to keep up-to-date with new software releases, even when they don't, they certainly are not using twenty-seven-year-old software.

You can achieve the same look without formatting with grids and tables if you are feeling wary; it just takes longer, so ultimately the decision is up to you.

Performance/Career Highlights

In completing the resume questionnaire, you gathered evidence of achievements and contributions in your work and quantified them whenever you could. Now is the chance to choose 2–4 of these (depending on the depth of your experience) as standout contributions. Capture them in confident statements:

Performance Highlights

35% increase in on-time delivery + 20% reduction in client complaints

Effective Operations Management demands understanding every department's unique problems and timelines. Building these considerations into daily activities helped:

- Finance & Supply Chain, saved $55,000 in last three quarters
- Increased productivity, with a 35% increase in on-time delivery

These on-time delivery increases were achieved with improved communications, connecting Purchasing, Supply Chain, Customers, and Customer Service:

- Delivered 20% reduction in client complaints

Professional Experience

Company Names

Each job needs to be identified with an employer. There is no need to include specific contact information, although it can be useful to include the city and state. When working for a multidivision corporation, you may want to list the divisional employer.

Employment Dates

A resume without employment dates considerably underperforms a resume that has dates, and those dates need to be accurate because they can be checked. With a steady work history and no employment gaps, you can be very specific:

January 2007–September 2011

If you had an employment gap of six months in, say, 2008, you can disguise this:

MBO Inc.   2006–2008

XYZ Inc.   2008–present

I am *not* suggesting that you should lie about your work history, and you must be prepared to answer honestly and without hesitation if you are asked.

If you abbreviate employment dates, be sure to do so consistently. It is quite acceptable to list annual dates, rather than month and year. Remember, when references get checked, the first things verified are dates of employment and leaving salary; untruths in either of these areas are grounds for dismissal with cause, and that can dog your footsteps into the future.

Layout for Dates and Jobs

If you don't have problems with too many jobs in your work history, you want the dates to jump out because it makes information gathering easier for the reader. The best way to do this is to right justify dates like this:

Microsoft   **2009–Present**

If you have had promotions while with a company, you want to make this jump right off the page and this is the way you would do it. In our example the job hunter has held four progressively more responsible jobs in ten years, so the listing first captures the full scale of growth and then goes into the detail of each job as identified by title and dates.

Microsoft   **2009–Present**
Senior Business Analyst   2012–Present
Sales Operations Associate   2010–2012
Sales Compensation Analyst   2009–2010
DATES in the above must be vertically aligned, last entry is out of alignment

Senior Business Analyst   **2012–Present**
(Job detail would follow here)

Continuity of employment is clear, as is consistent professional growth, and we can see that each job is going to be handled in turn.

Individual Jobs

Each section of the resume represents another opportunity to communicate your unique achievements and contributions. Replace time-worn descriptions in the Professional Experience section . . . :

- *Before:* Responsible for identifying and developing new accounts.

  . . . with strong action statements:

- *After:* Drove advances in market share and revitalized stalled business by persistently networking and pursuing forgotten market pockets—lost sales, smaller, untapped businesses/prospects overlooked by competition.

The area where you address your responsibilities and achievements in each job, *as they relate to the customer's needs you identified during TJD,* is the meat of your resume. When working on this part of your resume, constantly refer to your TJD to remind yourself of the details target employers are most likely to want to read about and the keywords and phrases that will help your resume perform in recruiters' database searches.

The responsibilities and contributions you identify here are those functions that best relate to the needs of the target job. They do not necessarily correspond with how you spent the majority of your working day, nor are they related to how you might prefer to spend your working day. This can perhaps best be illustrated by showing you part of a resume that came to my desk recently. It is the work of a professional who listed her title and duties for one job like this:

"Motivated a sales staff of six, recruited, trained, managed. Hired to improve sales. Sales Manager increased sales."

The writer mistakenly listed everything in the reverse order of importance. She's not focused on the items' relative importance *to a future employer,* who, above all, will want to hire someone who can increase sales. She also wasted space stating the obvious about the reason she was hired as a sales manager: to improve sales. Let's look at what subsequent restructuring achieved:

Sales Manager: Hired to turn around stagnant sales force. Successfully recruited, trained, managed, and motivated sales staff of six. Result: 22 percent sales gain over first year. Notice how this is clearly focused on the essentials of any sales manager's job: to increase income for the company.

"Hired to turn around stagnant sales force": *Demonstrates her skills and responsibilities.*

"Successfully recruited, trained, managed, and motivated a sales staff of six. Result: 22 percent sales gain over first year": *Shows what she subsequently did with the sales staff, and exactly how well she did it.*

By making these changes, her responsibilities and achievements become more important in the light of the problems they solved. Be sure to match your narrative to employers' needs and to the priorities of that target job. Avoid exaggeration of your accomplishments. It isn't necessary.

Achievements

Business has very limited interests. In fact, those interests can be reduced to a single phrase: making a profit. This is done in just three ways:

1. By *saving money* for the company
2. By *increasing productivity*, which in turn *saves money* and provides the opportunity to *make more money* in the time saved
3. By simply *earning money* for the company

That does not mean that you should address only these points in your resume and ignore valuable contributions that cannot be quantified. But it does mean that you should *try to quantify your achievements whenever you can.*

Pick 2–4 accomplishments for each job title and edit them down to bite-sized chunks that read like a telegram. Write as if you had to pay for each entry by the word—this approach can help you pack a lot of information into a short space. The resulting abbreviated style will help convey a sense of immediacy to the reader. I'll use an example we can all relate to:

Responsible for new and used car sales. Earned "Salesman of the Year" awards, 2014 and 2015. Record holder: Most Cars Sold in One Year.

Here's another example from a fundraiser's resume:

- Created an annual giving program to raise operating funds. Raised $2,000,000.
- Targeted, cultivated, and solicited sources including individuals, corporations, foundations, and state and federal agencies. Raised $1,650,000.
- Raised funds for development of the Performing Arts School facility, capital expense, and music and dance programs. Raised $6,356,000.

Now, while you may tell the reader about these achievements, never explain how they were accomplished; the key phrase here is "specifically vague." The intent of your resume is to pique interest and to raise as many questions as you answer. Questions mean interest, interest means talking to you, and *getting conversations started is the primary goal of your resume*!

Prioritize your accomplishments, and quantify them whenever possible and appropriate.

You can cite achievements as part of a sentence/paragraph or as bullets, for example:

Collections:

Developed excellent rapport with customers while significantly shortening payout terms. Turned impending loss into profit. Personally salvaged and increased sales with two multimillion-dollar accounts by providing remedial action for their sales/financial problems.

Collections:

Developed excellent rapport with customers while significantly shortening payout terms:

- Evaluated sales performance; offered suggestions for financing/merchandising, turned impending loss into profit.
- Salvaged two multimillion-dollar problem accounts by providing remedial action for their sales/financial problems. Subsequently increased sales.

Whenever you can, keep each paragraph to a maximum of four or five lines. This ensures that the finished product has plenty of white space so that it is easy on the reader's eyes. If necessary, split one paragraph into two.

Endorsements and Excerpts from Performance Evaluations

You don't see these on resumes very often, but they can make a powerful addition. They are most effective when supporting quantified achievements. These endorsements are not necessary, though, and while they can make a good addition to your resume, they shouldn't be used to excess. One or two are adequate, although I have seen successful resumes where each job entry is finished with a complimentary endorsement.

Here are a couple of examples of how to do them well:

- Sales volume increased from $90 million to $175 million. Acknowledged as "the greatest single gain of the year."
- Earnings increased from $9 million to $18 million. Review stated, "Always has a view for the company bottom line."
- **Professional Performance**

Year	Projection	Sales	Percentage
2011	$240,000	$425,000	177%
2010	$90,000	$106,200	128%
2009	$102,000	$114,000	121%
2008	$114,000	$123,120	117%
2007	$185,000	$192,816	109%
2006	$120,000	$121,000	102%

Charts and Graphs

A picture is worth a thousand words, so if you can use a graphic to make a point, it opens up the page and is infrequent enough to get attention. Here is an example of a graphic insert that shows increasing sales achievements. Compare this statement of achievement . . . :

Revenue Growth—Maintained consistent, year-over-year increase through fluctuating economies

. . . with:

Revenue Growth—Maintained consistent, year-over-year pattern of increasing revenues through robust and downturn economies, from $50,000 to $1.2 million as illustrated below:

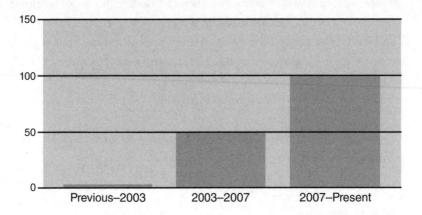

Avoid exaggeration of your accomplishments. It isn't necessary.

Education

Educational history is normally placed wherever it helps your case the most. The exact positioning will vary according to the length of your professional experience, and the importance of your academic achievements to the job and your profession.

If you are recently out of school with little practical experience, your educational credentials might constitute your primary asset and should appear near the beginning of the resume.

After two or three years in the professional world, your academic credentials become less important in most professions, and move to the end of your resume. The exceptions are in professions where academic qualifications dominate—medicine and law, for example. The highest level of academic attainment always comes first: a doctorate, then a master's, followed by a bachelor's degree. For degreed professionals, there is no need to go back further into educational history; it is optional to list prep schools.

It is normal to abbreviate degrees (PhD, MA, BA, BS, etc.). In instances where educational attainment is paramount, it is acceptable to put that degree after your name. Traditionally, this has been the privilege of doctors and lawyers, but there is absolutely no reason that your name shouldn't be followed, for example, by MBA.

List scholarships and awards. More recent graduates will usually also list majors and minors (relevancy permitting—if it helps, use it; if it doesn't, don't). The case is a little more complicated for the seasoned professional. Many human resources people say it makes life easier for them if majors and minors are listed, so they can further sift and grade the applicants. That's good for them, but it might not be good for you. The resume needs to get you in the door, not slam it in your face. So, as omitting majors will never stop you from getting an interview, I suggest you err on the side of safety. Leave them off unless they speak directly to the target job.

If you graduated from high school and attended college but didn't graduate, you may be tempted to list your high school diploma first, followed by the name of the college you attended. That would give the wrong emphasis: It says you are a college dropout and identifies you as a high school graduate. In this instance, you would list your college and area of study, but omit any reference to graduation or earlier educational history.

Employers really appreciate people who invest in their future and there's proof from the U.S. Department of Education to back it up. Of high school graduates who enrolled in any associate's degree program but didn't graduate, 48 percent received better job responsibilities and 29 percent received raises! If they actually graduated, it gets even better: 71 percent gained improved job responsibilities and 63 percent got raises.

Clearly, being enrolled in ongoing education looks good on a resume; you have nothing to lose and everything to gain by committing to your career. Being enrolled in courses toward a degree needn't be expensive, and all other things being equal when, say, a BS is required, "BS Accounting (Graduation anticipated Sept 2017)" can help you overcome an otherwise mandatory requirement.

Don't puff up your educational qualifications. Research has proven that three out of every ten resumes inflate educational qualifications. Consequently, verification of educational claims is quite common. If, after you have been hired, your employer discovers that you exaggerated your educational accomplishments, it could cost you your job.

Ongoing Professional Education

Identify all relevant professional training courses and seminars you've attended. It speaks to professional competency and demonstrates your *commitment* to your profession. It also shows that an employer thought you worthy of the investment. Technology is rapidly changing the nature of all work, so if you aren't learning new skills every year, you are being paid for an increasingly obsolescent skill set. Ongoing professional development is a smart career management strategy.

Accreditations, Professional Licenses, and Civil Service Grades

If licenses, accreditations, or civil service grades are mandatory requirements in your profession, you must feature them clearly. If you are close to gaining a particular accreditation or license you should identify it:

"Passed all parts of C.P.A. exam, September 2016 (expected certification March 2017)."

Civil service grades can be important if you are applying for jobs with government contractors, subcontractors, or any employers who do business with state or federal agencies.

Professional Associations

Membership in associations and societies related to your work demonstrates strong professional *commitment*, and offers great networking opportunities. See this year's edition of *Knock 'em Dead: The Ultimate Job Search Guide* for strategy and tactics in using these associations to find job opportunities. If you are not currently a member of one of your industry's professional associations, give serious consideration to joining.

Note the emphasis on "professional" in the heading. An employer is almost exclusively interested in your professional associations and societies. Omit references to any religious, political, or otherwise potentially controversial affiliations unless your *certain* knowledge of that company assures that such affiliations will be positively received.

An exception to this rule is found in those jobs where a wide circle of acquaintance is regarded as an asset. Some examples might include jobs in public relations, sales, marketing, real estate, and insurance. In these cases, include your membership/involvement with community/church organizations and the like, as your involvement demonstrates a professional who is also involved in the community and speaks to an outgoing personality with a wide circle of contacts.

By the same token, a seat on the town board, charitable cause involvement, or fundraising work are all activities that show a willingness to involve yourself and can demonstrate *organizational* abilities through titles held in those endeavors. Space permitting, these are all activities worthy of inclusion because they show you as a force for good in your community.

Companies that take their community responsibilities seriously often look for staff that feels and acts the same way. For instance, you could list yourself as:

American Heart Association: Area Fundraising Chair

If you are a recent entrant into the workplace, your meaningful extracurricular contributions are of even greater importance. List your position on the school newspaper or the student council, memberships in clubs, anything that demonstrates your potential as a productive employee. As your career progresses, however, prospective employers care less about your school life and more about your work life, so once you are two or three years into your career, the importance of these involvements should be replaced by similar activities in the adult world.

Publications, Patents, and Speaking

These three capabilities are rare and make powerful statements about *creativity*, organization, determination, and follow-through. They tell the reader that you invest considerable personal time and effort in your career and are therefore a cut above the competition.

Public speaking is respected in every profession because it is such a terrifying thing to do, and I say this as someone who has spoken all over the world for two decades! Publications are always respected but carry more weight in some professions (academia). You will notice in the resume examples in this book that the writers list dates and names of publications but do not often include copyright information or patent numbers, because it isn't necessary information for a resume. Here's an example of how to cite your publications:

"Radical Treatments for Chronic Pain." 2002. *Journal of American Medicine.*
"Pain: Is It Imagined or Real?" 2000. *Science & Health Magazine.*

Patents take years to achieve and cost a fortune in the process (I know; I have two optical patents). They speak to vision, *creativity*, attention to detail, and considerable tenacity. They are a definite plus in the technology and manufacturing fields.

> As you are piecing your resume together, it will almost certainly go beyond the one- and two-page mark. Do not worry about this. Traditional page-count considerations are out of date, and besides, you haven't gotten to the editing stage yet.

Languages

With the current state of communications technology, all companies can have an international presence. Consequently, you should always cite your cultural awareness and language abilities. If you speak a foreign language, say so:

Fluent in Spanish and French
Read German

Read and write Serbo-Croatian

Conversational Mandarin

If you are targeting companies that have an international presence, I suggest you cite your linguistic abilities in your performance profile and perhaps again at end of the resume.

Military

Always list your military experience. Military experience speaks, amongst other things, to your determination, *teamwork*, goal orientation, and your understanding of *systems and procedures*. There are a number of major international corporations in which the senior ranks are heavily tilted toward men and women with a military background. In fact, the best boss I ever had was Colonel Peter Erbe, an ex-Airborne guy and one-time head of officer training at West Point. Everyone respects the *commitment* and the skills you developed in the military, and this can be a big plus in your career.

Personal Flexibility, Relocation

If you are open to relocation for the right opportunity, make it clear. It will never, in and of itself, get you an interview, but it won't hurt. Place this information within the first half page so that it is within scanning distance of your address.

Judgment Calls

Here are some areas that do not normally go into your resume, but might. Whether you include them or not will depend on your personal circumstances.

Summer and Part-Time Employment

This should only be included if you are just entering the workforce or re-entering it after a substantial absence. The entry-level person can feel comfortable listing dates and places and times. The returnee should include the skills gained but minimize the part-time aspect of the experience.

Reason for Leaving

The topic is always covered during an interview, so why raise an issue that could have negative impact? You can usually use the space more productively, so your reason for leaving rarely belongs on a resume.

However, if you have frequently been caught in downsizings or mergers or recruited for more responsible positions, there can be a sound argument for listing these reasons to counteract the perception of your being a job hopper. You'll see examples in the resume section.

References

Employers assume that your references are available, and if they aren't available, boy, are you in trouble! However, there is a case for putting "References Available Upon Request" at the end of your resume. It may not be absolutely necessary to say that references are there for the asking, but those four extra words certainly don't do any harm and may help you stand out from the crowd. Including the phrase sends a little message: "Hey, look, I have no skeletons in my closet." But only if space allows—if you have to cut a line anywhere, this should be one of the first to go.

Never list the names of references on a resume: Interviewers very rarely check them before meeting and developing a strong interest in you—it's too time-consuming. Additionally, the law (1970 Fair Credit and Reporting Act) forbids employers to check references without your written consent, so they have to meet you first in order to obtain your written permission.

FYI, you grant this permission when you fill out an application form. In fact, it is usually the reason you are given an application form to complete when you already have a perfectly good resume. There, at the bottom, just above the space for your signature, is a block of impossibly small type. Your signature below it grants permission for reference and credit checks.

References and Other Citations

There are almost fifty ways to identify and layout references, citations, publications, and patents on your resume. My best advice is to follow the layouts we use in the sample resumes.

Name Changes and Your References

If you have ever worked under a different surname, you must take this fact into account when giving your references.

A recently divorced woman I know wasted a strong interview performance because she was using her maiden name on her resume and at the interview. She forgot to tell the employer that her references would, of course, remember her by a different last name. The results of this oversight were catastrophic: Three prior employers denied ever having heard of anyone by the name supplied by the interviewer.

Names and Racial Bias

We recently did a resume for an American with a Spanish name. Let's say it was Gonzales. She was sending resumes out and getting a response of 1 in 20. She got engaged, and her new last name was going to be Carrington. She started sending resumes out with what was to be her new last name, and her response rate went up 900%.

We have had similar results when someone with a difficult-for-a-Westerner-to-pronounce first name, changes it to something more manageable. For example, we had a resume client who was a second-generation immigrant (in other words entirely American in every way). Her first name was Faramadish. I asked her for the correct pronunciation, and she said, "Oh just call me Farah; everyone else does." It made a difference in resume response similar to the earlier example.

This is a matter of personal choice, but using a name that your prospective employer can pronounce, and is therefore less intimidating, can help. A lot of people are doing this with good results. It isn't being deceitful; it's assimilating and doing what is in your own best interests.

If you choose to do this, when an offer comes and the company rep asks for references, answer with the list of references and identify the name you worked under at that company.

Marital Status

Some resume authorities think your marital status is important on the basis that it speaks to stability. However, with 50 percent of marriages ending in divorce and the average length of a marriage under fifteen years, your marital status will rarely win or deny you an interview. As reference to marital status is illegal (1964 Civil Rights Act), it is safe to omit. There are some areas where this issue is occasionally thought to be a valid criterion for consideration: outside sales, trucking, and some churches.

Written Testimonials

It is best not to attach written testimonials to your resume. Of course, that doesn't mean that you shouldn't solicit such references: You might consider using them as a basis for those third-party endorsements we talked about earlier; then, if asked at the interview, you can produce the written testimonials to support the claims made on your resume. This way, you get to use them twice to good effect. Testimonials can be helpful if you are just entering the workforce or are re-entering after a long absence; you can use the content of the testimonials to beef up your resume and your interview.

Personal Interests

If space permits, always include personal interests that reflect well on you as a professional and as a human being. References to personal activities that speak to your ethics (you volunteer for hospice, for example) or are tied to the job in some way are the most effective.

A Korn Ferry study once showed that executives with team sports on their resumes averaged $3,000 a year more than their more sedentary counterparts. Now, that makes giving a line to your personal interests worthwhile, if they fit into certain broad categories. If you participate in team sports, determination activities (running, climbing, bicycling), and "strategy activities" (bridge, chess, Dungeons & Dragons), consider including something about them. The rule of thumb, as always, is only to include activities that can, in some way, contribute to your chances of being hired.

Fraternities and Sororities

Changing times have altered thinking about listing fraternities and sororities on resumes. In general, I recommend leaving them off. Unless your resume is tailored to individuals or companies where membership in such organizations will result in a case of "deep calling to deep": Then, by all means, list it.

Closing Brand Statement

Using a closing brand statement provides a powerful reinforcement of the branding you have striven for throughout the document. A closing comment at the resume's end acts both as an exclamation point and a matching "bookend" for the brand statement at the beginning.

Most resumes are written in the third person, allowing you to talk about yourself with the semblance of objectivity. It can be effective to switch to a first-person voice to make it conversational and differentiate it from the voice of the rest of your resume.

For example:

I see performance management as a critical tool to ensure maximum profitability within the sales department; my consistency has always led to motivated, high-performance sales teams.

Or:

I understand customer service to be the company's face to the world, and I treat every customer interaction as critical to our success; leadership by example and conscientious performance management underlie my department's consistent customer satisfaction ratings.

Many people confuse the need for professionalism with stiff-necked formality. You'll find the most effective tone for a resume is one that mixes the formal with a little of the informal or conversational.

The effect of switching to a first-person voice at the end of the resume is that throughout the document a third party has been objectively discussing someone's professional background, and the first person jumps out at the end with a statement that shows your ownership of this document.

Integrating brand statements is a new idea and something many resumes do not have. Do it well and you can really stand out. But don't do it if you haven't fully defined your brand, or realize you have work to do before you have something worth branding.

You can also close with a third-party endorsement:

"I've never worked with a more ethical and conscientious auditor." —Petra Tompkins, Controller.

Such an endorsement acts as a closing brand statement: a bold statement clarifying the value of the product (that's you, the brand). It's a great way to end a resume. If you have just the right kind of endorsement, this could be the perfect place to use it.

What Never Goes In

Some information just doesn't belong in a resume. Make the mistake of including it, and at best, your resume loses a little power, while at worst, you fail to land the interview.

Personal Flexibility and Relocation Issues

If you are open to relocation for the right opportunity, make it clear, but conversely, *never state that you* aren't *open to relocation*. Let nothing stand in the way of generating job offers! You can always leverage a job offer you don't want into an offer you do. (Check out how in this year's edition of *Knock 'em Dead: The Ultimate Job Search Guide*.)

Titles Such As: Resume, CV, Curriculum Vitae, etc.

Their appearance on a properly structured resume is redundant. It makes clear that your resume needs more work. Such titles take up a whole line, one that could be used more productively. Use the space you save for information with greater impact, or buy yourself an extra line of white space to help your reader's eyes.

Availability

All jobs exist because there are problems that need solutions. For that reason, interviewers rarely have time for candidates who aren't readily available. If you are not ready to start work, then why are you wasting everyone's time? As a rule of thumb, let the subject of availability come up at the face-to-face meeting. After meeting you, an employer is more likely to be prepared to wait until you are available, but will usually pass on an interview if you cannot start now or in the reasonably near future—say, two to three weeks.

The only justification for including this (and then only in your cover letter) is that you expect to be finishing a project and moving on at such-and-such a time, and not before.

Salary

Leave out all references to salary, past and present—it is far too risky. Too high or too low a salary can knock you out of the running even before you hear the starting gun. Even in responding to a job posting that specifically requests salary requirements, don't give the information on your resume. A good resume will still get you the interview, and in the course of the discussions with the company, you'll talk about salary anyway. If you are obliged to give salary requirements, address them in your cover letter—and give a range; you may want to read the section on salary negotiation in the latest edition of *Knock 'em Dead: The Ultimate Job Search Guide*.

If you are obliged to give salary requirements, address them in your cover letter or use a separate Salary History page; you'll find an example in the samples chapter of this book, and you can find a template of this and more than 100 resume templates in the eBook *Knock 'Em Dead Resume Templates* at *www.knockemdead.com*.

Age, Race, Religion, Sex, and National Origin

Government legislation was enacted in the 1960s and 1970s forbidding employment discrimination in these areas under most instances, so it is wisest to avoid reference to them unless they are deemed relevant to the job.

Photographs

In days of old, when men were bold and all our cars had fins, it was the thing to have a photograph in the top right-hand corner of the resume. Today, the fashion is against photographs. Obviously, careers in modeling, acting, and certain aspects of the media require headshots. In these professions, your appearance is an integral part of your product offering.

The place for your headshot is on your social networking profile on LinkedIn and other networking sites. We'll discuss your social networking profile as another version of your resume shortly.

Health/Physical Description

You are trying to get a job, not a date. Unless your physical appearance (gym instructor, model, actor, media personality) is immediately relevant to the job, leave these issues out. If you need to demonstrate health, do it with your extracurricular interests.

CHAPTER 7

HOW TO GIVE YOUR RESUME PUNCH

FIRST IMPRESSIONS ARE important. Editing polishes your content and helps it deliver a greater punch.

The recruiters and hiring authorities who need to read and respond to your resume just hate the mind-numbing grind of it all. It's an activity that makes the eyes tired and the mind wander, so your resume needs to be visually accessible, as we have already discussed. Next, you need to make sure the words you use make sense, read intelligently, and pack a punch by speaking directly to your customers' needs.

You can assume that anyone who reads your resume has an open position to fill and is numb from reading resumes. Understanding exactly what this feels like will help you craft a finished resume that is most readily accessible to the tired eyes and distracted minds of recruiters and hiring authorities.

Imagine you are a recruiter for a moment. You read resumes for a good part of the day, every day. Today, you have just completed a resume database search and have twenty resumes to read. Now, if you didn't do this when I suggested it earlier, go read six resumes from the sample section without a break. Really try to understand each one, but don't spend more than sixty seconds on each.

Three things will happen in sequence: first a ringing in the ears, followed by fuzzy vision and an inability to concentrate. After about fifteen minutes at this, you'll realize why your focus on relevant content, clear layout, and compelling language for your resume are critical for getting it read and understood . . . and why those headlines are so appreciated.

Customize the Templates You Choose

While *Knock 'em Dead* resume layouts and templates are based on common sense and market-response monitoring, you are still free to customize layout. As a rule of thumb, the information most relevant to your candidacy should always come first. For example, when you have no experience, your degree might be your strongest qualification, so put it front and center. As experience increases with the passage of time, in most professions your education can become less important. This is why you will usually see education at the end of a resume, unless the job or the profession's particular demands require it up front. (There are some professions—medicine, education, and the law, for example—where essential academic and professional accreditations tend to be kept at the front of the resume. Bear this in mind if you work in one of these professions.)

However, the resume template you choose isn't sacrosanct; you can customize the layout to suit your needs. For example, you might decide that moving languages, special training, or other information typically found at the end of the resume increases the strength of your argument when placed first. If that makes sense, go ahead and do it.

Filling In the Template

Go through your chosen template and transfer the information you developed earlier, and almost immediately, you have a resume that begins to look like a finished product.

Tighten Up Sentences

Sentences gain power with action verbs. For example, a woman with ten years of law firm experience in a clerical position had written in her original resume:

I learned to use a new database.

After she thought about what was really involved, she gave this sentence more punch:

I analyzed and determined the need for a comprehensive upgrade of database, archival, and retrieval systems. I was responsible for selection and installation of "cloud-based" archival systems. Within one year, I had an integrated, company-wide archival system working.

Notice how verbs show that things happen when you are around the office; they bring action to a resume. Note that while they tell the reader what you did it and how you did it, they also support the branding statements that can open and close your resume.

Now look at the above example when we add a third party:

I analyzed and determined the need for a comprehensive upgrade of database, archival, and retrieval systems. I was responsible for selection and installation of "cloud-based" archival systems. Within one year, I had an integrated, company-wide archival system working. A partner stated, "You brought us out of the dark ages, and in the process neither you nor the firm missed a beat!"

Now, while the content is clearly more powerful, the sentences are clunky, too wordy, and need tightening.

Tight Sentences Have Bigger Impact

Space is at a premium, and reader impact is your goal, so keep your sentences under about twenty words. Always aim for simplicity and clarity:

- Shorten sentences by cutting unnecessary words.
- Make two short sentences out of one long one. At the same time, you don't want the writing to sound choppy, so vary the length of sentences when you can.

You can also start with a short phrase and follow with a colon:

- Followed by bullets of information
- Each one supporting the original phrase

See how these techniques tighten the writing and enliven the reading process from our law firm example:

Analyzed and determined need for comprehensive upgrade of database, archival, and retrieval systems:

- *Responsible for hardware and software selection.*
- *Responsible for selection and installation of "cloud-based" archival systems.*
- *Responsible for compatible hardware and software upgrades.*
- *Trained users from managing partner through administrators.*
- *Achieved full upgrade, integration, and compliance in six months.*
- *Partner stated, "You brought us out of the dark ages, and neither you nor the firm missed a beat!"*

Notice in this example that by dropping personal pronouns and articles, the result is easier to read. It also speaks of a professional who knows the importance of *getting to relevant information fast.*

Big Words or Little Words?

Recruiters and hiring managers know every trick in the book; they've seen every eye-catching gimmick, and they're not impressed. Two of the biggest mistakes amateur (and professional) resume writers make is using:

1. Big words; in an effort to sound professional you end up sounding pompous and impenetrable.
2. Adjectives; when you use adjectives to describe yourself (excellent, superior, etc.), the recruiter will often discount them, muttering, "I'll be the judge of that." You'll see examples in the resume section, but notice that the use of superlatives is kept under control and backed up with hard facts.

The goal of your resume is to communicate quickly and efficiently, using short sentences and familiar words; they are easy to understand and communicate clearly and efficiently. Remember: Short words in short sentences in short paragraphs help tired eyes!

Voice and Tense

The voice you use in your resume depends on a few important factors: getting a lot said in a small space, being factual, and packaging yourself in the best way possible.

Sentences can be truncated (up to a point) by omitting pronouns—*I, you, he, she, it, they*— and articles—*a* or *the.* Dropping pronouns is a technique that saves space and allows you to brag about yourself without seeming boastful, because it gives the impression that another party is writing about you.

"I automated the office"—becomes, "Automated office." At the same time, writing in the first person makes you sound, well, personable. Use whatever works best for you. If you use personal pronouns, don't use them in every sentence—they get monotonous and take up valuable space on the page. Use a third-person voice throughout the resume, with a few final words in the first person as a closing brand statement at the end of the document to give an insight into your values. You saw an example of a functional resume with just such a personal tone that worked almost magically for its owner.

Using the third person and dropping pronouns and articles throughout the body of the resume saves space and gives you an authoritative tone.

Resume Length

The rule used to be one page for every ten years of experience, and never more than two pages. However, as jobs have gotten more complex, they require more explanation. *The length of your resume is less important than its relevance to the target job.* The first half to two-thirds of the first page of your resume should be tightly focused on a specific target job and include a Target Job Title, Performance Profile, Professional Competencies, and perhaps Career Highlight sections. Do this and any reader can quickly see that you have the chops for the job.

If you are seen to be qualified, the reader will stay with you as you tell the story. Given the increasing complexity of jobs, the length and depth of your experience, and the need for data-dense resumes (which are overwhelmingly rewarded in database searches), it is idiotic to limit the length of your resume on the basis of outdated conventions from before the age of computers, let alone the Internet.

The worst—the most heinous crime of all—is to cram a seasoned professional's work history into tiny font sizes to get it onto one or two pages. Why? Here's a flash from reality: If you are a seasoned professional with a real track record requiring a complex skillset and are climbing the ladder of success, it's likely your readers are also successful, seasoned professionals. Use tiny fonts and you annoy everyone whose eyesight has been weakened by prolonged computer use, and that means everyone. Busy senior managers simply won't read your resume because it speaks to poor judgment and *communication skills*, both of which are mandatory for seasoned professionals.

Let form follow function with your resume. If it takes three tightly edited pages to tell a properly focused story and make it readable, just do it.

What's the alternative? Leaving stuff out means your resume is less likely to get pulled from resume databases or sell the recruiter on your skills when it does get read.

Assuming your first page clearly demonstrates a thorough grasp of the target job, you can feel comfortable taking that second and third page, if necessary, to tell a concise story. In the resume sample chapter, you'll see examples of justifiably longer executive resumes, requiring greater length to convey a concise message of ability in a complex job.

Worrying too much about length considerations while you write is counterproductive. If the first page makes the right argument, the rest of your resume will be read with serious attention. A longer resume also means that much more space for selling your skills with relevant keywords and more opportunities to establish your brand. However, you should make every effort to maintain focus and an "if in doubt, leave it out" editing approach.

If you have more than twenty years under your belt, many older skills from the first part of your career are now irrelevant. On the whole, the rule of one page for every ten years is still a sensible *guideline*. The bottom line is that your resume can be as long as it needs to be to tell a concise and compelling story. I have never, ever heard of a qualified candidate being rejected because her resume exceeded some arbitrary page count; it just doesn't happen.

Does My Resume Tell the Right Story?

As you write, rewrite, edit, and polish your resume, concentrate on the story your resume needs to tell. You can keep this focus in mind by regularly referring to your TJD, and then layering fact and illustration until the story is told. When the story is complete, begin to polish by asking yourself the following questions:

- Are my statements relevant to the target job?
- Where have I repeated myself?
- Can I cut out any paragraphs?
- Can I cut out any sentences?
- Can I shorten two sentences into one? If not, perhaps I can break that one long sentence into two short ones?
- Can I cut out any words?
- Can I cut out any pronouns?

If in doubt, leave it out—leave nothing but the focused story and action words!

Resumes Evolve in Layers

Resumes are written in layers. They don't spring fully formed in one draft from anyone's keyboard. They are the result of numerous drafts, each of which inches the product forward. As I was writing this edition of *Knock 'em Dead Resumes*, we worked with a public relations professional on her new resume. She completed a TJD and the resume questionnaire. Before we were finished, we had completed eight different versions, each evolving until we had a great finished product. It took about two and a half weeks, but then generated eight interviews in a week, proof again that 50 percent of the success of any project is in the preparation. You can see three of the eight evolving versions of this resume at the end of Chapter 2.

Proofreading Your Final Draft

Check your resume against the following points:

Contact Information
- Are your name, address, phone numbers, and email address correct?
- Is your contact information on every page?
- Is the email address hyperlinked, so that a reader of your resume can read it on his computer and reach out to you instantly?

Target Job Title
- Do you have a target job title that echoes the words and intent of the job titles you collected when deconstructing the target job?
- Is this followed by a short, one-sentence branding statement that captures the essence of the *professional you*? Only make brand statements when you really have something to brand.

Performance Profile
- Does it give a concise synopsis of the *professional you* as it relates to the target job?
- Does the language reflect that of typical job postings for this job?
- Is it prioritized in the same way employers are prioritizing their needs in this job?
- Is it no more than five lines long, so it can be read easily? If more, can you cut it into two paragraphs or use bullets?
- Does it include reference to the *transferable skills and professional values* that are critical to success? If they don't fit here, make sure they are at least in the core competencies section.

Professional Competencies
- Is all spelling and capitalization correct?
- Are there any other keywords you should add?
- Do you have experience in each of the areas you've listed?
- Can you illustrate your experience in conversation?

Career Highlights

- If you included a Career/Performance Highlights section, do the entries support the central arguments of your resume?

Professional Experience

- Is your most relevant and qualifying work experience prioritized throughout the resume to correspond to the employers' needs as they have prioritized them?
- Have you avoided wasting space with unnecessarily detailed employer names and addresses?
- If employed, have you been discreet with the name of your current employer?
- Have you omitted any reference to reasons for leaving a particular job?
- Have you removed all references to past, current, or desired salaries?
- Have you removed references to your date of availability?

Education

- Is education placed in the appropriate position?
- Is your highest educational attainment shown first?
- Have you included professional courses that support your candidacy?

Chronology

- Is your work history in chronological order, with the most recent employment coming first?
- With a chronological or combination resume, does each company history start with details of your most senior position?
- Does your resume emphasize relevant experience, contributions, and achievements?
- Have you used one or more third-party endorsements of your work if they are available and relevant?
- Can you come up with a strong personal branding statement to end the resume? One that supports the focus and story you have told? Perhaps read your resume and decide which combination of your *transferable skills* are most relevant, and come up with a statement of how this selection of *transferable skills* allows you to perform in the way you do.
- Have you kept punch and focus by eliminating extraneous information?
- Have you included any volunteer, community service, or extracurricular activities that can lend strength to your candidacy?
- Have you left out lists of references and only mentioned the availability of references if there is nothing more valuable to fill up the space?
- Have you avoided treating your reader like a fool by heading your resume, "RESUME"?

Writing Style

- Have you substituted short words for long words?
- Have you used one word where previously there were two?
- Is your *average* sentence no more than twenty words? Have you shortened any sentence of more than twenty-five words or broken it into two?
- Have you kept paragraphs under five lines?
- Do your sentences begin, wherever possible, with powerful action verbs and phrases?
- Have you omitted articles and personal pronouns?

Spelling and Grammar

Incorrect spelling and poor grammar are guaranteed to annoy resume readers, besides drawing attention to your poor *written communication skills*. This is not a good opening statement in any job search. Spell checkers are *not* infallible. Check the spelling and grammar and then send your resume to the most literate person you know for input on grammar and spelling.

At *www.knockemdead.com*, our resume service offers a grammar, syntax, and spellcheck by a professional editor who also understands resumes. We will vet your resume and return it to you in thirty-six hours with tracked changes and suggestions. You need some distance from your creative efforts to gain detachment and objectivity. There is no hard-and-fast rule about how long it takes to come up with the finished product. Nevertheless, if you think you have finished, leave it alone at least overnight. The next day, read your TJD document before reading your resume: Then you will be able to read it with the mindset of a recruiter and see the parts that need tweaking.

CHAPTER 8

RESUME CUSTOMIZATION, ALTERNATIVE RESUMES, AND FORMATS NEEDED FOR AN EFFECTIVE JOB SEARCH

WITH JOB SEARCHING the way it is today, you will almost certainly need more than one resume for your job search, and you may need to repackage your background into three of four different delivery vehicles.

You'll probably need:

- Customized resumes for specific openings
- One or more resumes for other jobs you can do and want to pursue
- An ASCII resume
- A resume for your social networking site

And you might decide you need a *business card resume* and an HTML or *web-based resume.*

Customizing Your Resume for Specific Openings

Your resume is a living, breathing document, and the *primary* resume you so carefully developed is never really finished. It evolves throughout your job search as you learn more about the skills and experience your marketplace needs, and as you learn to express your possession of these skills and experiences in ways most accessible to your customer base.

Most important, it evolves every time you customize that resume in response to a particular job posting. Before sending your resume in response to any job opening, you should evaluate it against the job description, and tweak it *so that it speaks clearly and powerfully to the stated needs of that job.*

You will notice that the *transferable skills* we talk about throughout the *Knock 'em Dead* series (*communication, critical thinking, multitasking, teamwork,* etc.) crop up frequently in job postings:

"Work closely with" means you are a *team player* and work for the good of the team and the deliverables to which you are collectively committed.

"Communication skills" means you listen to understand and that you can take direction in all circumstances. It also refers to verbal and written skills, dress, body language, your social graces, and emotional maturity.

"Multitasking" does not mean you rush heedlessly from one emergency to the next; it means that you carefully order your activities based on sound time management and *organizational skills.*

"Problem-solving skills" means you think through the likely effects of your actions before taking them, and that you know your area of expertise well enough to identify, prevent, and solve the problems it generates on a daily basis.

Tweak Your Resume for *Keyword* Resonance

Match the job posting against your resume to see that the words you use to describe certain skills match the words the employer is using.

Then think through how the job posting requirement of, say, "work closely with others," applies to each of the employer's specific skill requirements that require you interact with other people and other departments to get your work done. For example, an accountant working with accounts receivable might, on hearing "work closely with others," think about problem accounts and working with sales and the nonpaying customer, as well as working laterally and upward within the accounting department.

When you think through your work experience and discover achievements that speak directly to the stated needs of an employer, you can draw attention to your close match in either your resume or a cover letter.

Keywords in a Cover Letter

In a cover letter, these might appear as the company statement in quotation marks followed by an achievement in that area:

"Analytical/Critical thinking/Problem-solving skills"
- Thorough knowledge of the issues that impact productivity in Operations has resulted in a 35% increase in on-time delivery.

"Work closely with" and *"Communication skills"*
- Improvements in on-time delivery also made possible by improved communications with stakeholders: Purchasing, Supply Chain, Customer, and Customer Service, which also delivered a 20% reduction in client complaints.

"Multitasking"
- Effective Operations Management demands understanding every department's critical functions and timelines. Building these considerations into daily activities helped Finance & Supply Chain save $55,000 in last three quarters.

Keywords in a Resume

In a resume, you might decide to highlight relevant achievements with a *Performance Highlights* or a *Career Highlights* section on your resume, coming right after the *Professional Competencies* section.

This section will comprise a short sequence of bulleted statements, each addressing one of the company's stated requirements, and so emphasizing the fit between the employer's needs and your capabilities. Use an example to illustrate if you can do so succinctly.

However, in your resume, space might be at more of a premium than in your cover letter, and so you would use the achievements without the quotes:

Performance Highlights
35% increase in on-time delivery + 20% reduction in client complaints

Effective Operations Management demands understanding every department's unique problems and timelines. Building these considerations into daily activities helped:

- Finance & Supply Chain, saved $55,000 in last three quarters
- Increased productivity, with a 35% increase in on-time delivery

These on-time delivery increases were achieved with improved communications, connecting Purchasing, Supply Chain, Customers, and Customer Service:

- Delivered 20% reduction in client complaints

A Job-Targeted Resume for That Other Job

With just a few years' experience in the professional world, most people reach a point where they have experience that qualifies them for more than one job. You built your *primary resume* around the job for which the odds are shortest. But that doesn't mean there aren't other jobs you can do and want to pursue.

After your primary resume is completed, it is fairly easy to create a resume for any additional job you want to pursue. Given your completed primary resume, you already have a template to start with; plus the dates, layout, chronology, contact information, and possibly the employers are all going to remain the same. There's a methodology that quickly helps you refocus and edit your primary resume into a resume for that second or third target job:

1. Save a duplicate copy of your primary resume, and save it under the new target job title, because although the job is different, a great deal of the information and resume layout will remain the same.
2. Complete Target Job Deconstruction exercise on the next target job.
3. On the duplicate copy of your resume, saved under the name of the second target job, use the new TJD to edit out less relevant details and replace them with the higher-impact information that is more relevant to the new target job.
4. Edit and polish, and you have a customized resume for that second or third target job.

The Major Resume Formats and Why You Need Them

An online job search means that you will be able to customize your resume for specific openings, upload it to resume databases, and send it directly to a hiring manager or networking contact. Each of these major needs is served by having your resume prepared in three different formats:

1. MSWord
2. PDF
3. ATS Friendly

Your Resume in MSWord

You will be saving and using your resume in MSWord, PDF, and ATS-Friendly formats, but you always develop your original document in MSWord because it gives you the greatest flexibility for design, layout, color, and text enhancements.

I recommend you create your primary resume document in MSWord because if a job is worth applying to, then it is worth customizing your resume for that opportunity, and the aforementioned design flexibility gives you the greatest range of options for doing so.

However, MSWord has certain problems, which means the resume versions you use most in your search are likely to be PDF and ATS Friendly. Microsoft Word can have problems:

- Crossing from a PC platform to a Mac platform
- Moving from one version of MSWord to another
- Printing on one of the many thousands of printers available

An example of the problems you will encounter in sending out MSWord versions of your resume is a line at the bottom of one page jumping onto the top of the next page; sometimes Word even leaves the balance of that page blank. This does not support the professional image that will help advance your career. This only happens occasionally, but it does happen, and Murphy's Law tells us that it will only happen to you at the most damaging of times.

Create your resume in MS Word (use .docx when available) because this gives you the greatest flexibility for delivering your message in a clear and visually attractive way. However, once created you should keep this as a clean source document from which you will make copies to customize for specific openings, and to save the revised resume document in other formats—as we'll discuss. But you are not advised to send an MSWord resume in response to job posting openings, headhunters, or potential employers, unless specifically requested to do so.

MSWord Conversion Problems

Word can create problems when a transmitted document crosses from a PC to a Mac, or when the sender and the viewer are using different versions of MSWord—or any combination of these factors. Consequently, if you are specifically requested to send an MSWord version of your resume, you should be aware of the conversion problems over which you can exhibit some control.

Page Jumps

If you discover, while testing your resume by sending to and receiving from a variety of friends and colleagues, that the bottom line of a page is throwing off the whole layout of your document by jumping to the top of the next page, you have a couple of options, depending on your machine and version of MSWord:

- With your MSWord document open, you can insert a hard page break by going to the "Insert" menu along the top of your page and inserting a page break from the options offered in the drop-down menu under "Break."
- You can also key CTRL ENTER to insert a hard page break at the end of the page.
- If you like to use paragraph marks when writing you must remove these once the resume is finished. A stray paragraph mark at the end of a page could cause your resume to jump to an additional blank page,

Using Symbols

Resumes can be enlivened by using symbols, but you must be careful:

- To use symbols that increase comprehension rather than just serve as an attempt to prettify the document.
- To use symbols that are recognizable across computer platforms and resume-tracking systems.

Symbols that can enhance comprehension and be intelligible regardless of computer platform or software opening the document are called Unicode symbols. You can find all you need by searching for "Unicode symbols" on Google. (The symbols used in *Knock 'em Dead Resumes* are all compatible with these requirements.)

You can find a complete list of Unicode symbols and typography at *http://unicode-table.com/en/ - miscellaneous-symbols*, although this might be overkill for some people.

Margins and Printing Your Resume

Today's printers can handle margins of as little as 0.35 inches at the top and bottom of your resume and 0.5 inches on the left and right sides; this gives you more space to tell your story on a page and still have plenty of white space to make your message easily accessible to the eye. Sticking to these conventions, your resume should print on any standard printer.

If you have an older printer it might not be able to handle such tight margins—they sometimes require margins of 0.75 inches on all sides. If this applies to you, make sure you test print your resume out on a printer that can handle the tighter margins; all corporate printers are likely to be able to handle these tighter margins. If all else fails take it to a FedEx Office Print & Ship Center and print out a copy there.

PDF Resumes

Save a version of your resume in PDF—its an acronym for Portable Downloadable File; you'll find this option within the "Save As" dialog box within MSWord that pops up when you give your document a title. Click on format choices and choose PDF. The PDF format is a permanent, locked, and incorruptible format that cannot change no matter what device it is viewed or printed on; it will appear exactly as you send it. You should:

- Use a PDF to send as an email attachment to networking contacts, recruiters, headhunters, and potential hiring managers.
- *Never* use a PDF for uploading your resume to databases, because ATS (Applicant Tracking Systems) have difficulty accessing the locked information.

When sending an attached PDF resume by email, mention the attachment in the body of your email: "My resume is attached in a PDF document."

ATS-Friendly Resumes

Resume databases are a fact of life, and during a job search you are likely to upload a version of your resume into these databases a number of times. Recruiters access these databases using applicant tracking system (ATS) software.

What is an ATS-Friendly format? Basically it is a version of your resume saved in MSWord 97-2003, and stripped of most of its formatting (you'll find this option within the "Save As" dialog box within MSWord that pops up when you give your document a title).

Most ATS software can read a properly formatted resume in MSWord but in case you apply to a company that has an older system we continue to recommend the SATS-Friendly format, in the older version of MSWord. In the example here you will see a resume in a single font size, left justified, stripped of columns, color, and many of the other niceties of formatting.

Jen Ellis

Branson, MO 65615   417-234-3640   j.ellis@gmail.com

Underwriter – Senior Credit Analyst – Loan Closer / Banking & Mortgage Lending Industry

Professional Profile
Branch Manager & Loan Officer with 12 years of experience managing branch banking and lending activities, improving business processes, and leading a team of financial services professionals who generate approximately $9 million in loans each year.

Professional Skills

Banking Products & Financial Services	Strategic Business Planning	New Business Development
Mortgage Lending & Underwriting	Economics, Accounting, & Finance	Staff Training & Supervision
Asset Management / Portfolio Valuation	Statistical Analysis & Market Trends	Teamwork & Collaboration
Asset Preservation & Loss Prevention	State & Federal Regulatory Compliance	Verbal & Written Communications
Loan Applications & Processing	Requirements Elicitation	Lead Generation / Prospecting
Credit Administration / Credit Analysis	Financial Statements & Financial Audits	Customer Accounts Setup
Credit Quality / FICO Credit Scores	Data Entry & Database Management	Customer Relationship Management
Loan Reviews, Approvals, & Closings	Spreadsheets, Flat Files, & Databases	Exceptional Customer Service
Documentation for Funding	General Ledger Accounting	Cross-Selling Opportunities
Collateral Analysis for Secured Loans	AR/AP, Billing/Collections, & Payroll	Critical Thinking & Sound Judgment
Data Verification / Fraud Analysis	Investigative Research	Organization & Time Management
Data Integrity, Security, & Confidentiality	Loss Prevention & Claims Mitigation	Ability to Manage Multiple Priorities

Computer Skills
Microsoft Office Suite: Word, Excel, PowerPoint, Access, Outlook, SharePoint

Performance Highlights
- Strategic Business Leader who leverages financial data and market trends analysis to drive business decisions.
- Credit Administrator proficient in interviewing clients, gathering financial information, processing loan applications, analyzing and interpreting credit quality for loan approval or denial, and closing asset-based loans. Train, coach, and mentor branch banking employees in best practices for selling bank products and providing exceptional customer service.
- Compliance Resource for fair lending and responsible banking laws. Solid understanding of Community Reinvestment Act (CRA), Interagency Fair Lending Examination Procedures (IFLEP), and CRA Examination Procedures (IEP).
- Loan Manager with knowledge and experience in asset management/valuation. Capable of managing multimillion-dollar real estate portfolios. Experience working with distressed properties and reviewing collateral reporting packages comprised of accounts receivable aging, inventory reports, sales journals, cash receipts registers, accounts payable listings, and other financial reports. Meticulous in analyzing field examination findings, reconciling all pertinent information to the bank's loan system, administering loan status reports, and overseeing billing and collections.

Professional Experience
Branch Manager / Assistant Branch Manager   May 2003 to Present
WELLS FARGO   Branson, MO

Promoted from Assistant Branch Manager to Branch Manager in July of 2004. Serve in a business development and sales role. Offer personal and real estate loans as well as credit insurance. Generate $9 million in loans each year, provide exceptional customer service, and build strong customer relationships.

- Recruit, hire, train, supervise, and evaluate performance of branch employees working in lending and loan collection.
- Monitor and direct loan activities. Analyze and deter risks associated with personal and real estate loans. Perform due diligence and conduct thorough credit risk assessments to provide an accurate risk profile and portfolio analysis pertinent to sustaining portfolio value and branch growth.
- Meet with clients to determine loan needs and discuss rates, terms, and underwriting requirements. Assist clients in loan application process. Analyze loan applicants' financial data to determine credit worthiness, including income, property valuations, credit report, credit history, etc.

Use your ATS resume version to cut and paste information into employer or commercial resume database dialog boxes. If you want to cover all the bases, you can upload an MSWord 2013 /.docx version as well.

TXT versus ATS Friendly

We used to use .txt versions of a resume for uploading to resume databases, but ATS-Friendly formats have made the less attractive .txt format obsolete for these purposes.

In the unlikely event that a database, employer, or recruiter asks for a .txt or .rtf (Rich text format) version of your resume, you can create one in sixty seconds: Make a copy of your ATS resume and save it; this will open the "Save As" dialog box. Click on format choices and you'll find both .txt and .rtf as options; click on the one you need and you are finished.

Employer-Preferred Formats

We have discussed the logical and generally preferred ways to format and deliver your resume, but there are two instances that trump everything I have said: the stated submission requirements of a database or an employer.

Always check to see how that database or employer wants your resume delivered. They will invariably define a specific format. Whatever is requested, or suggested, is the format you use in that instance.

Color in Resumes

Adding color to your resume is a very popular idea. In a visual world a little color does make a resume pop. You can use color in your PDF and .docx resumes, but ATS can still have difficulty with color. So, if you choose to use color, you will remember to remove it from the ATS version of your resume.

Color makes an impression but you don't want to overdo it. At the *www.knockemdead.com* resume-writing service we offer a maximum of two colors, although personally I think one color is adequate.

Web-Based or HTML Resume

A web-based/HTML resume is a "nice to have," not a "must-have." Don't even think about it until you have a properly constructed and branded resume that portrays you exactly as you wish to be seen and have created formats in .docx, PDF, and ATS Friendly.

An HTML, web-based, or e-portfolio resume is essentially a website dedicated to extolling your professional credentials. Apart from a simple resume, it can have additional features such as video and sound.

It is one of those approaches touted as the next big thing, but your LinkedIn profile can achieve everything your own website can. There are a handful of instances when this option might be viable: If you work in the arts, education, certain areas of communications, or technology, the ability to include audio and video clips, music, and pictures can be a plus. It also works in areas of technology where you need to control the bandwidth to ensure the quality of the viewer experience that presents your skills and credentials. Your time is better spent building a LinkedIn Profile (or better yet, let me build one for you), which achieves the same thing and delivers greater discoverability with less effort.

Your Resume and Database Discoverability

Your resume will go into databases, and to be found once uploaded it must contain the right balance of relevant information. We started the resume-building process with understanding employer priorities and the words they use to explain those priorities, through a process we call TJD or Target Job Deconstruction.

You used this information as a general guideline for the story your resume needs to tell, then you made a special effort to see that these TJD-identified priorities and the keywords that express them appear in a number of places throughout your resume:

- Target Job Title
- Performance Profile or Summary
- Professional Skills section
- Within the context of the jobs in which those skills have been developed and applied

ATS software is now able to recognize keywords in context and rewards resumes that use keywords within the context of their application at work so make every effort to do this.

On the job-hunting side of the desk we now have technology in the form of products that help evaluate your resume's performance in relation to specific job postings. At *www.knockem dead.com* we have this software embedded in the site, so come and check your how well your resume is likely to perform in database searches.

Updating Your Resume

Once you have landed in the new job and are starting the next steps of your career, you need to keep your work and achievements tracked on a weekly or monthly basis in your resume folder. I suggest this because you might remember something special you did this week for a few months, but if your next job change doesn't happen for a number of years, you'll have to work to drag up the events. If you keep a record of your work in your resume folder on a regular basis, it will make updating your resume for the next step that much easier.

When do you need to update your resume for a job search? Most people leave it until the last minute, but this is too important a document to rush into publication. My best advice is that you need to update the resume about ninety days before you pull the trigger on a job search.

Your Social Networking Profile

There are many options for social media sites, but for professional networking there is one dominant site on which you must have a presence: LinkedIn. Because more than half of the professional American workforce are already members, this makes it attractive to recruiters. A long-time friend and recruiter compared using LinkedIn to "shooting fish in a barrel." Another said it's a "honey pot."

With well over half a billion professionals around the world using LinkedIn for networking (and half of them in North America), you would be crazy to ignore it. There are two reasons for a social networking site: to find people and to be found. As a professional working in a world without any reliable job security, having a presence on a social media site like LinkedIn keeps you visible not just when you are job hunting but on an ongoing basis. This means you will have the opportunity to build ever-growing networks of similar professionals, recruiters, and headhunters. Even if you aren't interested in the job, knowing of a company that hires people like you is useful intelligence. Always be polite, professional, and helpful whenever you can with those recruiters and headhunters; you might not need them now, but six months or a year from now?

When recruiters are looking for someone like you, they use keywords and phrases from the job posting that they are working from; the relevance of your profile determines:

• Whether you will be found amongst those 400 million-plus other LI users
• Whether the recruiter follows his review through with a contact

First Things First

As you look at the headlines and categories of a LinkedIn profile, does the flow of information requested remind you of anything? Perhaps the exact flow that a *Knock 'em Dead* resume follows? We were in business way before LinkedIn existed, although I am in no way implying that they mimicked our flow. Rather I want to make two points:

1. The similarities should give you considerable confidence in what you are doing.
2. You can get a fast start on creating, or upgrading your profile, by cutting and pasting sections of your ATS-Friendly resume into the appropriate section of the LI profile.

However I want you to do something else first: Upload your resume to your profile so that it can be seen and downloaded by others. To upload your resume, follow these steps:

1. Click **Profile** at the top of your homepage.
2. Move your cursor over the Down arrow next to the **View Profile As** button and select **Import resume**.
3. Click **Choose file** or **Browse** to locate your resume on your computer.
4. Click **Upload resume**. You'll be taken to a page where you can review the information extracted from your resume.
5. Double-check all fields to be sure the information is completed and correct.

Click **Save**.

How to Create a Killer LinkedIn Profile

The profile you create will give you visibility with search engines and enable others to find you: It's like having a big-ass billboard on the side of a highway traveled by the people you want to be visible to. Additionally, recruiters, headhunters, and hiring managers who have already seen your resume often like to check out your social profile(s) to find out more about you. This is why—once you are satisfied that your resume and profile echo the same messaging—I suggest adding a link on your resume to your LI profile.

Your LinkedIn profile, and any other social networking profiles you subsequently develop, are your public face and your most important passive marketing tool, keeping you constantly visible to the very people who quite possibly hold the keys to the next step in your career.

It All Starts with Your Headshot

Your headshot appears at the top left of your LinkedIn profile, and it's the first thing recruiters or anyone else who visits your profile sees. Upward of 90 percent of Human Resources pros say they check out social media profiles, especially LinkedIn and Facebook, before inviting a candidate in for an interview. As the face you show to the world, your headshot is the face of your brand.

This means the wrong headshot could hurt your chances of making the cut. Five out of every ten social media profile headshots make me want to laugh, cry, or lose my lunch. I see headshots that are too close (you want to minimize wrinkles or acne), too far (I need to see your face), too sexy, too casual, grinning like a congenital imbecile, or scowling like a mass murderer. These problem headshots show a lack of appreciation for how important this first impression really is.

Every Picture Tells a Story

Headshots aren't just for celebrities anymore; they have become a critically important part of establishing a credible professional image for all of us. Like it or not, your headshot tells a story, so make sure yours is telling the right story.

We all make judgments based on visual first impressions; with search results, a profile with a headshot will get many more clicks than a profile without one, and the people who come to your profile will form an opinion based on your headshot before they read anything you have written. How professional and accessible your headshot makes you look will also color the impressions of anyone who then reads your profile. It's safe to say that getting your headshot right is extremely important.

Are You Trying to Get Hired or Dated?

We all have different personas at work and at play, so a killer headshot for your Match.com profile could be the kiss of death for your LinkedIn profile. Your social media profile gives the reader visual clues as to who you are and what your self-image is. Your appearance and facial expression provide the clues, and these are communicated through your headshot. It will happen whether you want it to or not, so the only smart choice is to make sure your headshot presents a confident professional. If you're seen as both professional (which implies competence) and friendly, you will encourage acceptance of the claims made within your profile, whereas a too casual or too sexy shot will call your judgment of professional issues into question.

Can You Get Away with a DIY Headshot?

As long as you look professional, the headshot doesn't have to be done by a professional, but headshots aren't snapshots and you should dress for yours as you would for a job interview.

You can probably get a friend/lover/partner to shoot a bunch of photos of you against a plain background and it will come out as an acceptable candid shot. Since we all need these shots in our professional lives, a competent headshot photography partner should be easy to find.

The beauty of a digital camera is that you can take as many shots as you want, pick the best one, and maybe even do some basic cleanups. Shoot straight on and then experiment with distance. Once you've settled on a distance (between four and eight feet for many cameras), experiment with angles to see which is most flattering; adjust the lighting to get the most complimentary result.

You need the best headshot you can generate for immediate use, but bear in mind that summer is the best time to upgrade your social media headshots: You look happier and more relaxed because it's summer, and for paler skins any kind of tan makes you look healthier and more attractive.

Your Headline

After your headshot, the next thing recruiters notice is your headline. This headline should say who you are and what you do; it is important to give recruiters focus, and this is one of the areas the search engine rates as important in establishing your ranking in searches. (Ensuring that your ranking in searches is high is called search engine optimization or SEO.) This headline is limited to a 120-character thumbnail description about you and works as a brief biography of the person behind the headshot. You have just these 120 characters to say who you are, so your headline should include your Target Job Title and the keywords that most succinctly capture what you do. You might consider the branding statements you established as your professional special sauce at the end of the CDQ discussed in Chapter 3. You increase the odds of these working well by doing searches on LinkedIn for your own target job title and looking at how the people who show up on the first few pages of results build a winning headline. Use this insight to adapt what you have to offer to synchronize with your findings.

Summary

This should include information that will maximize your *discoverability* when a recruiter searches for someone like you. Information in your Summary section should be geared to drawing a concise picture of your professional capabilities—not your hopes and dreams but your *capabilities*, because you get hired based on your credentials, not your potential.

The summary on your LinkedIn profile (as on other social networking sites) provides more space than you would usually use in the Summary or Performance Profile section of a job-targeted resume. However, if you have already built a resume according to *Knock 'em Dead* guidelines, you will have a Performance Profile that reflects the skills, experience, priorities, and word choices employers use to define the job they need to fill. If so, just upload the resume and change it to a first-person voice. If you *don't* have a *Knock 'em Dead* resume, identify the raw materials for the Summary in your TJD exercises (see Chapter 2) and then write six sentences that succinctly capture your capabilities in each of the employer priority areas.

The summary and work experience sections of your LinkedIn profile accommodate a considerable word count. However, anything you write needs to be accessible to the human eye, and long blocks of text become visually inaccessible very quickly, especially to recruiters who are scanning briefly rather than reading. Consequently, you need to make sure that no paragraph is more than six lines of unbroken text. You can also use bullet points to share important information and deliver visual variety.

Some career "experts" suggest writing about your hobbies here. That's silly. No recruiter cares about your personal interests until they know you can do the job, so such information is irrelevant to recruiters, a waste of this valuable selling space, and will cost you readers. Besides, LinkedIn has provided a space for this, where it belongs: at the *end* of your profile.

Instead, use any remaining available space to list critically important skill sets for your work. There is a place for peer-reviewed professional skills later, but listing them here is very helpful to recruiters, and you certainly won't diminish the discoverability of your profile by mentioning these skills more than once.

A First- or Third-Person Voice?

While your resume invariably uses a third-person voice, a social media profile has evolved as a longer, more revealing, and personal document, and many people think you should use a first person voice, " I did this, I did that, etc."

I disagree with this thinking, because talking about your responsibilities and accomplishments in first person can make you sound boastful. There is a saying from the world of architectural design that "form follows function"; it applies here. You want a presence on LinkedIn to build networks of professional contacts and to be discovered by recruiters and headhunters; to me this says that the universally adopted rule for professional resumes should apply here.

We always give our clients the option and recently we were doing a profile for a man who owns a couple of investment companies but whose main focus was sitting on company boards as a board member and external advisor; in response to the question he replied,

"OMG, third person please, if we used first person with my background I'd sound like a narcissistic buffoon. No one wants to work with someone like that."

Contact Information

The whole point of having a social media profile is to be in closer contact and better *communication* with your professional world. To this end LI offers multiple ways for others to connect with you; most importantly is the In mail function. As well, you need to have adequate connection information on your profile.

There are two places for this—the most important comes right after your name and headline and before your Summary. The section is referred to as "Contact Info." If you are smart, you will put your personal email address in here. I'm sorry to say that about a quarter of the connection requests I receive everyday lack an email address.

There is also the opportunity to add contact info at the end of your profile, and you should replicate all appropriate contact info here. With email addresses at start and finish of your profile you make contact that much easier for people who want to communicate with you, perhaps by opening doors of opportunity—help them as much as you can.

Work Experience

The experience section of your profile begins with your current job and work experience. Again, you can cut and paste the entry from your resume first, then add to this with additional information that you feel is relevant.

Review your entries to see if there is additional experience you would like to add. You have plenty of space here, so as long as your headline and entries for each job start with the most important information as determined by your TJD—making your profile more discoverable and a more tempting read for recruiters—you can continue to add additional supporting information until you run out of space.

Whatever you do, don't be lazy and just list your current job: That gives the impression that you have only had the one. LinkedIn will tell you that you're twelve times more likely to be found by recruiters when you have more than one job listed—perhaps because those other jobs allow you to weight your profile with enough relevant keywords in each job's headline to increase your discoverability in recruiters' database searches.

The inclusion of keywords in each job's headline and in the details of that work experience helps make you more visible. This helps recruiters see your claims of professional competency in context and will dramatically increase the frequency of keyword usage. Do this with each job and your discoverability will steadily rise in the results of recruiters' searches.

Special Projects

If you want to add greater detail about your work, perhaps the story that goes behind special achievements or description of an important project, then you can add these experiences (as many as you like) to each job as Special Projects. Now this is a nice option, but don't get carried away and detail the minutiae of your every working moment. Keep in mind that your goal in a job search is to get into *communication* with the people who can hire you as quickly and frequently as you can, so your LI profile is a marketing device to attract recruiters and start a conversation. This means that too much information can help rule you out of consideration before a conversation even occurs. As a rule of thumb think *moderation*, and in this context it means telling potential employers what you can do but never how you did it—that's for conversation.

Professional and Technology Competencies

LinkedIn has a Skills area that allows you to identify up to fifty different skills. Using your Target Job Deconstruction document to determine the skills your customers seek in someone with your professional title, you should add a list of *professional skills* to your LinkedIn profile.

Getting and Controlling Skill Endorsements

Once your profile is visible to the public, people can endorse you for each of these skills (a favor you can initiate and return). The more endorsements you have of your skills, the more discoverable you become to recruiters. Adding skills to your LinkedIn profile has the same benefits as adding it to your resume: It makes your profile more visible in database searches and your skills more readily accessible to readers.

You can post up to fifty skills in the dialogue box; however, you will also want your contacts to endorse you for these skills, so listing fewer skills can mean more endorsements for each, and more endorsements help your discoverability. As your networks grow, they'll certainly include others who are in transition, and mutual skill endorsements can help you both.

Your visibility in LI database searches does not depend on how many skills you have listed, but rather the volume of endorsements you have for those skills: Ten skills with 100 endorsements each is much better than fifty skills with ten endorsements each, not only for the database algorithms but for the message it sends to the reader.

On the personal settings page you can also decide if you want to permit others to add skills to your list or not. It is best to keep control of what appears on your profile so do not allow this option.

Education

Start with your highest educational level and work backward. While your educational attainments will usually stop with postsecondary education in your resume, with a LinkedIn profile you might want to consider listing high school as well: This increases your networking opportunities. Just a week before the time of writing, I received a connect request from a high school friend living half a world away, whom I'd lost touch with many years ago.

Certifications

Add all your professional certifications; they demonstrate that either your employers, or you personally, have seen fit to invest in your ongoing professional education. They also speak to money that a new employer doesn't have to invest. Additionally, they can be used by recruiters as search terms, making you more discoverable.

Interests

Finally, the place where it is appropriate to add something about your outside interests! If someone has read this far, learning that I enjoy history, historical fiction, kayaking, swing, rhumba, and country dancing, am an obsessed collector of phonographs, prohibition-era cocktail shakers, Emancipation art, and am the world's worst bass player might be of interest, because it allows the reader to see a three-dimensional person; but coming earlier in my profile it would only be a distraction.

Associations and Awards

Include membership in any associations or societies. List profession-related organizations and professional awards first, then follow with groups and awards related to your personal interests.

Reading List

You should include professionally relevant materials here; it is not the venue to share that you have read all three volumes of *50 Shades of Grey*. It isn't relevant to your professional persona and sends entirely the wrong message for a professional audience.

Spelling, Punctuation, and Grammar

The same considerations you applied to spelling, punctuation, and grammar in your resume also apply here. If you have problems creating your profile or editing it, at *www.knockemdead .com,* we create LinkedIn profiles for our resume clients and also offer a separate social networking profile editing service, similar to the one we offer for resumes.

Recommendations

LinkedIn likes your profile to have at least three recommendations and doesn't recognize it as complete until you do. This is in your best interests too, as recommendations from colleagues, coworkers, and past managers give your profile depth and increase your appeal to recruiters. The easiest way to get recommendations is to do them for your colleagues and then ask them to reciprocate. LinkedIn will send a recommendation to the recipient and ask him (a) if he would like to upload it, and (b) if he would like to reciprocate. If he doesn't reciprocate within a couple of days, send a personal request. You don't need to tell someone he *owes* you a reference in return for yours, just that you'd appreciate it.

If you are returning to the workforce after an absence, you can use recommendations from volunteer work. Also, you can reach out to people who gave you written recommendations and ask them to be duplicated on LinkedIn. You can make things easier by sending such people an email with a copy of the recommendation.

Link Your Resume to Your Social Media Profile

Once your profile is complete and supports the story told in your resume, upload the resume as directed. Linking to your resume is useful because a resume is still the most succinct vehicle for sharing your professional skills, and recruiters will use it for their records and to review with hiring managers.

Your resume should also have a mutual link to your LinkedIn profile (beneath your hyperlinked email address), so that HR or the hiring manager can click through and gather more insight into your potential candidacy.

Privacy and Saving Your Work

Building your profile may take a week before you have it exactly right, so you should know that every time you change a sentence on your LinkedIn profile and log out, LinkedIn can automatically send a change of status to your network. As you may make many changes to get it right, you don't want your contacts notified every few minutes. To avoid this, do three things:

1. Write your early drafts on a Word document with headings that match the site's profile subject headers. Then make changes to your heart's content without any danger of unwittingly sharing your edits with the world. When you do upload, you'll invariably still want to tweak your copy and so still want to maintain privacy.
2. Go to *Settings* from the drop-down menu under your name on the top right of your homepage and look for *Privacy Controls.* Choose *Private* while you are making profile changes. This will keep your changes private until your profile is complete and you release it for public display.
3. Save everything in the final published draft in a Microsoft Word document. This will give you a complete social media profile ready for fast adaptation when you join other social networking sites. Back up your work, because if you don't, somewhere along the line you are going to lose it.

You can also use the *Public Profile Settings* to customize your existing LinkedIn URL to make it more attention grabbing and informative—perhaps reflecting your job title.

LI Personalized URL Address

LinkedIn automatically gives your profile an address along the lines of *https://www.linkedin .com/in/Jim-Dowe-715594236*; this allows others to find you and you to refer people to your profile but you can do better. LI allows you to create a personalized URL for your profile to shorten it up and remove the numbers after your name.

Your name is okay, but something that speaks to your job like "TopAccountant" or "HCIexpert" is much better, because LI profile addresses and email addresses are often the very first thing a recruiter or hiring manager sees, so an address that helps identify your professional persona is a distinct benefit. Obvious profession-oriented addresses, such as the above are usually taken, but you can find plenty of ideas for personalizing your LI profile URL in our earlier discussion where we talked about how to create an email address for professional use that is focused on your profession.

You can find details at LinkedIn for customizing your profile here: *www.linkedin.com/help/linkedin/answer/87.*

LinkedIn Badge

LinkedIn now has a badge that can be configured to your LI URL address; it is available in various configurations. Here is one of them:

If you are reading a digital version of the book, you can see this link in action. Click on the badge and it will take you straight to my profile. LinkedIn has made creating and using a badge very easy (about 60 seconds). How to make it happen for your resume is here: *www.linkedin.com/profile/profile-badges.*

Once this is done you can download the LI profile button that is customized to your address and add it to your resume. This is an important step in the integration of your resume and social media. But, the messaging of both must be consistent so do not do the LinkedIn profile until your resume is completed.

Here's a YouTube video that shows you how to customize your LinkedIn URL: *www.youtube.com/watch?v=GIsZJ-6HTRg.*

LinkedIn Networking Tactics

You can learn much more about networking and how to leverage your social networking presence in the latest annual edition of *Knock 'em Dead: The Ultimate Job Search Guide* and in *Knock 'em Dead Social Networking.*

HTML/Multimedia Resume Considerations

An HTML or multimedia resume can be a sensible option if you work in a field where visuals and sound and/or graphics represent critical skills. A good percentage of resume banks and social networking sites accept HTML resumes; plus a simple HTML resume can be created by using the "Save as HTML" command, which you can access in Microsoft Word when you save and name your documents.

If you want to create a small website, you can create a much richer experience for the viewer, adding audio and video and other bells and whistles if they will help. You can add a hyperlink in your standard resume, or in your cover letter/email, that takes the reader to your web-hosted resume. This has the advantage of allowing the viewer to see your background positioned exactly as you wish it to be, with the enrichment of additional media.

HTML and Multimedia Design Considerations

- Don't be seduced by design capabilities for the sake of their flashiness; remember the needs of your customer and your communication goals. Use technology to make life easier for the visitor. For example, your email address can be a hyperlink, so that clicking on it immediately launches the user's email to contact you.
- If the HTML resume ends up being a complex document with graphics, sound, and video, layout is going to be a major consideration. You don't want the mission-critical topics— performance profile, core and technical competencies, education, work samples, etc.—to get lost in the glitz. It is all too easy to get caught up in the aforementioned glitz of building a website, because it's just a convenient and fun way to put off the real grunt work of building your resume.
- Provide a hyperlink that allows the user to print out that beautifully formatted PDF version of your resume.
- Don't start from ground zero; find an example you like and copy it.

Is an Interactive Portfolio/Web-Based Resume a Waste of Time?

Much depends on your situation and what you are trying to sell and to whom. It's a nice thing for anyone to have, but not mandatory unless:

- Your profession is web based
- Your work involves visual and auditory components
- Your work is technology based with a communications component
- Demonstrating technological savvy is a plus for your branding

Since an online portfolio is the most complex resume document you can create, you want the core content of the site to be finished before you start creating this version with all its bells and whistles. The most practical approach is to get your Microsoft Word resume completed, along with the necessary ASCII text versions. Once you've done your due diligence as you develop the other versions, and have your job search up to speed, you can decide if you need to develop this third variation.

Some disadvantages include:

- Adding graphics, visuals, video, and audio is a time-consuming process, and can be expensive if you hire someone to do it for you; most professionals don't need to present themselves in this way.
- If you want an HTML or web-based resume, you'll need to build a website or have one built. This website will then have to be hosted somewhere and you'll have registration fees, hosting fees, and announcement fees (elementary optimization); if this is a foreign language to you, as a website owner you'll have to learn it, because all these things cost money. Apart from paying to have such a site built, these costs are usually small, but they are ongoing and add up over time.
- If you want to build it yourself without any experience, there is a learning curve involved.
- Because the content is more complex, these documents take longer to open and work through, so the content needs to be compelling if you are going to hold anyone's attention.
- You will build a web-based resume because you hope to *send* people to see it. You can't expect recruiters to flock to it, since there is fierce competition to achieve a reasonable search ranking in the world of resumes. So unless you spend a small fortune on optimization, you can't realistically expect much traffic; it is more a place to which you send recruiters.

For most people, having a LinkedIn Profile will be a perfectly adequate substitute for a personal website. On top of this, I know a lot of corporate recruiters and headhunters, and they almost all express a bias against these websites—people who use them are seen as desperate; they'll try anything to get a job. The exceptions are the circumstances mentioned above where the profession makes such a initiative relevant and useful.

The Business Card Resume

The first time you hear about a business card resume, it can sound like a gimmick, and you should know better than to waste valuable job search time pursuing gimmicks. That said, business cards are an accepted sales tool the world over, and for a job hunter they're so much less intrusive than carrying around a wad of resumes under your arm.

If you want to try a business card resume, you must consider the severely limited space available to you and use that space wisely:

Front of the Card

- List critical information: Your name, Target Job Title, telephone number, and email address.
- Use legible, businesslike (Times Roman, Arial) fonts.
- Make it readable. Limit the word count so that you can maximize font size to increase readability; better to have one legible email address than add a social network address and have them both be illegible.
- No one in a position to hire you can read an 8-point font, and reminding someone that he/she is old and has failing eyesight . . . not a good sales pitch.

Back of the Card

Space is minimal, so less is more and readability is everything; the words you choose must communicate *both* your understanding of the job and your ability to deliver when you are doing that job:

1. Repeat your Target Job Title.
2. This is followed by a two-word headline on the next line: Performance Profile.
3. Follow this with a single short sentence that addresses the #1 deliverable of your target job. The #1 deliverable in your job (and all jobs) is—say it with me now—the identification, prevention, and solution of problems within a specific area of professional expertise. It is ultimately what we all get hired to do.
4. Finish with a social network address that delivers a comprehensive professional profile to any interested reader, such as your LinkedIn profile, your web-based resume, or any other URL that delivers the full story on your professional capabilities.

As an example we can all relate to, an accounting professional who worked in accounts receivable, might have the rear side of a business card resume that looks something like this:

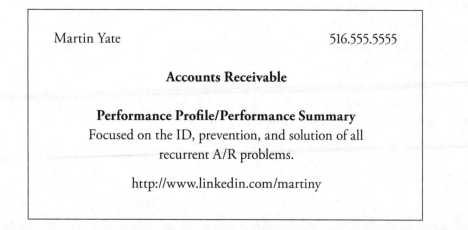

Martin Yate   516.555.5555

Accounts Receivable

Performance Profile/Performance Summary
Focused on the ID, prevention, and solution of all
recurrent A/R problems.

http://www.linkedin.com/martiny

Notice that by starting this mini-resume with a verb, you not only show understanding of what is at the heart of this job, you also deliver a powerful personal brand statement by telling the reader what to expect.

Resume for Promotions

We tend to think of our resume as a tool to get a new job at another company, and forget that we can use it to get a promotion where we already are.

You need a job-targeted resume for pursuing internal promotions because:

- No one is paying as much attention to you as you would like.
- It shows an employer you are serious about growth.
- It's a powerful way to get yourself viewed in a different light.
- It puts you on a par with external candidates who will have job-targeted resumes.
- It puts you ahead of these candidates, because you are a known quantity.
- When you have the required skills, it's much easier to get promoted from within.

Promotions come to those who earn them, not as a reward for watching the clock for three years. Thinking through what's really needed for your next step up the ladder, building the skills to earn that promotion, and then creating a resume that positions you for the job, is smart strategic thinking.

Your promotion campaign starts with determining a specific target job for the next logical step up the ladder, and then understanding the requirements for someone holding that job title.

Collect job postings for that next step and deconstruct the target job's specific deliverables. Once you have a crystal-clear idea of what is needed to succeed in the target job:

- Identify areas for skill development.
- Determine how you will develop these skills.
- Volunteer for assignments that build these skills and give you practical experience that can become part of your resume.

Once your skills have reached 70 percent of those required for the new job, you can start building a resume targeted to that promotion.

Proofread and Test-Email All Versions of Your Resume

Before you send any version of your resume, proofread it carefully. Send your electronic cover letters and resume attachments to yourself and to a friend or family member. Ask them for printouts of your practice email messages and resumes to ensure that what you intended to send is actually what was received, and can be printed out. Often, this exercise will help you find mistakes, bloopers, or larger problems incurred during the conversion process. If you find typos at this late stage, reward yourself with a smack upside the head for being sloppy. The most common and annoying problem is that the contact information you carefully put at the top of the second page now appears halfway down it; these are the important mistakes you can easily catch with this exercise.

CHAPTER 9
READY TO LAUNCH

WHY EVERYONE HATES reading resumes and what you can do about it. Here are some powerful construction strategies to simultaneously make your resume information dense and visually accessible to tired, distracted recruiters and hiring managers.

You are in the home stretch, giving your resume the final polish before releasing it to a very discriminating public. It has to be:

- Job focused and data dense to beat out the competition in the resume database wars.
- Typographically clean, and visually accessible to accommodate the recruiters' initial scan.
- Headline rich and textually concise to deliver a compelling message.

Make this happen and your resume will get pulled for review from the resume databases. It will then get serious attention from recruiters and hiring managers.

The Importance of Immediate Impact

Your resume will get between five and forty seconds of initial attention, and the more accessible it is to the tired and distracted eyes of recruiters and hiring managers, the closer the attention it will receive. You'll improve the chances that your resume will receive attention if you:

1. *Make it readable.* Stop worrying about page count. In resumes, as in everything, *form follows function*; use the space you need to tell the story you need to tell. Use 11- and 12-point fonts that are easier on adult eyes. You do not have to use 9- and 10-point fonts only a twenty-year-old can read in order to cram everything on one or two pages. (Tip: Twenty-year-olds are almost never in a position to hire you.)
2. *Check your headlines.* They help a reader achieve and maintain focus. The first page of your resume always needs to start off strong, and there is no better way of doing this than with headlines that help accessibility and comprehension.

Target Job Title
(What the resume is about)

Performance Profile
(A snapshot of what I can do)

Professional Competencies
(The key professional skills that help me do my job well)

Technology Competencies
(Optional: the technical skills that help me do my job well)

Performance Highlights
(Optional: my outstanding achievements as they relate to the job)

Professional Experience
(Where and when everything happened)

3. *Check Professional Competencies and Technology Competencies.* These are the hard skills that enable you to do what you do. Each word or phrase should act as a headline of capability and topic for discussion.
4. *Performance/Career Highlights.* This is an optional section, provided that your experience has the achievements to support it.

A first page with these headlines and job-focused content in readable fonts will draw in the reader.

Fonts and Font Sizes

You can use one font throughout your resume, but never use more than two fonts in your resume: one for headlines and the other for the body copy. The most popular fonts for business *communication* are Arial and Times or Times New Roman. They probably look boring because you are so used to seeing them, but you see them so much because they are clear and very readable. Bottom line: They work. The biggest criticism of these fonts is their lack of flair and design value. Below are some other fonts that are good for headlines and body copy, since they are readable and almost universally recognized by printers (obviously a plus if you plan on having someone actually read your resume). The nature of each font is unique and the actual size of each is going to vary. Don't be a slave to 12-point: Sometimes 11-point might work with a particular font. Just don't use a smaller font size to keep your resume to one or two pages. Your resume must be easily readable by those tired and distracted eyes.

Avoid or minimize capitalized text, as it's tough on the eyes. Many people think it makes a powerful statement when used in headlines, but all it does is cause eyestrain and give the reader the impression that you are shouting.

Good for headlines:
Arial
Times/Times New Roman
Century Gothic
Verdana

Gill Sans
Lucida Sans

Good for body copy:

Arial	Georgia
Times/Times New Roman	Goudy Old Style
Garamond	

Each of the above is in 12-point font, but you can see that the nature of each font is unique and the actual size of each is going to vary.

Avoid "script" fonts that look similar to handwriting. While they look attractive to the occasional reader, they are harder on the eyes of people who read any amount of business correspondence. That said, in the resumes later in this book you will see examples of just this sort of font. For example, the arts, education, and (sometimes) healthcare are areas where the warmer and more personal look of a script font can work and still present a professional-looking resume. Use with discretion.

Avoid Typos Like the Plague!

Resumes that are riddled with misspeltings get siht-canned *fast*. How annoying is that last sentence? You have a spellchecker; use it.

A couple of years back, I counseled an executive vice president in the $400k-per-year range. He was having problems getting in front of the right people. The first paragraph of his resume stated that he was an executive with "superior communication skills." Unfortunately, the other twelve words of the sentence contained a spelling error! Fortunately, we caught it. In an age of spellcheckers, this sloppiness isn't acceptable at any level.

A word of caution: The spellchecker can't catch everything, so you'll have to do some editing work yourself. For example, spellcheck won't catch the common mistyping of "form" for "from" because "form" is a word. Similarly, your spellchecker can't help you, but educated people will immediately recognize a cretin who doesn't know *too* from *to* and *two*, *your* from *you're*, or *it's* from *its*.

Once you decide on font(s), stick with them. More than two fonts will be vaguely disquieting to the reader. You can do plenty to liven up the visual impact of the page and create emphasis with **bold**, *italic*, ***bold italic***, <u>underlining</u>, sizing of words, and highlighting, used judiciously.

Remember that spellcheckers aren't infallible either and will confuse words and their appropriate usage, so get someone you trust to check it over as well. You can also use our *Knock 'em Dead* editor for a typographical and grammar check; just come to the resume services page at the website.

Proofing the Print Resume

Even in the age of email and databases, you will need print versions of your resume. For example, you should always take printed copies to your interviews: This guarantees each interviewer will have your background laid out in the way you want it. Print it out now to ensure that the onscreen layout matches that of the printed document. Make sure the pagination of the printed copy works the way you intend. Double-check the printed copy for:

- Layout and balance
- Typos and grammatical errors
- Punctuation and capitalization
- Page alignment errors
- That everything has been underlined, capitalized, bolded, italicized, and indented exactly as you intended

Print it out on as many different printers as you reasonably can. Why? Depending on the printer, you can find fonts performing differently. That's one of the reasons for using *Times* and *Arial*: They print without problems on every printer.

Appearance Checklist

Let the resume rest overnight or longer, then pick it up and review it with fresh eyes, immediately after you have reread your TJD.

- What's your immediate reaction to it? Is it clear who and what this document is about? Does it clearly address the needs of your TJD? Are the lines clean?
- Does the copy under each of your headlines tell a convincing story?
- Does the first page of the resume identify you as someone clearly capable of delivering on the job's requirements?
- Have you used only one side of the page?
- Are your fonts readable, in the 11- to 12-point range?
- Does the layout accommodate the reader's needs, rather than outmoded concerns on resume length?
- Are your paragraphs no more than five lines long? Are your sentences fewer than twenty words long?
- Are your sentences short on personal pronouns and long on action verbs?
- Is there plenty of white space around important areas, such as Target Job Title and your Opening and Closing Brand Statements? Recruiters and managers may be reviewing resumes on handheld devices, and plenty of space helps readability.

The Final Product

The paper version of your resume should be printed on standard, 8½" x 11" (letter-size) paper. Paper comes in different weights and textures; good resume-quality paper has a weight designation of between 20 and 25 pounds. Lighter paper feels flimsy and curls; heavier paper is unwieldy. Most office supply stores carry paper and envelopes packaged as kits for resumes and cover letters.

As for paper color, white, pale gray, and cream are the prime choices. They are straightforward, no-nonsense colors that speak directly to your professionalism, assuming you want to be perceived as straightforward and no-nonsense. I'm assured that some of the pale pastel shades can be both attractive and effective. Personally, I think that on a first meeting, most professionals don't come off as strongly as they might when dressed in pink.

Cover letter stationery should have the same contact information as your resume and should *always* match the color and weight of the paper used. Again, it's part of the professional branding issue that underlies all the little things you pay attention to in a job search.

Set up letterhead for your cover letter stationery, using the same fonts you used on the resume. The coordinated paper size, color, weight, and fonts will give your resume and cover letter a cohesive look.

CHAPTER 10
THE RESUMES

I HAVE INCLUDED resumes from a wide range of jobs so that you will be able to find a resume telling a story similar to yours. However, *resume layouts are tailored not to the job but to the person and his or her story.* So when you see a resume layout that works for you, use it: Don't be restrained because the example is of someone in another profession.

Zoe Blake

4332 Judge Street   (631) 579-5357
Elmhurst, NY 11373   zoe.blake@gmail.com

Accounting / Finance

PERFORMANCE PROFILE

A highly astute, energetic, and team-spirited 2012 accounting graduate seeking opportunity to contribute to an organization's goals and objectives. Accurate, precise, and ethically responsible in all work-related assignments. Quick learner with an eagerness for learning and expanding accounting capabilities. Proven ability in identifying problems and implementing innovative solutions.

✓ Recent college graduate with proven analytical and critical thinking skills.
✓ Disciplined with a desire to succeed as evidenced by working 20 hours per week while attending college full-time.
✓ Exceptional skills in written documentation and verbal communication.
✓ Effective interpersonal and leadership skills supported by an enthusiastic, team player attitude.
✓ Foreign Language—proficient in Chinese.
✓ Technology: MS Word, Excel, PowerPoint, Access, Database, and Adobe Photoshop; Internet savvy.

PROFESSIONAL SKILLS

- Customer Service Skills
- Accounts Payable
- Accounts Receivable
- Budget Forecasting
- GAAP
- Inventory Analysis
- Bookkeeping
- Journal Entries
- Financial Presentations
- Management Skills
- Cost Control
- Market Research

EDUCATION

Bachelor of Science in Accounting/Finance, Michigan State University, E. Lansing, MI   2016
Relevant Course Work: Intermediate Accounting I, Intermediate Accounting II, Accounting Theory, Accounting Principles, Government Accounting, Income Tax, and Auditing.

ACTIVITIES

Volunteer Income Tax Assistance (V.I.T.A.)
Prepared income tax returns for low-income families and internationals.

EXPERIENCE

Michigan State University, E. Lansing, MI   January 2014–Current
Student Manager, Dining Services
- Calculate weekly payroll for all employees.
- Conduct store management as well as accounting and financial presentations for daily business performance to enhance utilization of funds.
- Supervise daily sales operations and training for new hires to maintain quality and efficiency.

Student Employee   January 2012–December 2014
- Provided high-quality customer services and efficiently carried out monetary transactions.
- Assisted with opening and closing accounting procedures for Starbucks Coffee shop and campus deli store.

Student Worker, Rivers Center   January 2010–December 2012
- Arranged services to meet a large portion of the leisure, recreational, conference, and meeting needs on campus.
- Managed procedures of business conferences and banquets for campus needs.
- Successfully promoted student-faculty interaction and learning outside of the classroom environment.

HOLLY BOYETTE

42 Sand Drive, Jacksonville, Florida • 904-839-6943 • auditeagle@gmail.com

Auditor

Performance Profile

Top-performing CPA with five years of comprehensive public accounting and auditing experience in domestic and international settings. Progressively responsible positioning with a top-ranked accounting firm serving a wide range of clients. Broad knowledge of IFRS and US GAAP with the ability to work productively and deliver results in pressure-intensive situations.

♦ Strong analytical and critical thinking skills with a consistent record of anticipating problems and finding solutions, while exhibiting superior judgment and a balanced, realistic understanding of issues.
♦ A willing and eager learner who is constantly updating knowledge and skills. Completed all four parts of the CPA exam within four months while working full-time. Passed all exams on the first try.
♦ A lead-by-example, self-motivated mindset; able to set effective priorities and implement decisions to achieve immediate and long-term goals and meet operational deadlines.
♦ Builds and maintains excellent client relationships to ensure customer satisfaction.
♦ Fluent in English, French, and Afrikaans.

Professional Competencies

✓ Certified Public Accountant	✓ US GAAP	✓ Audit Methodology
✓ Chartered Accountant	✓ IFRS	✓ Financial Audits
✓ General Accounting Operations	✓ Sarbanes-Oxley Compliance	✓ Business Development
✓ Analytical	✓ Resource Management	✓ Communication
✓ Organizational	✓ Project Management	✓ Presentation
✓ Troubleshooting	✓ Staff Training & Development	✓ Report Writing

Professional Experience

Hepburn & Associates LLP, Jacksonville, FL   2009–Present
International assurance, tax advisory services firm. 35,000 employees and $4B in global revenue.

AUDITOR   2014–Present

♦ Working collaboratively and independently, conduct client engagements from start to finish, including planning, executing, directing, and completing financial audits and managing to budget. Supervise three to five interns and audit associates.
♦ Charged with assurance services, including assisting Senior Audit Associates, Audit Managers, and Audit Partners in performing external audits of public and private companies.
♦ Maintain excellent client relationships to ensure customer satisfaction; partner with all levels of client management and staff to effectively perform audit services.
♦ Proactively work with key client management to gather information, resolve audit-related issues, and offer recommendations for business and process improvements.
♦ Perform tests of controls including Sarbanes-Oxley Compliance and substantive procedures of audit. Compose project performance and budget reports for managers, partners, and clients.
♦ Prepare and review journal entries in accordance with GAAP; research errors and perform balance sheet reconciliations.
♦ Provide strategic support to Junior Audit Associates, advising, reviewing, and assisting with work.

BUSINESS ADVISORY SERVICES ASSOCIATE   2011–2014

Selected to work on confidential investigative project with one of the largest banks in the United States.
- Accountable for review and test of controls of bank's credit agreements in terms of their own and government credit guidelines.
- Involved in team and client discussion for review comments and recommendations.
- Performed review and quality control assessment of colleagues' and junior team members' work.
- Provided strategic support to Junior BAS Associates, advising, reviewing, and assisting with work.

AUDIT ASSOCIATE   2010–2011

Offered full-time permanent position with Hepburn & Associates in FL as result of performance excellence.
- Tasked with assurance services, including assisting Senior Audit Associates, Audit Managers, and Audit Partners in performing external audits of public and private companies.

SENIOR TRAINEE ACCOUNTANT   2009
JUNIOR TRAINEE ACCOUNTANT

Assisted with audits while acquiring experience for Chartered Accounting program.

Education

~Certified Public Accountant   2012
~Proposal Writing, University of Phoenix, Phoenix, AZ   2012

Professional Organizations / Affiliations

American Institute of Certified Public Accountants (AICPA)
British Institute of Chartered Accountants (SAICA)

Computer Skills

Software: Microsoft Access, Word, Excel; SharePoint; J.D. Edwards; AS400 (eServer iSeries/400)
Operating Systems: Microsoft XP, Windows7

Languages

Fluent in English, French, and Afrikaans, verbal and written

Kanji Mosoui

Boston, MA 02108   617.324.XXXX   finance_focused@gmail.com

QUALIFICATIONS FOR BANK OF AMERICA INTERNSHIP

➤ Committed to a career combining formal education in economics with practical work. Experienced with analyses for project management, including budgets, labor resources, and timelines.

➤ Prepared and delivered numerous presentations on project status to city and PG&E officials. Researched and presented options to property owners and investors for construction materials.

➤ History of taking on responsibility and successfully managing personnel for multimillion-dollar projects. Excellent communication with individuals, businesses, municipalities, and professional firms.

➤ Conversational Spanish.

Education

SAN JOSE STATE UNIVERSITY, San Jose, CA

Masters, Economics   Anticipated Dec 2017

Bachelor of Arts, Economics   Graduated 2016

Leadership Experience

PHI DELTA THETA, San Jose State, CA   2014 – 2016

Consecutively **Treasurer, House Manager, Vice President, President**

Professional Experience

CONFIDENTIAL, San Jose, CA   2010 – 2014

Installer of wet and dry underground utilities for new developers and municipalities

Project Manager

- Managed $3.6M project to install new underground dry utilities and new street lights on Main Street in Santa Cruz. Worked with city, PG&E, telephone and cable companies. Project took approximately 1 1/2 years for planning, execution, and completion. Averaged approximately 15 full-time crew, including both union and non-union.

DAVÉ CONSTRUCTION, San Jose, CA   2009

Residential and investment property new construction and renovation

Construction Manager / Project Manager

- Functioned as general contractor for construction of new $2M, 4,700-square-foot residential property. Hired and managed approximately 300 subcontractors and vendors over the course of the project.
- Obtained building permits, and worked with general contractors and clients on architectural plans. Oversaw daily construction, and handled accounting, including paying all subcontractors.
- Worked with owner to convert 1,000-square-foot home to 3,200 square feet. Same duties noted as above. Sale of home resulted in net profit of almost $400K for property owner.

Excellent references available

JAMES MARTIN

Atlanta, GA 30305
678.348.2484 | james.martin@comcast.net
Linked in profile

REGULATORY COMPLIANCE SPECIALIST

Protecting companies from financial and legal risk through the development of compliance policy.

Compliance expert offering 15+ years of related experience in banking capital markets, brokerage and investment firms, and insurance sector, ensuring strict adherence to legal and financial regulations to alleviate risk exposure, facilitate smooth audits, and enable company profitability. Adept at maintaining pulse on company operations to monitor, investigate, and ensure fulfillment of regulatory obligations and alignment of compliance policies. Advise key decision makers on regulatory and compliance requirements to aid in development of strategic solutions that support new programs.

Registered investment advisor whose wide-ranging expertise spans Investment Advisers Act of 1940, US Commodity Futures Trading Commission/National Futures Association (CFTC/NFA), Municipal Securities Rulemaking Board (MSRB), Financial Industry Regulatory Authority (FINRA), Dodd Frank, and Securities and Exchange Commission (SEC) laws and regulations. Thrive in evolving, high-pressure environments where swift, effective resolution of identified risk is paramount.

PROFESSIONAL SKILLS

Regulatory Compliance	Due Diligence	Performance Management
Legal Analysis	Staff Development	Fiduciary Responsibility
Risk Assessments	Team Leadership	Anti-money Laundering (AML)
Controls	Account Surveillance	Know-Your-Customer (KYC)
Negotiations	Mediations/Arbitrations	Training & Development

PERFORMANCE HIGHLIGHTS

- Played pivotal role in alleviating AML concerns through automation of new international account forms, remediating over 500 HH in 3 months.
- Thwarted reputational and financial damage of firm by uncovering and remediating adverse practices among select financial advisors via conducting surveillance on personal trading and researching patterns.
- Increased volume of licensed support staff through implementation of Series 7 training program as well as raised number of certifications held by financial advisors by offering incentives and training program for office staff.

PROFESSIONAL EXPERIENCE

Suntrust Bank | Atlanta, GA   1998 – 2015

Administrative Manager, Vice President – Global Wealth Management (1999 – 2015)
Appointed to ensure branch adherence to internal and regulatory agency requirements as well as to provide guidance on trading strategy policies, including options, commodities, derivatives, and structured investments.

Monitored office activities, from trading to complaint resolution, and facilitated biweekly performance management meetings, liaising with senior compliance executives.

Administrative Manager, Vice President – Global Wealth Management, continued

Guided branch to earn satisfactory FINRA and branch audit ratings. Supervised 250 employees and negotiated employee disciplinary actions and client complaints via mediation or arbitration.

- Spearheaded smooth transition of million-dollar wealth management teams from competition to Merrill Lynch platform.
- Bolstered office productivity by analyzing product profitability, helping financial advisors better understand products to increase their payout.
- Championed 1st successful internal audit with no significant findings, examining recordkeeping, trade tickets, correspondence, structured investments, trading activity, and client activity to ensure compliance.
- Fostered numerous strategic business relationships, forging alliance between Bank Street College of Education and branch office for summer intern program as well as proposing partnership between Carver Federal Bank and Atlanta-based African American Financial Advisors.
- Implemented and led annual September 11th Memorial Project, fostering team building and boosting morale among staff members.

Financial Advisor   1998 – 1999

Managed portfolios for more than 100 clients, facilitating financial seminars and providing financial planning expertise for individual, corporate, institutional, and nonprofit clients.

EARLIER CAREER

Bank South | **Compliance/Quality Control Associate**	1997 – 1998
Kirshbaum & Berman | **Compliance Associate**	1996 – 1997
South East Securities International | **Compliance Associate**	1994 – 1996
South East Securities International | **Sales Associate, Fixed Income Government Agency Dealer Desk**	1990 – 1994

EDUCATION

Bachelor of Business Administration: Georgia Southern University
Law Coursework (18 months): University of Georgia

PROFESSIONAL LICENSES

Series 3
Series 4
Series 7
Series 9
Series 10
Series 63
Series 65
Certified Financial Manager

PROFESSIONAL AFFILIATION

India Exports, Inc., Executive Assistant to Executive Director, Mentor

Sylvana Cecchini

Hartford, Connecticut   203-341-2434   syl.cecchini@att.net

Senior Credit Analyst with MBA and 10 years of investment banking experience.
With Expertise in Credit Evaluation, Risk Analysis, & Risk Mitigation

Credit Review, Analysis, & Structuring	Underwriting & Portfolio Management	Bonds/Securities Market
Corporate & Industry Research	Risk Infrastructure Advisement	C-Level Communications
Financial Analysis & Reporting	Risk Assessment/Risk Assignment Plans	Global Business Relationships
Presentations & Negotiations	Investment Banking/Corporate Lending	Tax Laws & Regulations

Performance Highlights

- **CPA** with substantial experience managing all aspects of credit analysis, credit risk, credit approval processes, including corporate/industry research, financial statement review, credit evaluation, and risk mitigation for multibillion-dollar portfolios of blue-chip corporations.
- **Communicator** with the ability to condense complex financial data into a readable format and present evidence-based opinions regarding financial health and credit worthiness of new and existing bank clients.
- **Integral part of investment banking teams** that:
  - **Financed the first geothermal power plant in Indonesia** out of a bank in Japan.
  - **Built banking relationships** with some of the largest oil and gas corporations in Southeast Asia.
  - **Loaned funds to diverse corporations and structured finance transactions in Oceania and Asia** including key markets of Australia, Singapore, Indonesia, Thailand, Malaysia, Philippines, Vietnam, Hong Kong, India, and New Zealand.
- **Worked for the Malaysian Ministry of Finance** as a part of the startup team that implemented the framework for operations of the first Malaysian financial guarantor of Malaysian bonds and Islamic securities market (sukuk) valued at US$5 billion annually.

Professional Experience

CONNECTICUT COMMUNITY BANK, West Hartford, CT   September 2011–Present
Senior Analyst, Credit Division

PEOPLE'S UNITED BANK, Hartford, CT   September 2009–August 2011
Head, Portfolio Risk

FARMINGTON BANK, Farmington, CT   January 2008–July 2009
Vice President, Credit Research

CONNECTICUT CREDIT, Wethersfield, CT   November 2004–December 2007
Credit Analyst, Department of Industrial and Consumer Products

JONES TAX PREPARATION SERVICES, Rocky Hill, CT   April 2003–October 2004
Tax Preparer

Education

Master of Business Administration, MBA–*UCONN*, Storrs, CT 2013
Bachelor of Accounting–*Central Connecticut State University*, New Britain, CT 2003

Personal Data
Languages: Fluent in English, Italian, and Portuguese

Professional Affiliations
Society for Certified Public Accountants

Caroline Olivero, CPA

2405 Buttercup Drive
Kansas City, KS 66103

913-863-4320
cpa66103@gmail.com

Financial Analyst

Performance Summary

Senior-level Accountant, Financial Analyst, and Internal Auditor with more than 15 years of experience in accounting and finance. Skilled in gathering and analyzing data, confirming accuracy, and performing monthly review of financial information. Quick, decisive, and highly effective financial strategist with proven success ensuring compliance with federal, state, and internal regulations and policies. Maintains the overall integrity of accounting and financial systems. Skilled in coordinating with regional finance teams on statement preparation. Able to prepare financial statements and summarize results for management and key stakeholders. Impeccable integrity and work ethic.

Professional Skills

Financial Analysis	Variance Analysis	GAAP	SAP & PeopleSoft
Financial Close	Sarbanes-Oxley	FCPA	Staff Leadership
SOX/non-SOX Controls	Communication	Relationship Development	Report Development
Account Reconciliations	Financial Statements	Internal Controls	Documentation
Microsoft Office Suite	Issue Resolution	Financial Reports	Compliance

——Professional Experience——

International Paper Company, Brunswick, GA   2013 – 2017
World's largest pulp and paper producer with $26B in annual revenue and 61,500 employees worldwide.

Senior Financial Analyst

Assisted in performing internal control reviews of Beverage Packaging Division manufacturing facilities in North America, Asia, and Latin America. Provided assistance with development and implementation of audit control activities for the division. Ensured audit programs were compliant with International Paper's SOX compliance program by coordinating with the compliance group. Developed new process narratives and Visio flowcharts for identification of control deficiencies and improvement of audit efficiency for Latin American locations. Prepared 2005 and 2006 GAAP financial statements and footnotes for division audits in preparation for divestiture, including coordination with external auditors and management.

- Coordinated with International Paper Accounting Staff in preparation of GAAP consolidated financial statements for Liquid Packaging Division.
- Coordinated with the International Paper's SOX compliance group to ensure compliance with SOX compliance program.
- Developed and implemented audit procedures used by the Liquid Packaging Division subsequent to acquisition by coordinating with International Paper's Internal Audit Group.

FedEx Express, Atlanta, GA   2008 – 2013
The largest business unit within FedEx, which has $43B in annual revenue and 300,000 employees worldwide.

Senior Accounting Research Analyst

Provided maintenance of the accounting data for long-term aircraft leases, including ensuring all leases were accrued on straight-line basis and amortizing gain on sale-lease aircraft. Reviewed expense line items for leased property and equipment expense, as well as long-term aircraft lease expense, including analyzing account variations, obtaining explanations for business reason for variation, and reporting findings to management. Provided quarterly summary of accounting information for management review. Prepared monthly summary of underutilized leased property.

- Selected to research accounting matters for the Corporate Accounting Group through preparation of a quarterly summary of accounting-related information for management review. Report summarized new or proposed EITF issues, FASB and AcSEC exposure drafts or proposals, and new or proposed SEC rulings that affected FedEx Express.

Coca-Cola Enterprises, Atlanta, GA   1997 – 2008
One of the world's leading beverage companies with $8B in annual revenue and 13,250 employees.

Senior Financial Analyst   1999 – 2008

Charged with providing management and support for the operating budget within the Mid-South Division. Traveled to various center locations and coordinated with Branch Managers, Division, and Corporate Management to ensure budget reflected expenditures.

- Spearheaded new method of analyzing contract profitability with local and primary schools, as well as colleges and universities. Project included downloading sales reports and incorporating into NPV analysis.

Senior Accountant   1997 – 1999

Prepared entries for month-end close, performed analysis, and provided explanations for various operating expense variances for management. Designed and delivered ad hoc reports. Provided management and training for senior accountant and staff accountant. Reconciled balance sheet accounts, including third-party marketing accounts, bank accounts, and division payroll account. Prepared federal and state tax packages for submission to the corporate tax department.

- Assisted in the implementation of a systematic method of accruing invoices by developing a database application utilized to track invoices and follow up on outstanding items.

—— **Education and Complementary Experience**——

Bachelor of Science, Finance, Texas A&M University, College Station, TX

Certified Public Accountant (CPA)

Meredith Sommers

24 Summerwood Terrace NE Kenwood Drive
Scarsdale, NY 10583

914.241.2434
meredith.sommers@gmail.com

Healthcare Sales Management

Performance Profile

Achievements: Percentage of Plan by Year

Year		%	Year		%
Year	2015	99%	Year	2010	153%
Year	2014	126%	Year	2009	183%
Year	2013	147%	Year	2008	99%
Year	2012	136%	Year	2007	166%
Year	2011	127%	Year	2006	85%

Eighteen years of Medical/Healthcare sales and a proven track record of consistently outperforming sales quotas, developing new business, building strong customer relationships, and effectively managing time and territory. Proficient and persistent in all stages of the sales cycle. Uncompromising commitment to management and customer service excellence balanced by the highest degree of integrity in all relationships and transactions.

Proven abilities include:

- ✓ Excel in prospecting, qualifying, developing, and closing sales opportunities.
- ✓ Experienced sales trainer in corporate classroom settings in addition to field training.
- ✓ Expert in consultative and solution selling with proven ability to capitalize on sales opportunities.
- ✓ Ability to gain cooperation and buy-in of multiple decision-makers in complex business environments.
- ✓ Strong healthcare IT industry knowledge and experience.
- ✓ Visionary strategist with the ability to articulate solutions to customer problems and maximize revenues.
- ✓ Strong ability to work effectively, independently, and collaboratively with internal and external sales teams.
- ✓ Change agent with expertise in indentifying business needs and delivering innovative solutions.
- ✓ Exceptional customer relationship management skills.
- ✓ Notable efficiency, organizational skills, and ability to multitask projects and set priorities.
- ✓ Strong communication and presentation skills.

Core Skills

Contract Negotiations	Margin Enhancement	Lead Generation	Presentations
Consultative Selling	Business Development	Change Agent	Prospecting & Closing
Revenue Growth	Cost Containment	Customer Retention	Team Building
Solution Selling	Key Account Management	Training & Educating	OEM/E-commerce

Professional Experience

Plastech, New York City, NY   2011 – Present
Manager of Business Development - Integrated Healthcare Solutions IT/VAR/Healthcare

-continued-

Selected to build Plastech's Integrated Healthcare Solutions market share and revenue within the $25 million IT/VAR channel. Established strategic vision and developed team of Business Development Healthcare representatives. Managed new product integrations, new partnerships, and new product solutions.

- Instrumental in building new and existing national distribution channels and vertical business partners.
- Completed certification and validation of 87+ EMR/EHR/Practice Management Software integrations with company's products leading to peripheral bundles, assessment add-in, and multiple purchasing channels, creating 33% new organic growth revenue in EMR category sales in 2011.
- Initiated, negotiated, and created Dell partnership resulting in $329K of new organic sales in 2014.
- Essential role in hiring team of new Healthcare Business Development managers. Designed strategy, trained new hires on the Healthcare industry, set direction, directed team, and managed multiple projects simultaneously.
- Negotiated, procured, and managed new distributor partner, SYNNEX. Drove SYNNEX sales of DYMO products from zero dollars to over $5 million in sales from 2012 to 2016.
- Awarded "Quota Buster Award" 2013; $1.4 million in growth for a territory total of $4,895,854.

Centor Inc., Newark, NJ   2005 – 2011
Surgical Sales Specialist
Quickly re-established Centor market presence in a territory that had been vacant for over two years. Managed and led all sales activities in hospitals, military bases, and surgery centers. Collaborated with local architects, hospital C-level administrators, and hospital military and surgery center department leaders to develop an in-depth understanding of customer needs and align focus and scope of territory management.

- Successfully developed new revenue-generating customer base with no prior information or CRM content data; generated $540K in new sales.
- Closed sale on first Bariatric Surgery Center in KC with all Centor equipment.
- Earned prestigious "Summit Award" for No. 1 Region 2006.
- Increased sales 83% from $157K to $1.3M.
- Completed year 2005 in top 10 of the Centor President's Club.

Technology

Operating Systems: Mac OSX, Windows; Software: SalesForce.com, Microsoft Office Suites and Windows, MS Word, Excel, PowerPoint, Office Communicator, Adobe Acrobat 8 Pro, SAP, Sales Perspectives, ACT, Gold Mine

Education

Bachelor's of Science, Business Administration, Bryn Mawr College   1986
Bryn Mawr, PA

Professional Development

Growth Partnering Sales: Value-Added Strategies for the 21st Century   2005
Allergan Sponsored

Gemba Kaizen Training, Kankakee, IL   2003
Kaizen Certificate of Completion
Esselte – Centor Sponsored

Rex Moore

Charlotte, NC 28078

Linked in profile

704-341-3424
rex_moore@att.net

Managed Care Coordinator

Performance Summary

Unique blend of academic achievement with strong knowledge and practical experience within the healthcare industry. Selected for internship at Wake Forest University School of Medicine within the Division of Dermatology for management of multiple projects while gaining understanding of Academic Medical Centers. Experienced in providing customer service and support for Medicare and Medicaid members by assisting with questions on benefits, billing, and physician research. Leverage outstanding customer service, analytical skills, strategic planning, and communication skills.

——Professional Skills——

Healthcare Knowledge	Analytical Skills	Communication	Technology
* Medicare	* Data Analysis	* Team Collaboration	* Microsoft Office/PowerPoint
* Medicare Fraud & Abuse	* Strategic Planning	* Customer Service	* Data Entry
* HIPPA & EDI Standards	* Report Development	* SPSS	* OSX Mountain Lion
* Academic Medical Center	* Issue Resolution	* Patient Support	* Mentoring & Leadership

——Education—

M.S., Health Administration, Wake Forest University   **2015**
Student Association of Health Managers

B.S., Major Psychology • Minor Business Administration, Armstrong Atlantic State   **2013**
Dean's Scholarship, Dean's List, Alpha Phi Omega, Service Fraternity

CMS MLN Web Courses:
HIPPA and EDI Standards Uniform Billing
Medicare Fraud and Abuse: Prevention, Detection and Reporting, and Medicare Parts A–D

——Professional Experience——

BestCare Partnership, Charlotte, NC   2013 to Present
A global customer service provider for BestCare members, with offices in the United States, Mexico, and Philippines.
Customer Service Representative

Provide support to BestCare Dual members and NC Medicaid members by answering a variety of questions on benefits, billings, and payment denials. Complete research on physicians, hospitals, and medical equipment companies for members. Utilize Care Connector, BestCare, and Coverage Navigator to locate providers, review benefits, plan formularies, and provide general information.
- Achieved a quality score of 92% by following approval processes and researching information prior to answering member questions.
- Expanded personal knowledge of Medicare and NC Medicaid regulations and guidelines.

Wake Forest University School of Medicine, Winston-Salem, NC   Summer 2012
Intern
Managed multiple projects within Dermatology and Medical Oncology.

Asheville Institute of Addiction Recovery, Asheville, NC   Summer 2011
Intern
Gained strong knowledge of addictions and recovery, including the 12-step process. Attended group and individual meetings. Communicated with staff, physicians, and patients.

Hillary Sanders

34 Mountain Pass Trail
Portland, OR 97201

in View my profile

541.431-4342
OrthoSales@outlook.com

Orthopedics Account Manager

PERFORMANCE PROFILE

Top-producing medical device sales professional with 12+ years' experience and proven track record of surpassing sales quotas, developing new business, via effective time and territory management. Extensive orthopedic knowledge of reconstructive, trauma, orthobiologics, hand, foot, and ankle technologies. Strong business acumen with the ability to execute the sales cycle, leading customer to action. Ability to build relationships with physicians, surgeons, and other healthcare professionals. Excellent interpersonal, cross-functional teams, networking, presentation, negotiation, and closing skills.

- Ability to handle customer questions and objections in a way that is consistent with product indications and sales training methodology.
- Increases territory growth by building and maintaining strong business relationships with key accounts and key opinion leaders.
- Adheres to all policies and SOPs regarding interactions with healthcare professionals, including product handling and complaints, expense reporting, sales activities, and training.
- Strong organizational and time management skills with the ability to think strategically and analytically.
- Maintains training in sales skills, product features, benefits, competitive data, and industry trends.

PROFESSIONAL SKILLS

*Strategic Sales Development	*Consultative Selling Techniques	*Post-Sale Follow-Up
*Surgical Case Coverage	*Customer Acquisition	*Presentation Skills
*Customer Solution Skills	*Maintains Sales and Product Training	*In-Service Training
*Product Demonstration	*New Production Introductions	*Policies & Procedures
*Orthopedic Device Sales	*Customer Relationship Management	*Full Sales Cycle Skills
*Exceeds Sales Quotas	*Clinical Knowledge	*Professional Work Ethics
*Inventory Management	*Industry Trends & Territory Analysis	*Product Portfolio

PROFESSIONAL EXPERIENCE

Vista Orthopedics, Portland, OR   2012–Present
Sales Representative

Manages sales territory by planning and implementing sales strategies to retain current business and converting new business in the orthopedic sales climate. Promotes and presents company's medical-device products at hospitals, doctor's offices, surgical centers, and other healthcare facilities to raise awareness of latest medical devices offered. Provides customer base with excellent post-sale follow up.

- Attained sales quota of $1.3M+, subsequently receiving 2009 Quota Achiever award.
- Converted new customers, resulting in increased sales of $400K.
- Increases sales growth within sensitive pricing accounts by conducting customer needs analysis to aid customer in identification of product benefits.

- Develops and maintains key customer relationships within territory.
- Manages inventory turns by implementing best strategy for utilizing inventory.

Vista Agency Osteologic, Portland, OR   2007–2012
Sales Representative

Vista Orthopaedics Idaho and Nevada branches become part of Vista Agency Osteologic, one of the largest agencies within Vista with a total of $60M in sales.

- Quota Achiever award (2006); total sales $1M+ resulting in a 47% growth.
- Managed $10M territory; worked independently and as team of three sales representatives to achieve quotas and meet agency target sales goals.
- Demonstrates ability to identify and close new customers while managing existing accounts.
- Created sales strategies for territory resulting, in increased sales.

Vista Osteonics, Omaha, Nebraska   2005–2007
Sales Representative

Producer of orthopedic implants for reconstructive, trauma, and spine surgery. Hired to manage sales territory generating $6M in sales. Responsible for Immanuel Hospital services, including assisting current sales representatives in increasing sales by helping with customer relationship management, building relationships with new surgeons, contributing to day-to-day operations of covering cases, and setting up instruments and implants for surgeries.

- Increased sales by $26K + for a total of $558K+ in total sales; first year 100.12% to quota.
- Established relationships with current and potential customers by establishing a reputation for strong product knowledge.
- Converted competitive business by identifying needs not met by competitors, resulting in increased sales.
- Assisted company sales representatives in achieving quotas and meeting organizational goals.

CORPORATE AWARDS / RECOGNITION

Quota Achiever: 102% to Quota (2009)   Quota Achiever: 108.9% to Quota (2007)
Quota Achiever: 101.5% to Quota (2008)   Quota Achiever: 100.12% to Quota (2006)

EDUCATION

Pacific University Oregon, Forrest Grove, OR   2005
BA Business Administration

PROFESSIONAL DEVELOPMENT
Sponsored by Vista Orthopaedics

Customer Centric Selling   Gallup Strength Finder
Vista Revision Training   Vista Reconstructive Product Training
Vista Product Trauma Training   Vista Orthobiologic Training

Superior references available

Gayle Ramirez-Chung

Trenton, NJ 08601   609.567.1569   opthalmictech@sbcglobal.net

OPHTHALMIC TECHNICIAN/ DOCTOR ASSISTANT

Building organizational value by assisting with diagnostic and treatment-oriented procedures

Technical Skills:

Precise Refracting/Workup
Scribing
Goniometry
Sterile Techniques

Procedures & Treatments:

Chalazion Surgery
Glaucoma Treatments
Conjunctivitis
Diabetes Monitoring
Retinopathy of Prematurity
Macular Degeneration
Strabismus
Cataracts
Palsy
NLD Obstruction
Blepharoplasty

Equipment:

A Scans
Lasers
Tonometry
Slit Lamp
Lensometry
Keratometer
Visual Fields
Topography

Performance Summary

Personable and capable professional experienced in conducting diagnostic tests; measuring and recording vision; testing eye muscle function; inserting, removing, and caring for contact lenses; and applying eye dressings. Competently assist physicians during surgery, maintain optical and surgical instruments, and administer eye medications. Extensive knowledge in ophthalmic medications dealing with glaucoma, cataract surgery, and a wide variety of other diagnoses.

Professional Experience

AUGUSTA EYE ASSOCIATES, Decatur, Georgia — 2010 to Present
Technician/Assistant for a cornea specialist in a large ophthalmic practice. Perform histories, vision screenings, pupil exams, and precise manifest refractions. Assist with a variety of surgical procedures. Quickly build trust and rapport and streamline processes to ensure physician efficiency.

GUGGINO FAMILY EYE CENTER, Atlanta, Georgia — 2006 to 2010
Taught customer service techniques and promoted twice within 2 months to an **Ophthalmic Doctor Assistant** for a pediatric neurology ophthalmologist performing scribing, taking histories, preparing patients for examination, and educating patients on treatment procedures.

DAVEL COMMUNICATIONS, Atlanta, Georgia — 1999 to 2006
Recruited as a **Regional Account Manager** and promoted within 3 months of hire to **National Account Manager**. Contributed to the company doubling in size within 10 months; maintained a 100% satisfied customer retention rate.

Education

Bachelor of Science, Organizational Communication — 1998
University of Georgia, Athens, Georgia

Certification

Certified Ophthalmic Assistant (COA)

Hillary Sanders

34 Mountain Pass Trail
Portland, OR 97201

541.431-4342
OrthoSales@outlook.com

Orthopedics Account Manager

PERFORMANCE PROFILE

Top-producing medical device sales professional with 12+ years' experience and proven track record of surpassing sales quotas, developing new business, via effective time and territory management. Extensive orthopedic knowledge of reconstructive, trauma, orthobiologics, hand, foot, and ankle technologies. Strong business acumen with the ability to execute the sales cycle, leading customer to action. Ability to build relationships with physicians, surgeons, and other healthcare professionals. Excellent interpersonal, cross-functional teams, networking, presentation, negotiation, and closing skills.

- Ability to handle customer questions and objections in a way that is consistent with product indications and sales training methodology.
- Increases territory growth by building and maintaining strong business relationships with key accounts and key opinion leaders.
- Adheres to all policies and SOPs regarding interactions with healthcare professionals, including product handling and complaints, expense reporting, sales activities, and training.
- Strong organizational and time management skills with the ability to think strategically and analytically.
- Maintains training in sales skills, product features, benefits, competitive data, and industry trends.

PROFESSIONAL SKILLS

*Strategic Sales Development	*Consultative Selling Techniques	*Post-Sale Follow-Up
*Surgical Case Coverage	*Customer Acquisition	*Presentation Skills
*Customer Solution Skills	*Maintains Sales and Product Training	*In-Service Training
*Product Demonstration	*New Production Introductions	*Policies & Procedures
*Orthopedic Device Sales	*Customer Relationship Management	*Full Sales Cycle Skills
*Exceeds Sales Quotas	*Clinical Knowledge	*Professional Work Ethics
*Inventory Management	*Industry Trends & Territory Analysis	*Product Portfolio

PROFESSIONAL EXPERIENCE

Vista Orthopedics, Portland, OR   2009–Present
Sales Representative

Manages sales territory by planning and implementing sales strategies to retain current business and converting new business in the orthopedic sales climate. Promotes and presents company's medical-device products at hospitals, doctors' offices, surgical centers, and other healthcare facilities to raise awareness of latest medical devices offered. Provides customer base with excellent post-sale follow-up.
- Attained sales quota of $1.3M+, subsequently receiving 2009 Quota Achiever award.
- Converted new customers, resulting in increased sales of $400K.
- Increases sales growth within sensitive pricing accounts by conducting customer needs analysis to aid customer in identification of product benefits.

- Develops and maintains key customer relationships within territory.
- Manages inventory turns by implementing best strategy for utilizing inventory.

Vista Agency Osteologic, Portland, OR   2003–2009
Sales Representative

Vista Orthopedics Idaho and Nevada branches become part of Vista Agency Osteologic, one of the largest agencies within Vista with a total of $60M in sales.
- Quota Achiever award (2006); total sales $1M+ resulting in a 47% growth.
- Managed $10M territory; worked independently and as team of three sales representatives to achieve quotas and meet agency target sales goals.
- Demonstrated ability to identify and close new customers while managing existing accounts.
- Created sales strategies for territory, resulting in increased sales.

Vista Osteonics, Omaha, NE   2000–2003
Sales Representative

Producer of orthopedic implants for reconstructive, trauma, and spine surgery. Hired to manage sales territory generating $6M in sales. Responsible for Immanuel Hospital services, including assisting current sales representatives in increasing sales by helping with customer relationship management, building relationships with new surgeons, contributing to day-to-day operations of covering cases, and setting up instruments and implants for surgeries.
- Increased sales by $26K+ for a total of $558K+ in total sales; first year 100.12% to quota.
- Established relationships with current and potential customers by establishing a reputation for strong product knowledge.
- Converted competitive business by identifying needs not met by competitors, resulting in increased sales.
- Assisted company sales representatives in achieving quotas and meeting organizational goals.

CORPORATE AWARDS / RECOGNITION

Quota Achiever: 102% to Quota (2015)   Quota Achiever: 108.9% to Quota (2012)
Quota Achiever: 101.5% to Quota (2014)   Quota Achiever: 100.12% to Quota (2011)

EDUCATION

Pacific University Oregon, Forrest Grove, OR   1999
BA, Business Administration

PROFESSIONAL DEVELOPMENT
Sponsored by Vista Orthopedics

Customer-Centric Selling   Gallup Strength Finder
Vista Revision Training   Vista Reconstructive Product Training
Vista Product Trauma Training   Vista Orthobiologic Training

Superior references available

NICOLE SILVER

341-D Lilac Court ♦ Tacoma, WA 98409 ♦ 253-634-3424 ♦ n.silver@comcast.net

Pharmacy Manager
Dedicated to promoting health and safety by pursuing the highest quality of pharmacist's care.

Performance Profile

Licensed Pharmacist with an outstanding record of progressive accountability in pharmacy and pharmacy practice settings, including retail, hospital, sales, and long-term care. In-depth knowledge of all pharmaceutical operations, as well as computerized drug distribution systems, drug utilization evaluation, complex equipment and delivery systems, emerging medications, and multi-state pharmacy regulations.

♦ A strong and trusted individual with a high standard of credibility and ethics who subscribes to a straightforward, hands-on style in getting the job done.
♦ Calm, flexible, and focused in deadline-driven, urgently paced, and demanding environments.
♦ Superb interpersonal skills and proficiency in building and maintaining strategic business/client relationships while interfacing positively with people of all levels and backgrounds.

Professional Competencies

✓ Project Management	✓ Report Preparation	✓ Technically Savvy
✓ Customer Development/Service	✓ Marketing & Sales	✓ Problem Resolution
✓ Professional Presentations	✓ Performance Improvement	✓ Negotiation
✓ Relationship Building	✓ Financially Astute	✓ Long-Term Care
✓ Multi-site Management	✓ Staff Training/Development	✓ Innovation

Professional Experience

Pharmatech, Inc., Tacoma, WA   2004 – Present
Pharmatech, a Fortune 400 Corporation, provides a broad array of pharmacy-related services.

SENIOR DIRECTOR OF OPERATIONS - West Division   2014 – Present
AREA DIRECTOR   2011 – 2014
GENERAL MANAGER   2004 – 2011

SENIOR DIRECTOR OF OPERATIONS - West Division   2014 – Present
Charged with the provision of operational resources to Western Division pharmacies, which includes 47 pharmacies in 13 Western states.

♦ Assist in division's multi-pharmacy budgeting process of $1B in annual sales and approximately 3 million dispensed prescriptions.
♦ Captured nearly $300K in annual savings by coordinating and executing stat delivery reduction initiative.
♦ Partnered with regional management to develop and execute multi-phase plan that boosted performance and profitability of pharmacy that generated $120M in annual revenue. Initiative resulted in 6% increase in revenue, 3% increase in operating profit, and multiple improvements in performance indicators.
♦ Created purchasing scorecard that identified sites needing improvement, such as inventory accounting for nearly 70% of expense. Scorecard was launched/implemented countrywide at all sites.
♦ Partner with Divisional Compliance Officer to identify regulatory goals and corresponding operational processes and best practices.

- ◆ Facilitate high-level, consistent patient care through provision of pharmaceuticals in challenged pharmacy sites.
- ◆ Collaborate with operations managers and pharmacy managers to exceed customer expectations and ultimately support customer development and sales efforts.
- ◆ Research, evaluate, and implement new technologies, including eMARs, CPOE, e-Prescribing, and automation across 11 western states.

AREA DIRECTOR   2011 – 2014

Accountable for multi-site, multi-state management of 5 pharmacies, 250 employees, and annualized revenue of $66M. Developed budgets and performance/financial objectives.

- ◆ Capably managed 5 multi-state pharmacies to ensure financial and operational success as well as compliance with federal, state, and local regulations.
- ◆ Analyzed and assisted in consolidating Walgreens Corp SeniorMed subsidiary acquisition, capturing additional $42M in annual revenue to Pharmatech nationwide.
- ◆ Implemented hub/spoke model for Colorado pharmacies, resulting in efficiencies and significant cost reductions for Colorado service area.
- ◆ As Pharmatech State Board of Pharmacy liaison, served as member of special committees, including Technician Certification committee.

GENERAL MANAGER   2004 – 2011

Managed financial and budgetary factors to achieve annual goals, ensured regulatory compliance of pharmacies for annual State Board of Pharmacy inspection success, and recruited, selected, trained, and coached all personnel.

- ◆ Captured $400K in annual revenue by coordinating training, implementation, and evaluation of IV program.

University Hospital, Portland, OR   2001 – 2004
STAFF PHARMACIST

Education

BS, Pharmacy, Oregon State College of Pharmacy, Corvallis, OR

Professional Development

Essentials of Business Development, Part I, Oregon State College
Corporate Finance, Oregon State College
Microsoft Office Certificate, Penn-Foster

Professional Licenses

Washington Pharmacist License #143293

Professional Organizations / Affiliations

Washington Pharmacists Association
Oregon State Pharmacy Association, former Vice President
Chi-Beta Honor Society, former Vice President various board and corporate committees

Computer Skills

Operating Systems: Windows OS, Mac OS, OmniDX, Oasis
Software Applications: Microsoft Word, Excel, PowerPoint, Project, Access; SharePoint; eMARs; CPOE; e-Prescribing

Corporate Recognition

Pharmacy of the Year, 2007
Most Improved Pharmacy, 2004

Warren Davis

12 Mountain Terrace
Butte, MT 59701

(406) 436-3851
warren.davis@gmail.com

Radiology Technologist

Performance Profile

Detail-oriented and quality-focused radiologic technologist with hands-on experience in managing fluoroscopy guidelines and radiation safety, fluoroscopy equipment, X-ray image intensifiers, image recording equipment, and diagnostic imaging services. Outstanding patient rapport and exceptional patient satisfaction. Works cooperatively with members of the healthcare team to maintain standards for professional interactions.

- ✓ Maintains and improves high-quality, cost-effective department operations.
- ✓ Mechanical aptitude and manual dexterity while operating complicated diagnostic equipment.
- ✓ Flexible and able to perform tasks with minimum to no supervision.
- ✓ Comprehensive knowledge of methods and techniques of preparing patients for X-ray imaging.
- ✓ Good knowledge of latest X-ray equipment and standards; produces high-quality diagnostic film.
- ✓ Plans efficient patient exam workflow; good time management skills.
- ✓ Detail oriented; multitasker.
- ✓ Technology: Proficient in radiology/hospital information systems including IMPAX, Allscripts, Novius, and Virtual Radiologic.

Areas of Expertise

Fluoroscopy	Diagnostic Equipment
Radiation Safety	High-Quality Diagnostic Film
X-ray Image Intensifiers	ICU and NICU
Mechanical Aptitude	IMPAX, Allscripts, Novius, Virtual Radiologic
Patient Positioning Skills	Image Recording Equipment
Diagnostic Imaging Services	Maintain and Troubleshoot Imaging Equipment

Professional Experience

Sisters of Mercy Hospital, Butte, MT   2012-Current
Radiology Technologist
- Accurately operates radiologic equipment to produce quality X-rays to diagnose and treat illness and possible injuries as directed by the radiologist.

-continued-

Radiology Technologist (continued)

- Ensures and executes physician's orders by using two point identifiers to ensure each patient receives the correct imaging procedures to eliminate unnecessary exposure and ensure the correct diagnosis.
- Determines the best method of obtaining optimal examination and regulates patient flow to keep from creating a backlog of patients, virtually eliminating the need for off-duty personnel.
- Maintains documentation requirements to ensure that technical data is entered timely and accurately.
- Accomplished the ability to work independently weekend nights caring for ER patients in a 180-bed general medical and surgical acute care facility. Performs all stats on patients and morning portables in ICU and NICU.
- Obtains patient cooperation and helps reduce patient anxiety by explaining procedures and establishing a comfortable environment.
- Consistently safeguards patients by executing radiation protection techniques through patient shielding skills and knowledge of applicable exposure to minimize radiation to patients and staff.

Education

Associate Degree, Radiologic Technology   2012
Montana Tech, Butte, MT

Certifications/Licensure

American Registry of Radiologic Technologists (ARRT)   Current
Montana Radiologic Technology (LSRT)   Current
BLS/CPR Certified   Current

Excellent references available on request

ShaQuan Jones, RN, BSN

Linked in profile

4343 B Lee Towers, Richmond, VA   s_jones@att.net   804-234-0501

Registered Nurse, BSN

PERFORMANCE PROFILE

Compassionate healthcare professional with 14 years' experience as a registered nurse in a clinical setting providing comprehensive cardiac care. Experienced in advanced cardiac care as a nurse clinician. Provides high-quality nursing care and unsurpassed patient service.

- ✓ Uses systematic approach to nursing practice; maintains professional ethics.
- ✓ Facilitates outcome-based compassionate care to patients and families.
- ✓ Exceptional skills in written documentation and verbal communication; conflict resolution.
- ✓ Demonstrates independent critical-thinking skills and sound nursing judgment.
- ✓ Effective interpersonal and leadership skills supported by an enthusiastic team player attitude.

PROFESSIONAL SKILLS

- Clinic Management
- Telephone Triage
- Patient Evaluations
- Coordinates Services
- Focused Patient Care

- Diagnostic Assessment
- EKG/Stress Testing
- Holter/Event Monitoring
- Implantable Devices
- Procedural Tests

- Pharmacological Management
- Diagnostic Results
- Discharge Procedures
- Infection Control Standards
- Patient Education/Safety

EDUCATION

Bachelor of Science in Nursing (BSN), University of Virginia, Charlottesville, VA   2006
Associate of Arts Degree, University of Virginia, Charlottesville, VA   2004

LICENSURE

RN License – State of Virginia, License #: R 110234 2   Current

PROFESSIONAL CERTIFICATIONS/CONTINUING EDUCATION
Certifications
Virginia Tech, Richmond, VA   2016
- Basic Cardiac Life Support for Healthcare Providers (BLS)
- Advanced Cardiac Life Support Provider Course (ACLS)
- IV/Infusion Therapy Certification

Continuing Education
Eastern Schools, American Nurses Credentialing Center (COA)   2015
- Cardiovascular Nursing: A Comprehensive Overview

National Center of Continuing Education, American Nurses Credentialing Center (COA)   2010
- End of Life Issues and Pain Management

PROFESSIONAL EXPERIENCE

Southern Heart and Vascular Institute, Fredericksburg, VA   2014 – Present
Registered Nurse, Cardiology
Services include Cardiology, Cardiac Surgery, Electrophysiology, and Interventional Cardiology.

- Managed satellite outpatient clinic under the direction of more than seven cardiologists.

- Performed as nurse liaison between hospital and clinic; demonstrated effective time-management and leadership skills for maintaining daily flow of clinic operations.
- Assisted physicians with in-office procedures including EKG, Exercise Stress Testing, Holter/Event monitoring, and pacemaker evaluations.
- Scheduled inpatient procedures including Echo, Stress, Angiography, PTCA, and EP studies.
- Performed hospital inpatient evaluations and assessments including angiogram checks, sheath pulls, discharge planning, and patient education.
- Consulted with attending cardiologist to review positive findings, abnormal test results, and patient concerns.
- Provided patient education and enrollment in specialized clinics for lipids, heart failure, pacemaker, amiodarone, anticoagulation, and rehab management; patient advocate to cardiac support groups.

Southern Neurological Clinic, Richmond, VA   2006 – 2014
Registered Nurse, Neurology
Southern Neurological Clinic specializes in comprehensive diagnostic testing and treatment of neurological diseases. Specialties include Adult and Pediatric Neurology, Neuropsychology, Electroneurodiagnostics, EMG and Nerve Conduction Studies, Sleep Center, and Headache Management.

- Functioned as clinic's Registered Nurse responsible for providing individualized care to patients and families in accordance with the neurology clinic standards, policies, and procedures.
- Managed patient flow throughout the clinic and assisted providers in evaluation and treatment of neurological patients.
- Applied skilled telephone triage.
- Provided follow-up communications of lab/test results and medication management.
- Documented medical history, vital statistics, and test results in patient medical records.
- Facilitated communication between patients and physicians to ensure patient comprehension of treatment plans and compliance with healthcare regimen.
- Collaborated with other healthcare departments to facilitate patient care.

University of Virginia Medical Center, Charlottesville, VA   2006
Senior Nursing Assistant, Medical/Surgical
University of Virginia Medical Center is among the most respected teaching institutions in the nation. Staffed by nationally and internationally renowned orthopedic surgeons, it provides personalized orthopedic care that combines excellence, service, compassion, and innovative research.

- Implemented orthopedic nursing care under the management of a "team nursing process" covering 4 to 7 high-acuity patients per shift.
- Applied understanding of mechanical principles necessary for using hospital equipment and instruments; applied knowledge of hospital recordkeeping.
- Maintained infection control standards and provided safe physical environments to assist in patient comfort and recovery; assisted with comprehensive discharge planning and patient education.

AFFILIATIONS

Sigma Theta Tau National Honor Society, University of Virginia, Charlottesville, VA

Virginia Nurses Association / American Nurses Association

COMMUNITY/VOLUNTEER ACTIVITIES

Place of Hope and Kids Against Hunger, Richmond, VA
- Prepared and served meals for homeless shelter; disaster aid relief.

John Chen

Atlanta, GA 30305   404-459-8482   chen.hr@gmail.com

Linked in profile

HUMAN RESOURCE ANALYST
Dedicated professional with integrity, resourcefulness, and sound judgment

Performance Summary
3 years of exceptional client service and support. Works with professionals of all levels and builds trusting relationships. Outstanding communication skills. Ability to solve problems with ease and sound judgment. Skilled in analyzing data and giving presentations. Incredibly organized, detailed oriented, and committed to producing quality work. Ability to adjust to evolving situations and shifting priorities in a calm and balanced way. Pursuing MS in Human Resource Management.

Professional Skills

Research & Analysis	Problem Solving	Strategic Planning
Communication Skills	Organizational Skills	Interpersonal Skills
Teamwork	Leadership	Relationship Building
Presentations	Mediation	Negotiation
Administrative Support	Sales & Marketing	Newsletters & Reports

Peachtree Partners, LLC, Atlanta, GA   **2014–Present**
Real estate company that has a sales volume of more than $18 billion annually.
Licensed Real Estate Sales Associate
Assists buyers and sellers in all price points in residential Atlanta area, guiding them through the whole process of the buying and selling transaction. Works with all professionals on all levels. Anticipates and solves problems on a daily basis and strategizes on how to close the deal. Understands the delicate balance required to reach a positive outcome. Great client service, strong communication skills, and good organizational skills have been key factors to success.

- Manages the marketing and sales of residential properties, from studios to townhouses, in all price ranges.
- Analyzes data and properties and advises clients on the right investment.
- Creates presentations, a marketing plan, and a strategy for sellers.
- Educates and keeps clients updated on the real estate market.
- Negotiates the best price for clients.
- Manages the entire process of the sale of contract. Works with other parties, such as broker, other buyer/seller, real estate attorney, mortgage lender, and building management agent to close the deal.
- Maintains client relationships and builds trust. Result is repeat business and referrals.
- Manages confidential information.
- Mentors new brokers on how they can market themselves and offers guidance on their transactions.

Education
Atlanta Business School
M.S. in Human Resource Management—*starting Fall 2016. Expected date of graduation to be in 2018.*

Savannah College of Art & Design
B.F.A. in Film and Television

Computer Skills
Microsoft Office: Word, Excel, PowerPoint, Outlook

Community Activity
One of the organizers and leaders of Dogs on Tybee. Objective was to negotiate permitting dogs on the Tybee Island beaches. Negotiated with state officials, gave presentations to the City of Tybee, and managed social media activities and face-to-face networking events to generate gained community and media support.

Veronica Kent

Placentia, CA 92870   (562) 555-9012   ronnie.kent@sbcglobal.net

Linked in profile

Human Resources Generalist / Administrative Support

Flexible, disciplined, organized, and hardworking—the consummate small-office professional

Performance Summary

Human resources and accounts payable professional with over 15 years' administrative support experience. Recognized for outstanding discipline and leadership.

Skilled in all aspects of small-office human resources: payroll, benefits administration, accounts payable, customer service, sales support, collections, administrative support, purchasing, facilities management, event planning, and compliance.

Core Skills

- Human Resources
- Payroll Processing
- Benefits Administration
- 401k and Section 125 Plans
- Customer Service
- Employee/Vendor Relations
- I-9 and EEO Compliance

- Accounts Payable
- Invoice Discrepancies
- Payment Processing
- Purchase Orders
- Expense Tracking
- Journal Entries
- Auditing & Compliance
- Spreadsheets/Reports

- Administrative Support
- Collections
- Bank Deposits
- Internal/External Liaison
- Property Leases
- DMV Renewals
- Month/Year End, 1099s
- Event Planning

Technology Skills

- Windows 98/2000/XP/Vista
- Word, Excel, PowerPoint
- Outlook

- Corel Draw Graphics
- Digital Photo Graphics
- ACCPAC Accounting
- QuickBooks

- ADP Payroll, Time and Attendance
- Purchasing Software
- Internet Research

Accomplishments

- Reduced corporate liability and workers' compensation insurance costs by one-third; restructured liability insurance management programs to facilitate savings.
- Detected fraudulent activities from utility companies and enabled company to recover $14,000 in taxes and fees.
- Assisted in the implementation of company merger by reorganizing company policies and procedures, vacation/sick time, and payroll systems.
- Employee of the year nominations 1992, 1996, 2003, and 2010.

Professional Experience

Wireless Communications, L.A., CA   2013–Present
Wireless audio products for the professional and semi-professional audio markets.
Administrative Support Generalist

- Support for an Independent Sales Contractor, selling Airfonix products to distributors nationwide.
- Related experiences: administrative support, customer service, contracts and proposals, accounts payable/receivable, expense tracking, bank reconciliation and deposits, email, and Internet research.

Telecom Networks, Huntington Beach, CA   2004–2013
Independent business communications providers in the United States.
Human Resources Generalist/Accounts Payable Specialist

Managed full range of human resource services including:

continued

192

- Benefits administration; experience includes maintenance of costs through vendor negotiations and implementation of alternative benefits program.
- Processed payroll for 250-employee company.
- General liability, workers' compensation, subcontractor, and payroll auditing and compliance.
- Responsible for all accounts payable functions, including monthly and yearly closeouts.
- Liaison between internal and external accounting functions.
- Processed DMV renewals for corporate vehicles.
- Managed petty cash accounts, processed bank deposits, and handled expense tracking and reports.
- Administrative support, accounts receivable/backup, property building maintenance/facilities management for three facilities, sales support/marketing, and purchasing activities.

McDonnell Douglas Corporation, Long Beach, CA   1996–2004
Aerospace manufacturer and defense contractor.
Administrative Assistant

- Coordinated daily quality-control efforts between the internal planning departments and management.
- Collaborated, as a key member of the Quality Support Team, along with the production line and management team to contribute to the main business goal, "First Time Quality and Customer Satisfaction."
- Performed daily office support duties.

Education

Fullerton City College, Fullerton, CA. *Continued Education*
Long Beach City College, Long Beach, CA. *Continued Education, units 97*
Long Beach City College, Long Beach, CA. *Associate Degree, General Business*

2015
1997–2012
2009

Personal

- St. Jude Cancer Center, Fullerton, CA. Critical care support group volunteer.
- Snail's Pace, Fountain Valley, CA. Coach and train beginning marathon runners.
- Eleven competitive marathons, seven half-marathons, 10k and 5k competitive runs.

"Every day I am determined to make a positive difference with my presence."

Superior references available

Yasuo Kuniyoshi MBA

Dallas, TX   214-965-7667   alwaysonbrand@comcast.net

E-Commerce Marketing Communications

Performance Summary

20+ years' experience in brand marketing: international, corporate, and entrepreneurial cultures. Practical problem-solving skills, and a deep well of experience to meet the challenges of this fast-paced function.

Project planning and management experience in high-stress scenarios where failure is not an option and the wrong decision could deliver substantial client loss.

- Consultative approach to assess client needs and provide "turnkey" solutions and programs that meet strategic goals.
- Strategic business sense, an uncompromising work ethic, and a burning desire to create consistently successful marketing solutions.
- Loyal support from clients, partners, managers, and business owners.
- Deep expertise in branding, management, and positioning product lines.
- Marketing messages that drive revenue and bring unique product "stories" to the community.
- MBA – Marketing.

Professional Skills

✓ Branding	✓ Needs Assessment	✓ Product Positioning
✓ Product Stories	✓ Strategic Rollouts	✓ Brand Development
✓ Brand Creation	✓ Project Planning	✓ Media Relations
✓ Brand Establishment	✓ Sales & Pricing	✓ Investor Sourcing
✓ Training Materials	✓ Sales Materials	✓ SEO
✓ Event Planning	✓ Event Promotion	✓ Charity Fundraisers
✓ Social Networking	✓ Distance Learning	✓ MarComm

Performance Highlights

Communications

- Built a packaged employee communication strategic rollout plan for *Montgomery General Hospital*, partnered with senior internal HR leaders, and directed launch timeframe for new employee subscription benefit (*PepPods*, an online emergency preparedness and personal home record system).
- Sourced and secured a $1 million investor for *Zigzag.net*. Marketed online learning management system to military and law enforcement professionals.
- For *Nation's Bank*, developed an interactive kiosk concept for banking clients to receive instant product and service information during peak periods. Praised by customers nationwide during rollout.

Marketing and Events Planner

- Created and launched the *AT&T* "*No More Excuses*" multimedia cell phone campaign, the most successful January campaign in company history.

Continued

Marketing and Events Planner, *continued*

- ◆ For *Mercy Health*, lined up musicians and artisans for children's entertainment, food and health-screening vendors, and launched direct mail campaign to the *Mercy Health Plan* members, resulting in an impressive 900-person turnout. Located creative team to design mascot *Percy's* character costume.
- ◆ Organized and launched a hugely successful *White Glove Car Wash* charity grand opening event, and donated a portion of the proceeds to the *Make a Wish Foundation*.

Multimedia Marketing Strategist

- ◆ Created the *Magistar* public corporate identity, including the marketing language on the corporate website, trade show participation strategy, and public relations presentations.
- ◆ Established strong rapport with *TMC Labs* editor who agreed to conduct an extensive product evaluation and testing, resulting in a rave product review for *Magistar* in the *Internet Telephony*.

Gifted Leader

Developed a turnkey fundraising program for immediate online client use complete with a fundraising micro-site, fundraising, sales, and pricing procedures, and training and sales support materials such as scripts and FAQs.

Improved the volume and quality of traffic to *ActiveMedia* client websites from search engines via "natural" search results, raising their resulting online rank, and improving their click-through numbers.

Professional Experience

THE RIVER BANK GROUP – Reston, VA	2015 – Present
Marketing Consultant	
MAGISTAR – Reston, VA	2010 – 2015
Director, Brand Marketing	
NATIONS BANK/BARNETT BANK, INC – Jacksonville, FL	2007 – 2010
Advertising Project Manager	
URBAN DESIGN, INC – Philadelphia, PA	2004 – 2007
Director of Marketing	

Education

MBA, Marketing Communications	2003
Phoenix	
Online Faculty at UNIVERSITY OF PHOENIX	2012 – Present

Develop and deliver online undergraduate courses in Marketing, Integrated Marketing Communications, Management, and Organizational Behavior.

Excellent professional references available

Chang Apanya

San Francisco, CA 94109   415-000-0000   techmarketing@gmail.com

E-Commerce Marketing

Performance Summary

Accomplished Senior Executive with a strong affinity for *technology* and a keen business sense for the application of *emerging products* to add value and expand markets.

Proven talent for identifying *core business needs* and translating into *technical deliverables*. Launched and managed cutting-edge Internet programs and services to win new customers, generate revenue gains, and increase brand value.

Unique combination of technical and business/sales experience. Articulate and persuasive in defining the benefits of e-commerce technologies, differentiating offerings, and increasing customer retention. Highly self-motivated, enthusiastic, and profit oriented.

Professional Skills

Sales & Marketing	Business Development	Strategic Initiatives
Business Planning	Project Management	Strategic Partnerships
Contract Negotiations	Relationship Management	Emerging Products
E-Commerce Technologies	Increase Brand Value	Customer Retention
Secure E-Commerce	Internet Services	Smart Card Technology

Technical Skills

E-Commerce	Encryption Technology	Payment Products
Firewalls	Smart Cards	Stored Value
Digital Certificates	Network Security	Internet Security
Dual and Single Message	Payment Gateways	Financial Systems
Authorization	Clearing & Settlement	Java
Key Management	Public Key Infrastructure	RF Communications

Professional Experience

ABC Credit Card Corp., San Diego, CA   2013 - Present

E-COMMERCE AND SMART CARD CONSULTANT

- Developed strategic e-commerce marketing plans for large and small merchants involving web purchases and retail transactions using a multifunctional, microcontroller smart card for both secure Internet online commerce and point-of-sale offline commerce.
- Combined multiple software products for Internet and non-Internet applications: home banking, stored value, digital certificates, key management, rewards & loyalty program.
- PCS/GSM cell phone, and contactless microcontroller with RF communications without direct POS contact.

E-COMMERCE AND SMART CARD CONSULTANT, continued

- Consulted on business and technical requirements to define new e-commerce products and essential deliverables for ABC Credit Card, valued at $2.5 M, supporting and enhancing Internet transactions.
- Analyzed systems relating to the point-of-sale environment in the physical world and at the merchant server via the Internet for real-time authorization, clearing, and settlement.
- Managed projects including the requirements management system for electronic commerce products affecting core systems: authorization, clearing, and settlement. Provided expertise about business and technical issues regarding SET and the Credit Card Payment Gateway Service.

Communications Technology Corporation, Miami, FL   2007 - 2012

MANAGER OF WESTERN REGION CHANNEL PARTNER PROGRAM

- Developed and maintained business relationships with Fortune 500 customers using client-server software for applications and contracts involving:
  - E-commerce and smart card technology for a variety of Internet/intranet products: home banking.
  - EDI, stored value, digital certificates, key management, perimeter defense with proxy firewalls.
  - Secure remote access.
- Negotiated an exclusive contract with one of the largest government and commercial contractors in the industry, projected to generate $2–$4 million over a 24–36-month period. Contract includes secure remote access, telecommuting, secure healthcare applications.

Avanta Corp., Miami, FL   1998 - 2006

SENIOR SOFTWARE ENGINEER / SOFTWARE INSTRUCTOR

Managed a software engineering group of 53. Developed in-house program that saved over $150,000 in training costs for state-of-the-art communications system software development.

  - Designed new programs and trained software engineers in object-oriented analysis and design using UML Solutions which were implemented in C++ in a UNIX environment.
  - Developed and maintained C and C++ communication software in a UNIX environment.
  - Created curriculum and course materials that reduced overall training costs by more than $150,000.
  - Coordinated and presented software training programs.

Education & Credentials

B.S., Electrical Engineering, University of Miami, Emphasis: Software Engineering, Minor: Psychology; President of the Sigma Sigma Fraternity

Top Secret Security Clearance with Polygraph

123 Main Street
Anywhere, VA 22222
Linked in profile

Nancy Wright

Home (555) 555-5555
Mobile (555) 333-5555
nancywright@yahoo.com

PR Manager • Account Director • Group Manager

Performance Profile

High-tech public relations professional with 13 years' experience, including nine in Silicon Valley, in the software, Internet, networking, consumer electronics, and wireless industries. Substantial experience in PR and strategic communications campaigns that lead to company acquisitions. Experienced in all aspects of strategic and tactical communications, from developing and managing multiple campaigns, accounts, and results-oriented teams, to developing and placing stories. Seasoned motivational speaker and freelance TV color commentator. Two-time Olympic gold medalist.

Core Competencies

High-Tech Public Relations	Media Relations	New Business Development	Market Research
Strategic Communications	Craft & Place Stories	Team Management	Build & Lead Teams
Executive Communications	Strong Writing Skills	Budget Management	Mentor
PR Messaging & Tactics	Media Training	Account Management	Client Satisfaction
Storytelling	Multiple Projects	Project Management	Organizational Skills
Collateral Materials	Story Placement	Detail Oriented	Thought Leadership
Leadership Branding	Counsel Executives	Acquisition Positioning	PR Counsel
Analyst Relations	Strong Editing Skills	Pitch Media	Social Media

Strategic Public Relations Leadership

Orchestrated PR campaigns that positioned companies as both industry leaders and sound investments. Developed and directed PR campaigns for four companies that were subsequently acquired within two years of the campaigns: *InfoGame Technologies* (creator of the first iProduct®, acquired by *ABC Network*), *Triiliux Digital Systems* (acquired by *Intel*), *LinkExchange* (acquired by *Microsoft*), and *The Internet Mall* (acquired by *TechWave*). Proven client satisfaction demonstrated in repeat business and account growth: over a span of ten years, contracted by former *InfoGame* execs to serve as communications counsel for *NextLink Technologies, ABC Network Systems*, and *AirPlay Networks*.

Executive Communications Management

Executive Communications Manager for iconic executive and public speaker, *Charles Smith, Group VP, Service Provider Sales, ABC Network Systems* (currently *senior VP* and *technology evangelist* for *ABC Network*). Developed communication messaging, strategy, and platform skills for VP, Group VP, and C-level executives.

Media Coverage

ABC World News Tonight, CNN, The Today Show, Associated Press, Baltimore Sun, Boston Globe, Business Times, Business Week, CNN.com, Fast Company, Financial Times, Forbes, Fortune Magazine, Inc., MSNBC.com, New York Times, Parade, San Jose Mercury News, SF Chronicle, USA Today, Wired, Wall Street Journal, AdWeek, CommsDesign, Computer Reseller News, Computer Retail Week, Computer Shopper, Computer World, CRN, CNET, EE Times, Embedded Systems Design, Internet.com, InfoWorld, InformationWeek, Internet.com, Internet Telephony, LightReading, Network World, Phone+, PC Magazine, Red Herring, TMCnet, VoIP News, VON and ZDNet, Dataquest, Forrester Research, Frost and Sullivan, Jupiter Communications, Yankee Group.

——Professional Experience——

Principal

2003-Present

Wright & Associates Public Relations, Richmond, VA

Develop and deliver strategic communications. Drive all PR strategies and tactics, messaging, media training, media relations, budget management, story creation, and placement for technology clients.

- Representative clients include *AirPlay Networks* (former *InfoGame* and *NextLink client*), *ReligiousSite.com* (founded by *eCompany.com* founder), and *PanJet Aviation*.

Principal
2001-2003

Three Kids Public Relations, Redwood City, CA

Developed and implemented all strategic and tactical aspects of public relations for Silicon Valley clients, including thought leadership, leadership branding, story creation and telling, media materials, stories, media relations, and publicity.

- *ABC Network Systems*—Executive Communications Manager to Charles Smith, Group VP at *ABC Network*, a highly pursued public speaker.
- *NextLink Technologies*—Company's first PR counsel. Repositioned obscure company, impaired by trademark dilution, into an industry leader by leveraging market's widespread knowledge and use of *NextLink's* industry-standard *GreatD* networking software.

Marketing Manager
2000-2001

ABC Network Systems, San Jose, CA

Directed internal, cross-functional marketing for *iProduct*, following ABC Network acquisition of *InfoGame* and its technology.

- Shortly after acquisition, ABC Network dissolved *InfoGame/Managed Appliances Business Unit (MASBU)*.

Public Relations Manager
1998-2000

InfoGame Technology Corporation, Redwood City, CA

Advised CEO and VP of marketing on all aspects of PR. Developed and implemented all strategies, tactics, and stories.

- Revamped the start-up's teetering image, which was ruining *iProduct* sales. After two press tours, garnered hundreds of additional stories in all top trade and consumer media with the *iProduct Reviews* program. Catapulted company into a leadership position in the Internet appliance industry, setting it up for acquisition. *iProduct* is now a household name.
- Managed and inspired cross-functional teams of marketing, operations, and customer service to work outside their job responsibilities to deliver excellent service to hundreds of editors beta-testing the *iProduct 2.0*.

Account Supervisor; Senior Account Executive; Account Executive
1996-1998

XYZ Advertising & Public Relations (acquired by *Fleishman-Hillard* in 2000), Mountain View, CA

Promoted annually for successful track record of positioning unknown companies as both industry leaders and solid investments/acquisitions. Designed and managed all PR strategy and activities for start-up, software, Internet, and networking companies. Managed teams of up to ten PR professionals.

- Repositioned, rebranded, relaunched, and reintroduced *InfoGame*, the *iProduct 1.0* and *2.0*, positioning them collectively as leading the nascent Internet appliance space.
- Accelerated *Triiliux* and its CEO out of obscurity and into undisputed leadership through media placement and top speaking engagements.
- Transformed unknown *LinkExchange* into a highly publicized leader in the Internet advertising arena. Placed hundreds of stories in both business and industry media.
- Launched *The Internet Mall*, landing continual coverage in all top Internet and business publications.

——Complementary Experience——

Motivational Speaker/Guest Celebrity
1989-Present

Coach audiences on how to use the Olympic model to set and achieve goals, and succeed in business and life. Representative clients: *IBM, Hardees, Speedo America, Busch Gardens, Alamo Rent-A-Car.*

Television Sports Commentator
1987-2000

Swimming analyst for *NBC, ESPN, FoxSports, SportsChannel, Turner Sports*, and others. Covered the Olympics. Half-time reporter for *Miami Heat* and *The College Conference.*

Awards & Achievements
Winner—Two Olympic swimming gold medals plus one silver and one bronze.
Recipient Southland Corporation's *Olympia Award* for academic and athletic leadership.
NCAA, USA, Southeastern Conference swimming champion and *26-time NCAA All American.*
Hall of Fame Inductee: *International Swimming Hall of Fame, University of Florida, Pacific Northwest Swimming, Washington State Swimming Coaches Association, Mercer Island High School.*

EDUCATION—University of Florida, Gainesville, FL; BS in Journalism, Minor in Speech.

Bilingual

Sarah Bernhardt

MBA

Perryville, VA 22033   703.276.8655   multimediasales@juno.com

ONLINE MULTIMEDIA SALES
Advertising, Communications, and Media

Performance Profile

High-performing sales professional with a 20-year track record of success with high-profile clients for *best-in-class* companies. Consistently **exceeding sales quotas**. Deep expertise in brand, management, and product lines positioning. **Gifted sales strategist and tactician,** excels in channel development.

Professional Skills

- Sales
- Recruitment & Selection
- Performance Appraisals
- Overcoming Objections
- P&L
- Brand Management
- College Relations

- Telemarketing
- Training & Development
- Separations
- Contract Negotiations
- Cost Containment
- Strategic Alliance/Partners
- Employee Communications

- Email Marketing
- Employee Retention
- Business Development
- Channel Development
- Relationship Management
- Diversity Strategies
- Sales Manuals

Excels in training and mentoring teams to outperform the competition. High level of personal and professional integrity, a passion for achieving organizational success, and a desire to always play on a winning team.

Professional Experience

POWER BUSINESS DEVELOPMENT – Ashburn, VA	2007 – Present
Account Manager	2014 – Present
National Ad Agency Channel Sales Representative	2010 – 2014
National Recruitment Sales Representative	2007 – 2010

Aggressively recruited to develop, revitalize, and nurture productive relationships with Fortune 1000 companies and government agencies such as *Inova Healthcare, BAE Systems, Lockheed Martin, FBI*, and *CIA*. Packaged and sold targeted multimedia integrated talent solutions and services.

Key Accomplishments

- ➤ **Multimedia Campaign Development.** Offered existing clients an opportunity to "fish in a different pond" by developing and recommending new and alternative multimedia account strategies targeted at niche and passive candidate markets. Packaged and sold nontraditional campaigns from nonprint sources targeted to key audiences.
- ➤ **Product Development.** Credited for designing and spearheading the execution of a cutting-edge hotjobs.com product offering whereby keyword searches served up product-related ads along the margins of the website, generating more than $50K in incremental revenue per year.
- ➤ **Increased Advertiser Revenue.** Through a combination of face-to-face visits to 13–15 domestic markets, the creation of various telemarketing programs, and email marketing campaigns, grew Easterner JOBS Advertising Unit by $10 million, an increase of 25%, representing one-third of all sales for the unit.
- ➤ **Sales Performance.** Consistently met and exceeded quarterly and annual sales revenue goals, up to 131% above quota.
- ➤ **Awards & Recognition.** Recipient of Presidents Club Year End Award for demonstrating a commitment to customers that is reflected in business performance, a high level of sales achievement, and customer satisfaction. Recipient of several prestigious awards including two Vice Presidents Club Awards, three Sales Achievement Awards, two Sales Excellence Awards, and a Publishers Award for Sales Excellence.

HOTJOBS.COM – Annandale, VA	1999 – 2007
Director of Client Services	2003 – 2007
Account Executive	1999 – 2003

Promoted and progressed rapidly through positions with increasing responsibility. Directed all aspects of sales, marketing, and operations functions, and managed full P&L ($10 million in revenue) for Washington D.C. office. Generated significant new client business and produced employer-branded recruitment and retention advertising campaign and execution strategies.

Key Accomplishments

- ➢ **Cost Containment.** Spearheaded key cost-containment initiatives, saving thousands of dollars, resulting in a Top 10 (out of 35) "managerial profitability" ranking for the Washington D.C. office.
- ➢ **New Business Development.** Partnered with the HotJobs sales channel in the design and implementation of a "business case building" sales contest, increasing HotJobs revenue by $2 million.
- ➢ **Sales Productivity.** Noted for driving $1 million in new business development in one year.
- ➢ **Process Improvement.** Spearheaded from conception to implementation an employee retention initiative. Launched monthly new hire performance appraisals (30/30's), which fostered a welcoming new hire experience, and drastically improved retention. Hired, trained, and supervised a staff of 12 account managers, and provided ongoing staff mentoring and support enabling them to grow company's client base.
- ➢ **High Expectation Client Relations.** Painstakingly researched and subsequently instituted the recommended solutions outlined in the business book classic *The Nordstrom Way: The Inside Story of America's #1 Customer Service Company* to maximize HotJob's customer satisfaction.
- ➢ **Employer Branding.** Partnered with senior-level Human Resources clients in the design and development of uniquely branded corporate recruitment advertising strategies. Recommended tactical approaches for campaign execution.
- ➢ **Marketing Solutions.** Presented competitively positioned employee communication solutions and executed delivery of solutions such as collateral development, diversity strategies, university/college relations, and creative ad design to maximize employee communication programs.

Education

Master of Business Administration
The Kogod School of Business, American University – Washington, D.C.
Fully financed way through Business School

Bachelor of Science in Marketing
Michigan State University – East Lansing, MI

Professional Affiliation

Member –ß National Society of Hispanic MBAs

Superior references available on request

CALISTA BOWMAN

Birmingham, AL 35209   205-634-4342   c.bowman@gmail.com

Linked in profile

Sales & Customer Service

"I drive new business with commitment, persistence, and focus."

Performance Summary

Top-producing Sales professional with 12 years experience capitalizing on market opportunities and delivering first-rate results in business-to-business markets. Strong agricultural manufacturing background and robust networking skills with a talent for prospecting, understanding customer needs, and integrating relevant value propositions into solutions.

♦ Dynamic performer with the ability to open new territories, create trusted business relationships, and identify, pursue, propose, and close new business opportunities.
♦ Uses progressive selling techniques by creating innovative, value-oriented presentations and strong rapport-building skills that foster and grow enduring customer relationships.
♦ Negotiates and structures business deals with self-motivation, initiative, and the business savvy necessary to meet the challenges of today's highly competitive marketplace.
♦ Outstanding capacity for developing and executing sales strategies and tactics that increase product awareness, market share, and profitability.

Professional Competencies

✓ Account Management	✓ Strategic Planning	✓ Networking
✓ Business Development	✓ Territory Development	✓ Negotiating
✓ Goal Achievement	✓ Market Development	✓ Agribusiness
✓ Conflict & Issue Resolution	✓ Informed Decision Making	✓ Communication
✓ Problem Solving	✓ Merchandising / Marketing	✓ Prospecting
✓ Time Management	✓ Dealer Training	✓ Presentation

Professional Experience

Bama Bearings, Huntsville, AL   2012 – Present
A total system solution provider, from bearings to seals and belts to gearboxes.
SALES REPRESENTATIVE
Built strong client relationships, cultivated and grew existing accounts while aggressively prospecting for new accounts.

♦ Grew key accounts 15% by commitment, persistence, and offering value-added training and services that resulted in becoming go-to vendor for problem resolution.
♦ Developed key refinery account into lucrative monthly maintenance contract.
♦ Helped establish and launch new product line for oilfield containment that delivered approximately $100K in sales in less than one year.
♦ Coordinated and scheduled new jobs; managed interdepartmental activities of related jobs.

Alabama Steel Supply, Inc., Mobile, AL   2007 – 2012
Alabama Steel is a manufacturer of agriculture machinery, farm bins, commercial bins, livestock equipment.
TERRITORY MANAGER
Charged with oversight of a five- to six-state sales territory. Developed a profitable multi-state territory from the ground up, selling a product line of steel buildings, grain bins, livestock equipment, and tractor-

related accessories, including Koyker Manufacturing loaders and Short-Line equipment. Accounts included independent retail stores, large chain stores, distributors, and contractors.

♦ Packaged various divisions within Sioux Steel products, resulting in increased primary and add-on sales; qualified/transitioned new vendor leads into repeat customers.
♦ Captured more than $2M in new territory sales and multitude of referrals during first two years of tenure.
♦ Designed and launched highly successful dealer/builder program with Fabric Membrane Building line.
♦ Utilized strong network of current and former customers, locals, and local agribusinesses to develop leads and establish new accounts.

Autauga Steel, Inc., Prattville, AL   2005 – 2007
Autauga Steel is an employee-owned company providing quality steel products worldwide.
DISTRICT SALES MANAGER
Established and managed a money-making multi-state/multi-province sales territory consisting of distributors, wholesalers, and retailers. Product line included metal buildings, custom fabrication, grain bins, and livestock equipment. Accounts consisted of independent retail stores, large store chains, and distributors.

♦ Developed numerous top 50 accounts and two top 20 accounts that produced a combined $2.5M in sales during recessionary period.
♦ Formulated strategic business plan, aggressively targeted competitors' weaknesses, proactively networked, and cultivated customer rapport to deliver wins that:
   ✓ grew territory by greater than 125% in six years;
   ✓ boosted sales in two territories by $3M and $1.5M respectively.
♦ Launched and managed dealer training program that educated dealer network and boosted sales.

Education
Loyola University, New Orleans, LA, BSME   2005

Certifications
♦ Microsoft Excel I & II Certification, Entre Tech Services
♦ SKF Certification

Ongoing Professional Education
♦ Martin Engineering Foundation training (conveyor components)
♦ 3D Customer Focused training process (customer service excellence)
♦ Numerous Manufacturing in-house training sessions and webinars

Computer Skills
♦ JD Edwards; Microsoft Word, Excel, Outlook; CRM software

Pauline Zamudio

6789 Starbright Lane
Seattle, Washington 98101

206.734.5634
techsales@ameritach.com

Technology Sales Management

Performance Summary

Strong background in sales, sales management, business development, and account management. Skilled in Enterprise Software Sales, Enterprise Content Management (ECM), Business Process Management (BPM), and Business Process Outsourcing (BPO). Increased sales by developing strong relationships with clients, staff, partners, and management from initial contact through implementation. Demonstrated talents in building name brand awareness.

- Exceptional ability to research, analyze, and translate information to diverse audiences.
- Skilled in development and implementation of marketing strategies that increase sales.
- Consultative sales, strong communication, negotiation, and needs assessment skills.
- Extensive experience selling to C-suite of large organizations.

Professional Skills

* Sales & Marketing	* Strategic Accounts	* Technical Sales
* Business Development	* Order Management	* Contract Negotiations
* Client Development	* Vendor Relations	* Business Process Management
* ECM	* FileNet	* Enterprise Document Generation
* Strategic Alliances	* Events	* Open Standards
* Relationship Management	* Platform Skills	* Government Programs
* Systems Integration	* Training & Development	* Business Process Outsourcers
* Cost Containment	* Document Management	* Business Process Analysis

Performance Highlights

- ✓ Created a niche market at Pyramid Solutions, providing a repeatable Business Process Management (BPM) solution for national financial services and mortgage industries, using FileNet technologies. Project profit margin increased by 35%.
- ✓ Awarded FileNet's "Innovative Solution of the Year" at Pyramid Solutions for development of a repeatable Business Process Management solution in financial services industry.
- ✓ Met and exceeded quota by 103% and added (4) new named accounts.
- ✓ Recognized as "Top Partner - Kofax Midwest Region" at Pyramid Solutions.
- ✓ FileNet Presidents Club Achiever 125% > of Quota.

Professional Experience

THUNDERHEAD INC.– ATLANTA, GA   2013 – Present
DIRECTOR NATIONAL ACCOUNTS

Software sales for 100% Open Standards–based Enterprise Document Generation for financial services and government programs. Negotiates contracts with new vendors and partners. Cultivates relationships from initial contact through implementation with partners, clients, staff, and management.

- Hired as first direct sales staff member for start-up operations in North America, gaining four named accounts in first year.
- Organized "Lunch & Learn" program for FileNet System Consultants and integration partners to provide product education.
- Established strategic partnerships with *UNISYS, BearingPoint, and IBM Global Services*, as well as several other system integrators.

TECHNICAL SOLUTIONS, INC. – NEW YORK, NY   2009 – 2013

DIRECTOR OF SALES & MARKETING

Charged with providing sales and marketing for systems integration and professional services organization. Increased brand awareness through development of comprehensive marketing materials. Analyzed business needs and implemented solutions that drove business growth. Created new pricing model and product structure.

Provided sales and deployment of ECM and BPM solutions nationwide. Managed relationships with *FileNet, Captiva, and Kofax*. Implemented Business Process Analysis methodology: analyze and document customer's current processes, and how the technology could streamline these processes. Customers included: *Flagstar Bank, Sun Trust, PMI, Comerica, Washtenaw County, Muskegon County, Oakland County.*

- Awarded FileNet's "Innovative Solution of the Year" for development of Business Process Management solution in financial services industry (2012).
- Exceeded quota by over 100% two out of four years.
- Earned membership in FileNet's ValueNet Partner Million Dollar Club (2011–2013).
- Developed and implemented new change management marketing program, assisting companies with installation of complex technology.

NEW SYSTEMS, INC. – NEW YORK, NY   2006 – 2009

REGIONAL SALES Manager

Directed and managed sales staff throughout the United States. Oversaw and managed budget of $6.2M. Created and implemented new value-based sales process for rapid prototyping technology. Developed and installed Rapid Manufacturing Application within the aerospace industry. Provided global sales support for *Ford Motor Company, DaimlerChrysler, and GM*. Trained sales and engineering staff members. Oversaw all regional operations, including deals and resources on a national basis. Established and managed relationships with Business Process Outsourcers (BPO).

- Reduced operating costs for field operations by combining facilities.
- Facilitated professional sales training boot camps.
- Discovered highly complex application, resulting in creation of InVisiLine braces.
- Transformed 3D Solutions sales force from product focus to solutions-oriented focus, through process analysis, training, and ROI models.
- Grew annual sales 15% by focusing sales teams on solution sales.

ABC CORPORATION – NEW YORK, NY   2002 – 2006

ACCOUNT EXECUTIVE

Promoted to Senior Account Executive in 2005. Provided direction and management to 14 staff members, charged with providing large enterprise document management and BPM solutions. Gained new channel partners with application providers and consulting vendors. Charged with selling $MM solutions to C-level executives at large organizations, including *GE Aircraft Engines, Medical Mutual of Ohio, Goodyear Tire and Rubber, Steelcase, Dow, Ford Motor Credit, U of M Health Systems, Comerica, Huntington Banks, and Key Banks.*

- Increased indirect sales channels by 100%.
- Awarded "Presidents Club" for exceeding quota by 125%.
- Earned "Rookie of the Year."
- Received "Eastern Region Top Producer."

Education

Bachelor of Science, Business Administration • The Ohio State University

– Columbus, OH

CHERISE JOHNSON

(617)321-8924 • c.johnson@gmail.com • 378 Miles Standish Court, Unit B • Cambridge, MA 02139

APPLICATIONS ENGINEER

PERFORMANCE SUMMARY

MIT Engineering PhD candidate with 5+ years of experience using simulation and project R&D skills in basic and applied research on membrane and separation technologies, including membrane system design, fabrication & testing, process development and optimization, and performance evaluation for industrial chemical engineering applications. Demonstrated record of developing membrane system devices and processes with direct business application for improved performance and reliability while decreasing costs.

➢ Develops and implements innovative solutions through experimentation and modeling that improve performance, reliability, and energy requirements to meet both technical and economical goals.
➢ Strong coursework and research using CFD and Aspen HYSYS as well as hands-on fieldwork to verify simulations.
➢ Lifelong learner who actively stays current with industry developments, shares knowledge, and contributes to new science in areas of personal and professional interest.

PROFESSIONAL SKILLS

Material Engineering	Project Management	Computational Programming	Problem Solving
Process Design Engineering	Large Process Systems	Mathematical Modeling	Engineering Standards
Membrane Module Design	Flow Visualization	Simulation Techniques	Data & Numerical Analysis
Economic/Cost Evaluation	Production Scale-Up	Multiphysics Flow Modeling	Client Relations

PROFESSIONAL EXPERIENCE

UNIVERSITY OF TOLEDO • Toledo, OH   **2011–Present**
GRADUATE RESEARCH ASSISTANT
While attending classes full-time, actively assist with a variety of commercially based research projects within the Chemical & Environmental Engineering Department. Support all stages of the research life cycle: hypothesizing and designing solutions, working onsite to test prototypes, collaborating with sponsors and research partners, and presenting results both orally and in writing. Additionally, serve as a mentor to new graduate students on lab processes, simulation skills, and research ideas.

Key Achievements:
▪ Successfully completed 2 main research projects and 2 side projects that led to development of new technologies and processes.
▪ Published 3 research articles in top-level scientific journals, with another 2 ready to submit.
▪ Proactively addressed technical difficulties with project partners and quickly provided solutions.
▪ Volunteered to support visiting professor with experimental design and instrument setup, spending at least 2 hours each day discussing progress, assisting with tests, and contributing to group discussions.

RESEARCH PROJECTS

MASSACHUSETTS INSTITUTE OF TECHNOLOGY
Research Project: Low-Pressure Membrane Contractors for CO_2 Capture
▪ In partnership with Membrane Technology and Research, designed, built, and tested a 500 m^2 prototype low-pressure, counter-flow, sweep membrane module for use in post-combustion carbon dioxide capture.
▪ Utilized CFD and PIV to evaluate design parameters; CFD to determine uniformity of flows, pressure drops, degree of counter-current flow, and CO_2 mass transfer within modules; and CT to visualize flows and mass transfer.
▪ Results will lead to development of first-of-its-kind, large-scale, membrane-based carbon dioxide capture processes that mitigate the effects of global warming while reducing energy cost by 50% due to pressure drop.
▪ Key contributor to biweekly update teleconference with research partner as well as quarterly research reports to DOE.

206

MASSACHUSETTS INSTITUTE OF TECHNOLOGY
Research Project: Development of Novel Carbon Sorbents for CO_2 Capture
- Partnered with research team from SRI in $1.8M project (cost shared with $1.35M DOE) to validate use of and develop process for using carbon sorbents to capture CO_2 in post-combustion application.
- Worked onsite at UT Energy Center for 130 hours of field testing and functioning as an active member of the SRI R&D project team.
- Performed parametric experiments to determine optimum operating conditions and evaluated technical/economic viability.
- System reduced CO_2 level from 4.5% to less than 0.05% while maintaining steady-state operation with 90% capture efficiency and more than 98% CO_2 purity in the product gas.

MASSACHUSETTS INSTITUTE OF TECHNOLOGY
Research Project: New Static Mixing Spacer Design for Flat Sheet Membrane Modules
- Optimized spacer geometry to remove boundary layer effect and control polarization without power consumption increase.
- Conducted experimental measurements of mass transfer coefficient and pressure drop.

MASSACHUSETTS INSTITUTE OF TECHNOLOGY
Research Project: Theoretical Analysis of Gas Separation Process in Polymeric Membranes
- Created novel theoretical model that successfully predicted properties of Robeson upper bound.
- Prepared thin polymeric membranes using solvent casting and phase inversion technologies.
- Performed gas sorption and permeation experiments using rubbery and glassy polymeric membranes.

EDUCATION & PROFESSIONAL DEVELOPMENT

College Education
- DOCTOR OF PHILOSOPHY (PhD) IN CHEMICAL ENGINEERING (*Expected July 2017*), MASSACHUSETTS INSTITUTE OF TECHNOLOGY
    ~ <u>Dissertation</u>: "Transport Modeling and CFD Simulation of Membrane Gas Separation Materials and Modules"
    ~ Recipient of The Elias Klein Founders' Travel Awards in 2011 at North American Membrane Society (NAMS) Conference
- BACHELOR OF SCIENCE IN POLYMER MATERIALS & ENGINEERING, CLARKSON UNIVERSITY
    ~ Senior Design: "Synthesis and Characterization of Polyurethane/Carbon-nanotubes Composite Materials by Using Electrospinning Technology"
    ~ Recipient of Excellent Dissertation for Bachelor Degree Award

Certifications – COMSOL Multiphysics
- COMSOL Multiphysics Intensive Training, COMSOL, Inc.
- COMSOL Multiphysics CFD Certification, COMSOL, Inc.
- COMSOL Multiphysics Chemical Reaction Engineering Certification, COMSOL, Inc.
- COMSOL Multiphysics Heat Transfer Certification, COMSOL, Inc.
- Solver Setting for Effective Analysis in COMSOL Multiphysics Certification, AltaSim Technologies, LLC

Certifications – Process Design and Simulation
- Process Design Engineering Training
- Aspen HYSYS Advanced Training: Process Simulation and Modeling
- Aspen HYSYS Basic Process Simulation Training

ADDITIONAL INFORMATION

Technical Skills
- <u>Commercial Multiphysics Simulation Software</u>: COMSOL Multiphysics
- <u>Process Simulation Software</u>: Aspen HYSYS, Aspen Custom Modeler (ACM)
- <u>Computational Programming</u>: MATLAB, VBA, Fortran
- <u>Analytical Techniques</u>: PIV, GC, XRD, FTIR, TGA, DSC
- <u>Design of Experiment Software</u>: Design Expert, Minitab 16

International Exposure
- Fluent in Mandarin

JOHN A. CHRISTOPHER
11 Barbara Lane • Simi Valley, California 80932 • (805) 816-3787 • fax (805) 792-9741 • jacla@aol.com

Applications
Adaptec Easy CD Creator
Adaptec Direct CD
Carbon Copy
Cc Mail
Clarify
HP Colorado Backup
MS Active Sync
MS Office Professional
MS Outlook 98 and 2003
MS Internet Explorer
NetAccess Internet
Netscape
Norton Ghost
Partition Magic
PC Anywhere
Rainbow
Reflection 1
Reflection X
Remedy-ARS
Symantec Norton Antivirus
Visio
Windows CE

Operating Systems
Microsoft Windows 2000
Microsoft Windows NT 4.0
Workstation and Server
Microsoft Windows ME
Microsoft Windows 95, 98
Cisco Router/Switch IOS
MS-DOS
UNIX

Hardware
Intel-based Desktops
Intel-based Mobile
Computers
HP Colorado Tape Backup
Cisco 2500 Series Router
Hewlett Packard Pro Curve
Switches
CD Writer

Protocols & Services
TCP/IP
DHCP
DNS
NetBEUI
Remote Access Service
WINS

Networking
Ethernet
Token Ring
Microsoft Networking

Network Architecture Specialist
Cisco Certified Network Associate

Performance Profile

Results-driven, self-motivated professional with solid experience supporting hundreds of users in multiple departments in the corporate environment. Recognized for outstanding support and services, process development, and project management. Able to manage multiple projects simultaneously and to move quickly among projects. Capable of leading or collaborating. Areas of expertise include:

- Network architectures and networking components
- Software and operating system deployment in corporate environments
- PC hardware installation/repair and disk imaging
- Troubleshoot complex operating system problems
- Call tracking, case management, solution integration

Accomplishments

- Reduced help desk calls by developing end-user training and knowledge database.
- Led migration for 3000+ client/server email accounts from HP Open Mail to MS Exchange.
- Developed data collection protocol for BLM Natural Resource Inventory.
- Mentored teammates on technical materials and procedures.
- Built relationships to quickly resolve business critical issues.

Certifications

Technical Certification for MS Network Support Program
CCNA – Cisco Certified Network Associate

Work History

Technical Support Engineer, ABC Technologies (Holt Services), 2014 – Present
Email Migration Specialist, ABC Technologies (Holt Services), 2010 – 2014
PC Technician, RBM (The Cameo Group), 2012 – 2014

Education

B.S., Soil Science: Environmental Mgt. – CA Polytechnic State University
Pacific Institute Workshop – Goal Setting, Achievement, Motivation
A.A., Mathematics, Mira Costa College

Awards and Honors

ABC Shining Star Award for Outstanding Customer Service
Outstanding Services to Technical Services Division
High Quality Customer Service Award, RBM Technical Support

John Stamos

San Francisco

(415) 652-9567
cloudmanagement@gmail.com

Data Center Engineer
"Trained to anticipate and deliver customer satisfaction."

PERFORMANCE SUMMARY

17+ years' experience in data center management and technical support. Lead storage engineer at a dedicated high-security site with 1,300 enterprise servers for a global provider of secure financial messaging services on behalf of Hewlett Packard. Manage schedules and workload of three rotating assistant engineers.

✓ Server technology and hardware replacement and upgrades: Hard Drive, CPU, RAM, etc.
✓ Worked across global groups ensuring worldwide redundancy/transparency for all platforms and configurations.
✓ Conversant in all relevant storage technologies & their business applications, adding $6M+ in new sales.
✓ Maintained customer main message flow availability at 99.999% for 10+ years.
✓ Executed incident-free 6-hour CTR contract with $500K nonperformance penalty for 10+ years.

TECHNOLOGY PROFILE

Hardware: Hitachi Data Systems (HDS, P9500, XP24000), HP 9000 Servers and Workstations, Itanium- and Intel-based Blade Servers, C-class Blade Enclosure, SN8000 B-series Brocade SAN Switches (DCX), B6200 D2D StoreOnce Backup System, 3Com switches, 3Par, and all major storage peripherals.

Operating Systems: Windows, HP UX, Brocade Fabric OS.

Applications: Remote Web Console (Hitachi Data Systems), Virtual Connect Support Utility, Brocade Fabric Manager, ICE (support ticket documentation tool), HP Common Desktop Environment, StorageWorks Library and Tape Tools (LTT), Insight Control Environment, SanXpert, Support Tools Manager (STM).

Hitachi Data Systems (HDS)	Environmental Assessment	System Security
Lead Storage Engineer	Event Monitoring Service (EMS)	Electrostatic Discharge
Preventative Maintenance	ElectroMagnetic Interference (EMI)	Disaster Recovery, Backups
C-class Blade Installation	Hardware Replacement and Upgrades	Application Support
Troubleshooting: Systems & Networks	Cabling and Testing	UNIX
Rack Layout, IO Card Layout	Diagnose and Repair Systems	Technical Support
Operational Readiness Deadlines	Server Installations	Server Locations
SN8000 B-series Brocade SAN Switches (DCX)	Configured Technical Computing Solutions	Cooling System/Air Distribution

PROFESSIONAL COMPETENCIES

ITIL - Processes	ITSM - Change Management	Customer Service
ITIL - Best Practices	ITSM - Customer/Business Relationship Management	Cost Management
ITSM - Capacity Management	ITSM - Reference Model - Business Assessment	Presentation Skills
Project Management	ITSM - Problem Management	Resource Tracking
Sales Support/Lead Generation	NI62 – High-Level Account Development	Inventory Control
Scheduling Management	Needs Assessment/Business Analysis	New Product Training
Ability to Work Independently	Executive Relationship Development	Policy & Procedures

-continued-

PROFESSIONAL EXPERIENCE

Mission Critical Hardware Specialist, Samsung, CA 2009–Current

Lead Storage Engineer for Hitachi Data Systems storage platform and the primary interface between HP and high-level customers. Leadership skills with the ability to mentor team to deliver results on time and within budget.

- Trusted advisor role: first point of customer contact for resolution of all issues.
- Proven ability to effectively coordinate with external vendors and internal staff; works well with others in a team environment.
- Prompted repeat business and submitted leads to the sales force increasing client base.
- Increased team productivity resulting in the ability to manage a large data center with the assistance of one other employee while reducing overtime by 50%.
- Implemented customer problem structure/flow increasing responsiveness and decreasing resolution time.
- Responsible for developing technical protocols and identifying process improvements techniques by using real-time data collection.

Field Engineer Technical Support, Hewlett Packard, Washington, DC 2001–2009

Conducted reactive field repairs and support for enterprise-level HP servers and storage. Troubleshot and resolved problems quickly to ensure uninterrupted operating capability.

- Provided 24/7 coverage for Government account including DEA, USPTO, and the Pentagon.
- Quickly learned new products and services for generating sales leads.
- Improved processes and performance in a deadline-driven environment.
- Chosen by management to advance to permanent customer interaction role.

Pre-Sales Technical Consultant, Hewlett Packard, Rockville, MD 1997–2001

Interfaced with technical customers to complete sales cycle and ensure that all needs of sales opportunities were fulfilled. Main contact for issue resolution related to product, pricing, and delivery.

- Configured technical computing solutions for government agencies to assist sales.
- Received and effectively assessed customer issues through meetings and other media.
- Proposed a variety of solutions with varying price points to meet customer needs.
- 100% of sales representatives under my watch achieved company sales quotas annually.

EDUCATION, PROFESSIONAL TRAINING, & CERTIFICATIONS

National Louis University, Chicago, IL 1996
B.S. in Business Management

Monroe Community College, Rochester, NY 1993
A.A.S. in Computer Science

HP D2D Gen 3 StorageWorks B6200 StoreOnce Install, Service, and Support	2016
3PAR InServ Storage Server Hardware Introduction	2015
HP StorageWorks VLS and D2D Solutions	2015
HIPAA Privacy and Security Awareness	2014

Mission Critical Certified Specialist

Certifying Body: Samsung

Mission Critical Mindset Assessment Specialist

Certifying Body: Hewlett Packard

"I have the cleanest computer rooms in the nation."

Doug York

Chicago, IL
773.345-4324 | doug@dougdesigns.com
Linked in profile

WEBSITE DESIGN • USER INTERFACE DESIGN • USER EXPERIENCE DESIGN

Professional Profile

UI / UX designer with 19 years of success designing user interfaces and user experiences for complex web, mobile, and cloud solutions. Trusted advisor who collaborates with business leaders and multidisciplinary teams comprised of product development, marketing, and IT professionals to create intuitive websites, streamlined user interfaces, and compelling user experiences. Fluent in Portuguese, Spanish, Italian, and English.

Professional Skills

Art Direction / Graphic Design	Web Development Project Management	Client Communications / Presentations
Website Design & Performance	Problem Identification & Resolution	Technology Assessments
Mobile & Cloud Solutions	UI Standards, Usability, Guidelines, & Specifications	Contract Negotiation & Administration
Servers / Website Security	User Interface Design & Interaction	Digital Strategy
Search Engine Optimization	Front-End Development	Storyboards, Page Layouts, & Site Grids
Website Development / Intranets	Prototype Creation & Usability Testing	Animated GIFs / Cinemagraphs
E-Commerce	Knowledge of Cross-Browser Quirks	Product Development / Content Marketing

Technology & Computer Science Skills

Design: Adobe Photoshop, Illustrator, Adobe Flash, Adobe Edge Inspect, Responsive Web Design, Usability, Accessibility
Development: HTML 5 – HTML, CSS3, JavaScript, Sublime Text 2 / Notepad++, and basic use of jQuery, PHP, MySQL; Joomla CMS Expert (Front-end development, administration, deployment, security, maintenance, and migration), Bootstrap v3
Website Performance Optimization: Server-side and client-side solutions
Browser Developer Tools: Firebug/Chrome/IE development tools
Servers: WHM/cPanel administration (advanced), Linux server administration (basic), and basic server security knowledge
Other: Adobe Premiere, Adobe Media Encoder (for DVD/Blu-ray and Web), Sony Vegas and Sound Forge, DVD Lab Pro 2, Adobe Lightroom, Adobe Acrobat Pro DC, Microsoft Office Suite (Word, Excel, PowerPoint, and Outlook), SEO, and research

Performance Highlights

➢ Proven leader in the design of practical user interfaces and user experiences for a wide range of solutions.
  - As a UI designer, provide user interface layout and design with special attention to visual appeal and interactive features. Collaborate with design teams, software application developers, network engineers, and other IT professionals.
  - As a UX designer, conduct user tests, face-to-face interviews, and field research. Create user personas, study detailed analytics, provide design layouts, lead prototype creation, and conduct usability testing. Work closely with internal stakeholders, including marketing, brand development, product development, and product management teams to understand the businesses' functional requirements from the UX perspective.
➢ Articulate spokesperson with the ability to explain creative design concepts and user journeys to nondesigners. Effectively communicate project and design rationale to technical and nontechnical people at all organizational levels.
➢ Outstanding customer service skills with a proven record of maintaining client satisfaction and retention.

Professional Experience

TECHMASTERS, INC.   Chicago, IL
Art Director, Website Designer, UI Designer, and UX Designer   1998 – Present

Techmaster, Inc. is a boutique website design and development agency known for innovative design and quick turnaround.

- Create attractive, highly functional user interfaces for websites, serving more than 200 corporate clients in South America, North America, and Europe.
- Serve as the single point of contact with clients. Actively participate in brainstorming and design execution meetings.
- Collaborate with clients' product groups, marketing teams, and IT staff to create and refine effective online marketing strategies for the clients' products/services.

- Meet with clients to gain an understanding of their business models, assess their needs, and derive insights about the clients' customers, including researching personas, competitive analysis, etc.
- Advise clients on the evolution of UI/UX solutions and emerging technologies. Identify and resolve issues as they arise.
- Design the user experience from concept through implementation across all online solutions, including active development on top of the chosen CMS solution.
- Manage overall quality of design deliverables for marketing online products/services. Deliver wireframes, information architecture, and high-fidelity comps.
- Lead the development and deployment of websites, intranets, and other online solutions.
- Manage 3–15 people, depending on the project size.
- Provide quick turnaround on client requests and resolve issues in a timely and accurate manner.
- Exercise meticulous care in creating/maintaining detailed documentation such as user experience road maps and style guides.

Selected Long-Term Client Projects

EXPLORE! LAND & SEA TRAVEL SERVICES – Art Director, UX Designer, and Web Developer   2008 – Present

Explore! is a holding company encompassing 8 different business groups in 22 countries with annual revenue of $7.5 billion in 2013.

- Designed/developed 3 versions of company's website. (The newest design, which is some of my best work, has not been released yet, but it can be viewed with a confidentiality agreement.) Designed/developed 2 versions of the company's intranet.
- Serve as a trusted advisor to the client. Provide UX design services, including active development on top of the chosen CMS solutions. Perform graphic design and video editing. Engineer quick solutions to internal and external communication challenges. Deliver wireframes, information architecture, and high-fidelity comps. Manage quality assurance and product documentation. Lead the development/deployment of online solutions (web, intranet, etc.).

CHASE TOWERS – Art Director, UX Designer, and Web Developer   2013 – Present

Chase Towers is a high-rise luxury condominium community with exclusive space at street level. Designed by Bernard Rice & Sons, Architects. The building won a sustainability award as the first project with LEED Platinum 3.0 precertification in Chicago.

- Designed a captivating online presence for Chase Towers par with the magnitude of the commercial real estate development. Delved deep into the architectural style of the building and worked to bring the grandeur of the client's vision for the website to life.
    - This two-phase project included creating a showcase sales website and turning the website into the building's intranet once Chase Towers was fully rented.
    - Chose the best technological platform for the foundation of the website. Developed demo prototypes and presented conceptual design to key stakeholders.
    - Created an interface that could easily change states and developed an information architecture that could hold both personalities, only showing the relevant interface at each phase of the project.
    - Delivered the design (user architecture, interfaces, and user experiences) from concept to final product.
    - Created the information architecture (IA) for the content.
    - Created and maintained internal documentation (text and screencast) for the products.
    - Completed both phases of the project perfectly within budget, even with performing additional requests from the client.
- Ongoing services include art direction, user interface design, information architecture, and improving the building's website and intranet, serving detailed information to all tenants about the building's amenities and internal processes, area transportation and commerce, and tenant-specific documents such as lease renewals, etc.

GEORGE, WIENER & SMITH, ATTORNEYS AT LAW – UX Designer and Web Developer   2012 – 2015

George, Wiener & Smith is one of the top 100 law firms in Chicago, with more than 30 practice areas and clients in all economic sectors.

- Provided user interface design, information architecture, and web development for the client.
- Worked closely with the advertising agency, art director, and the client to achieve a user interface that accurately reflects the client's brand. The project had a constrained budget and short deadline.
- Developed the company's website. Recommended the best technical solutions without sacrificing the required functionality.
- Deployed the solution with zero downtime, managed 2 developers, and completed the project on time and within budget.

MONEY MAN PAWN SHOPS – UX Designer and Web Developer   2015 – Present

Money Man is the largest privately owned chain of pawnshops in the greater Chicago area.

- As an outside consultant working for an external agency, designed a concise user experience information architecture while giving the agency's junior art director a crash course on responsive web design and usability.
- Provided user interface design, information architecture, and web development of the 2014 annual report website.
- Provide ongoing design of the user experience from concept through design/implementation across all target devices, including desktop, smartphones, and tablets. Find creative solutions to difficult interaction challenges. Actively participate in design team brainstorming and sketch sessions and develop demo prototypes. Develop front end and deploy final solution.

INTERNATIONAL BRANDING, LTD. – UX Designer and Front-end Developer   2012 – Present

International Branding is a global design and innovation consultancy with offices in 8 countries with locations in Paris, London, Warsaw, Hamburg, New York City, Sao Paulo, Shanghai, and Singapore.

- Work as an independent contractor. Collaborate with the clients' product groups to develop and implement user interfaces and information architecture for web and mobile applications that optimize user engagement and contribute to brand loyalty, customer retention, and website conversion (visit-to-order ratios) for retail commercial clients.
- Provide ongoing services including designing the user experience from concept through implementation. Actively participate in brainstorming and design execution meetings. Lead the development/deployment of online solutions (websites, intranet, among others). Create and maintain documentation for the products. Develop the front end and deploy online solutions. Provide quick turnaround on all issues and requests.

Education

Graduate – Shermer High School, Shermer, IL, 1997
B.S., Computer Science, C.W. Post University, Long Island

Hobbies and Interests

PC building with focus on water cooling and quiet computing

Marc Peyton

4542D Gwinnet Townhomes
Atlanta, GA 30317

Linked in profile

404-243-4245
marc.peyton@outlook.com

Copy Editor

"Helping writers become readable and publishers profitable."

PERFORMANCE PROFILE

11+ years' experience as a copy editor, with complete grasp of grammar, syntax, flow, meaning, and cohesion, including summary analyses and full analyses, press and media releases, and commentaries. Experienced in managing technical and editorial issues, with the ability to step up when full editorial skills are required. Fastidious about style and consistency while meeting deadlines with high-quality products.

- ✓ Strong communication skills, with the ability to work independently and as part of a team.
- ✓ Manages multiple deadlines in fast-paced environments with changing priorities.
- ✓ Resolves problems by recommending solutions to ensure high-quality products.
- ✓ Manages heavy workloads and assures completion of work according to schedule.
- ✓ Reliable and available to help those in need complete jobs on time and accurately.

PROFESSIONAL SKILLS

*Excellent Editing Skills	*Copyediting	*Proofreading Skills
*Collaborative Skills	*Customer Service Excellence	*Headline Writing
*Leadership Skills	*Strong Writing Skills	*Tracking Skills
*Technically Proficient	*Project Management	*Researches Facts
*Production Layout	*Desktop Publishing	*Trafficking
*Proofreads Galleys	*Vendor Interaction	*Newsletter Creation

TECHNOLOGY SKILLS

*MS Office (MS Word, Excel, PowerPoint)	*Outlook	*Product & Software Tester
*LinX	*MS Visio	*InDesign
*Photoshop	*Illustrator	*PageMaker

PROFESSIONAL EXPERIENCE

Dun & Bradstreet, Atlanta, GA   2006–Present
Copy Editor
A worldwide leader of financial market intelligence and one of the Big Three credit rating agencies. Publishes financial research and analysis for investors. Responsibilities include copyediting articles for grammar and house style. Article types include research updates and recovery reports. Performs summary and full analyses, press and media releases, and commentaries. Collaborates with analysts, manages workflow, resolves technical issues, and tracks projects. Strong competencies in public finance and corporate sectors.

- Honored with 11 ACE (Acknowledging and Celebrating Excellence) Awards for customer focus, teamwork, and spirit.

- Participated in alpha and beta testing of technology upgrades for internal software and client products, enabling employees to be more productive and resulting in improved customer experience.

- Participated in training initiatives, including individual training of new employees, contributions to instructional manual, and service on an interdepartmental committee tasked with ensuring quality of training and increasing productivity.

Assistant to Editor   2004–2006
Initially hired as a temporary worker for three days a week; hired full-time in 2005 due to excellent performance. Responsibilities included proofreading galleys and inputting corrections to galleys.
- Provided extra time and dedication to complete first note season in 2006.
- Charged with managing group completing summary analyses when editorial assistant and editorial manager were unavailable.
- Selected to provide training to temporary workers and permanent employees as needed to ensure superior performance.

Oglethorpe Group, Ltd., Atlanta, GA   2001–2004
Editor
Initially hired as a temporary employee, then moved into permanent editing position. Responsibilities included collecting information, writing and editing articles, designing and placing advertisements, handling production layouts, working with outside vendors including printing companies and advertisers, assisting with special projects, and providing administrative support to staff.
- Produced monthly, quarterly, and yearly publications for two professional associations and a for-profit subsidiary.
- Created the masthead for four-page newsletter for the for-profit subsidiary.
- Assisted in the transition from manual newsletter production methods to desktop publishing (PageMaker), resulting in improved services to clients.

CORPORATE AWARDS / RECOGNITION

Awarded 11 ACEs (Acknowledging and Celebrating Excellence)
   *Awards recognized top-quality customer focus, teamwork, and spirit at Dun & Bradstreet.

EDUCATION AND PROFESSIONAL DEVELOPMENT

Duke University, Durham, NC   2001
Bachelor of Arts   Major: Political Science; Minor: English

Situational Communication   2015
  D&B: Editorial Classes

Certificate: Digital and Graphic Design Production   2008
Relevant Coursework
 InDesign, Photoshop, Illustrator, Copyediting and Proofreading Fundamentals
Advanced Copyediting: 2007
Relevant Coursework
 Editing for Clarity
 Headline Writing for Commentaries
 Trimming Words for Tighter Writing
 Identifying, Translating, and Eliminating Jargon
 Actively Speaking: Spotting and Eliminating the Passive Voice

54 Blue Ridge Trail
Ellijay, GA 30536

Shawn Brandon

Linked in profile
706-243-4340
shawn.brandon@gmail.com

Director of Planning & Materials

Performance Summary

Supply Chain Leader with 17 years' experience in planning and purchasing for organizations with a Worldwide reach. Demonstrated talent in leading and managing unified teams, ensuring all company and personal goals are achieved. Technically astute, with skills in Kanban, SAP, BAAN, RetailEdge, and Microsoft Access.

Demonstrated knowledge in lean manufacturing. Substantiated history of developing and executing enterprise-wide processes and procedures that increase productivity, quality, and consistency by removing redundancies. Strategic planner with well-honed analytic and technical proficiencies; adept in Worldwide business initiatives and able to excel in fast-paced, complex, and ambiguous environments.

Professional Skills

Strategic Planning	Worldwide Supply Chain	Purchasing	Inventory
Turnkey Solutions	Metrics	Lean Manufacturing	Sourcing
Forecasting	Replenishment	Project Management	Procedure Development
Kanban	Re-Order Points (ROP)	Logistics	Life-Cycle Management
Procurement	On-Time Delivery (OTD)	MRP/ERP	Negotiations
Staff Leadership	APICS Certified	SAP	BAAN

"Shawn has a history of leading many successful projects that have improved customer satisfaction and enabled flawless execution." – Sharla Jones, Director of Worldwide Planning, Worldwide Supply Chain

—— Key Highlights ——

➢ Drove site availability to 98% by establishing daily meetings between Site Manufacturing Managers, Planning group, and Purchasing group.
➢ Key contributor of the migration of the Molecular Biology Lab, providing planning and setup of new SAP plant with a very aggressive timeline.
➢ Reduced expedited expenses more than 60%.
➢ Saved $107,000 in service agreements and system cost.

—— Professional Experience ——

Scientech, Alpharetta, GA   2014 to 2017
Formerly the Georgia Special Division of Applied Technologies and Resoursystems and joint ventures.
Director of Worldwide Planning

Selected to oversee the entire supply chain life cycle. Hired and managed 14 staff members, providing support for Worldwide planning and procurement, instrument master scheduling, indirect procurement, DC Kanban Administration, service logistics call center, and data maintenance. Directed project initiatives for business process re-engineering and optimization. Led teams on Kaizen events.

• Reduced inventory 30%, totaling more than $9 million in one year.
• Saved $107,000 by initiating early termination of service agreement with Life Tech supply chain.
• Realized $170,000 in annual transportation savings by providing distribution planning changes.
• Increased product availability from 93% to 96%.
• Led the Supply Chain separation of ERP cloning from Applied Technologies without impact on customer service.

Applied Technologies, Alpharetta, GA   2000 to 2014
Formerly Resoursystems, providing instruments and consumables for life sciences.
Senior Manager, Worldwide Planning, Alpharetta Consumables   2010 to 2014

Promoted to provide planning and Worldwide supply chain management within the Consumables Group. Analyzed and resolved complex products. Managed six staff members. Partnered with Product Management and Manufacturing on prioritizing products, providing strategic resolutions to supply issues, and reduction of losses. Utilized visual reporting tools to create reports. Provided executives with weekly summaries on concerns with the site.

- Assisted in transitioning manufacturing group to an abbreviated time schedule, an $800,000 annual savings.
- Recognized with *Platinum Award* for leading the Supply Chain for U.S. DC consolidation to Frederick, MD.
- Reduced turnaround time 50% and eliminated a $400,000 backlog.
- Cut overdue work orders 30% by establishing daily cross-functional meetings.
- Selected by the Director as a replacement before the purchase of Resoursystems.

Senior Manager, Worldwide Spares Planning and Service Logistics   2005 to 2010

Provided life-cycle management of Spares Planning. Oversaw Service Logistics throughout North America. Directed contingency strategy planning for supplier bankruptcy, which included leading organization discussions with Project Managers, Service Product Management, Finance, Senior Management, and staff to salvage product lines. Represented sites across the globe.

- Saved the company $2 million in inventory by developing alternatives to Lifetime Buys.
- Led an organization-wide program, *President's Initiative*, saving the company $1 million in revenue.

Manager of Worldwide Service Logistics and Service Inventory   2000 to 2005

Primary liaison for entire supply chain, providing process alignment across the organization and establishing territory boundaries for Europe and APAC. Streamlined process by implementing SOX-compliant Field Service cycle program, metrics, and self-help tools for Field Engineers. Served as Service Business Operations Manager, driving optimization for 28 staff members in Service Call Center, Service Administration, and Service Contract Administration functions.

- Reduced aging inventory by $750,000 and priority overnight shipments by 40%, with a total savings of $350,000 per year by designing and implementing self-help tools for Field Service Engineers.
- Served as a key speaker at a Worldwide Service Conference with more than 500 attendees.

"Shawn is a patient, fair, and organization team leader who brings together people of diverse skills and personalities to accomplish measurable goals." – Debbie Firestone, Founder and President of SaveAPeke

—— **Volunteer Experience** ——

SaveAPeke Pekingese Dog Rescue, Blue Ridge, GA, 2011 to Present
Animal rescue and adoption center
Volunteer

Provided implementation and maintenance of a Point-of-Sale Inventory Management System. Created technical documentation of the inventory management processes.

—— **Education and Professional Development** ——

Bachelor of Economics, University of Georgia, Athens, Georgia

CPIM Certification, APICS

Chris Eisenstein
MBA in Finance & General Management

San Mateo, CA 95008   415-555-0606   chriseisenstein@gmail.com

Electronics Manufacturing Management

"Chris is a strategic thinker, respected as a role model of integrity—he sets a good example for others to follow. Chris not only recognizes opportunities but takes decisive action to make the most of them. He knows how to get things done through channels."

Performance Profile
15+ years of electronic manufacturing services management experience involving operations, finance, supply chain, and project and materials management.
Includes 6 years managing cross-functional teams and customer relations. Skilled at evaluating complex issues, identifying key issues, creating action plans, and guiding execution. APICS certified: CPIM and CSCP.

Professional Skills
✓ Revenue & Profit Increases
✓ Cost Reduction & Cost Avoidance
✓ Process & Efficiency Improvement
✓ Customer Relationship Management
✓ Contract Development & Negotiation
✓ Team Building & Leadership
✓ Materials & Supply Chain Management
✓ P&L Management
✓ Metrics Management & Analysis

PROFESSIONAL EXPERIENCE

High-Tech Circuits, Inc., San Mateo, CA   2004–Present
Business Analyst, Business Unit Financial Analyst   2015–Present

Perform extensive analysis and reporting for a business unit group of 300+ employees. Key actions and accomplishments include the following:

- Revitalized the Time Clock project, which was behind schedule. Established close interaction with offsite project manager and completed assembly, installation, and testing ahead of schedule. Recognized for contribution to efficiency improvement and more effective plant operation.
- Compiled and updated quarterly customer QBR reports using Excel pivot tables and Access database information. In addition, generated and reported quarterly bonuses for employees.

Business Unit Manager   2012–2015

Managed a challenging $25 million/year account and approximately $18 million of materials to maintain profitability. Major areas included forecasting, contract negotiations, supplier performance, financial management, and HR issues. Developed and coordinated activities of cross-functional teams. Key actions and accomplishments include the following:

- Spearheaded revision and execution of full manufacturing contract within 4 months versus expected 6–12 months.
- Grew revenue 330% in fiscal year 2006.

Business Unit Coordinator   2009–2012

Managed accounts valued at $12 million per year. Interacted with customers to ensure high satisfaction. Contributed to cost-reduction and efficiency improvements that included developing Excel macros to use purchasing and inventory data more efficiently and an Access database to track ECN changes and impact.

Master Planning Supervisor   2004–2009

Established rules, procedures, tools, and techniques to move plant from prototype to volume production. Managed master scheduling for multiple programs, as well as work cell material management and metrics. Key actions and accomplishments include the following:

- Achieved smooth transfer of $30+ million program to another facility through detailed material transactions and planning.
- Reduced excess inventory by $400,000 and increased inventory turns 20%.
- Originally earned promotion from Master Planner position within less than a year.
-

Previous positions: Master Planner; Accounting Manager

Peterson Laminate Systems, Phoenix, AZ   1997–2003
Production/Scheduling/Inventory Manager

Served as a member of Plant Leadership Team and as High Performance Work Team coach for Shipping department. Additional actions and accomplishments include the following:
- Participated in Kaizen event that promoted continuous improvement and elimination of waste by initiating changes that included reducing product travel from 5,000 to 2,000 feet.
- Contributed to $500,000 inventory reduction and 98% on-time shipping record.

EDUCATION, AFFILIATIONS, & CERTIFICATIONS

Master of Business Administration–Finance & General Management
Boston University, Boston, MA
Bachelor of Science–Accounting
Northeastern University, Boston, MA

Professional Affiliations
Member, American Production & Inventory Control Society

Certifications
Certified in Production & Inventory Management (CPIM): earned in less than one year
Certified Supply Chain Professional (CSCP): earned in less than 6 months

Application Competencies
Access, Visio, SAP, ERP Word, Excel (including pivot tables and macros), PowerPoint, etc.

Exemplary professional references available on request

Cheyenne, WY 82003

307-243-4243

pat.paulson@gmail.com

ENVIRONMENTAL CONSULTANT

Navigating the intersections of business, technology, and ecological systems.

Devise appropriate compliance and risk mitigation strategies when regulatory issues impact clients. Recognized for project leadership, supporting all aspects from requirements gathering and proposal development to resource allocation, implementation, and final handover. Exhibit consultative approach, giving clients one-on-one attention and making project adjustments to meet their needs.

Experienced interface for corporations, concerned communities, and government agencies, including O&G, Technology, Pharma, and Department of Defense. Communicate technical concepts to nontechnical audiences. Demonstrate valuable technical expertise, working with ERPs, CRMs, and other databases to manage critical information.

PROFESSIONAL SKILLS

Environmental Assessment	Requirements Gathering	Risk Management
Air & Water Quality Issues	Project Management	Health & Safety Protocols (EHS)
Site Investigations & Remediation	Proposals & Contract Administration	Client Consultation
Permitting	Budgeting & Cost Control	Vendor Relations
Regulatory Compliance	Cost Estimates	Training & Mentoring
Scientific Data Collection & Analysis	Cross-discipline Communication	Team Leadership
Field Surveying & Sampling	Continuous Process Improvement	
	Quality Assurance	

TECHNICAL SKILLS

Scientific Modeling	RERP/CRM	Microsoft Excel
isee systems STELLA	Industrial & Financial Systems (IFS)	Microsoft Excel Solver Plugin
PRé SimaPro Life Cycle	4D	Technical Report Writing
Assessment	Microsoft Word	Intranet Administration

PROFESSIONAL EXPERIENCE

AQUA INDUSTRIA, San Diego, CA   2012 to Present

Leading provider of shipbuilding, ship repair and modernization, and industrial services.

Project Coordinator

Appointed to support 5 project managers with contract and change order management, materials, subcontracting, and quality assurance plans for FFP, T&M, hybrid, cost plus, and IDIQ contract vehicles. Engaged with client stakeholders to understand their requirements and respond to needs. Contributed to scoping and preparing cost estimates for proposals. Secured final customer and regulatory approval for project closeout. Balanced competing priorities while juggling project schedules and budgets. Maintained vendor relationships during project life cycle.

Heavily utilized ERP (IFS) for project setup and to generate detailed project reports. Updated intranet to distribute project data; maintained customer information in CRM (Treasure Chest). Co-managed hundreds of craft workers spanning 12 unions. Interacted with various private customers and federal agencies, including Department of Homeland Security (Coast Guard), Department of Defense (Navy, Military Sealift Command), and Department of Commerce (NOAA), to coordinate multimillion-dollar contracts. Supported compliance with health and safety requirements via administrative measures.

Interfaced with U.S. Coast Guard on federal contracts exceeding $90.8M. Delivered key support for completion of dockside availability initiative for Healy, ahead of contracted deadline.   *continued*

- Acquired experience analyzing and interpreting state permitting requirements and federal rules concerning labor.
- Facilitated timely implementation of projects and issuing of work orders by rapidly processing award packages.
- Ensured client satisfaction by integrating controls into work items (inspection test plan, QA/QC) and communicating status updates to client to proactively address any issues and obtain approval for solutions. Integrated growth work into contracts.
- Played key role in implementing new version of ERP (IFS) to increase project efficiency and enhance reporting, conducting system test to ensure functionality and reporting accuracy before go live.
- Improved monitoring of job charges and resolution of discrepancies by assisting in migrating to new timekeeping system.
- Reduced redundant handling of data, errors, and project setup time through creation of templates in ERP.
- Elevated job estimate accuracy by recommending direct estimation of jobs in ERP to avoid need for data transfer.
- Drove continuous process improvement within Lean Manufacturing and ISO 9001 certified environment.

SMYTHE PACIFIC SHIPYARDS, San Diego, CA — 2009 to 2012

Former provider of ship repair and fabrication services to government and commercial markets.

Project Administrative Assistant

Hired into permanent position following brief temporary role. Joined project execution team, performing project setup, change management, progress billing, and closeout. Acted as point of contact for clients, regulatory agencies, and subcontractors. Entered specifications into ERP to develop budgets and work breakdown structure for project controls, financial management, and reporting. Contributed to bid package preparation and researched government RFPs. Prepared and submitted condition found reports for client approval. Ensured timely project closeout process and reconciled financial discrepancies.

- Completed public works contracts exceeding $36M for clients at state (Department of Transportation, Washington State Ferries) and county level.
- Expedited project completion by streamlining data flow within estimation and project delivery processes.
- Played central role in obtaining release of funds held in retainage for public works jobs (performance bond).
- Enhanced tracking/progress system to monitor steps required to close out public works initiatives by creating clear, scalable closeout process for all jobs within shared spreadsheet for easy review and update by all project staff.
- Replaced extraneous, disorganized secondary archiving system with single, centralized solution to ensure that all projects followed same sequential index used during execution.

ROLLING RAPIDS DISTILLERY, Jackson Hole, WY — March 2004 to June 2005

Low-volume producer of premium craft spirits.

Production Specialist

Hired to participate in all phases of production, sales, and distribution (domestic/international) for premium product line. Ensured quality control of production to deliver best-in-class products. Interacted with state and federal regulatory agencies. Developed proficiency with specialized precision measuring tools. Gained exposure to material flows, water, and energy usage within production process.

- Contributed to new product development and production process innovation to facilitate efficiency while maintaining product integrity.
- Played active role in company winning coveted industry awards by contributing to creation of high-quality products.

EDUCATION

Master of Science in Natural Resources and Environment: Sustainable Systems (December 2013)
Graduate Certificate in Industrial Ecology (December 2013)
University of Wyoming, Laramie, Wyoming

Relevant Environmental Coursework: Water Quality Management, Water Resources Policy, Energy Markets and Policy, Statistics, Transportation Energy, Environmental Assessment, Environmental Law, Ecology, Land Use and GIS

Miranda Bradshaw

Hilton Head, SC
843.234.2434 miranda.bradshaw@hargray.net

EXECUTIVE ADMINISTRATIVE & CLERICAL SUPPORT • OFFICE ADMINISTRATION • ACCOUNT MANAGEMENT

Linked **in**.

Executive Assistant & Office Manager

Supporting Financial Reporting, Shareholders & Board of Directors' Meetings, Leasing & Sales Activities, and Facilities Management

Performance Profile

Advanced problem-solving skills with the capability to accurately multitask in fast-paced environments. Proven track record in operations with a broad-based background. Recognized as a consistent producer driven to exceed goals and improve workplace efficiency. Highly focused multitasker with the ability to prioritize and manage timelines effectively. Advanced user of complex technology with solid background in MS Office, database management, end-user training, and updating websites; Internet savvy. Solid foundation in all facets of business operations including administrative policies and procedures. Maintains excellent communication skills and a high level of confidentiality.

Professional Skills

Scheduling & Calendar Management	Account Management & Admin. Support	Staff Training & Supervision
Office Management & Organization	Correspondence / Presentations	Exceptional Customer Service
Project Management / Priority Setting	Confidentiality & Diplomacy	Supply Inventory & Requisitions
Sales & Marketing Support	Budget Administration & Expense Control	Meetings & Conferences Logistics
Computer Systems & Software Applications	Financial Reporting & Reconciliation	Problem Identification & Resolution
Filing, Faxing, & Mail Distribution	Project Management & Research Skills	Billing / Collections Management
Answering Multi-Line Phones	Client Relationship Management (CRM)	Vendor Relationship Management

Computer Skills

Microsoft Office Suite: Word, Excel, PowerPoint, and Outlook. Also proficient in Multi-Data Services software, Microsoft Front Page, LogMeIn software, Doc Record, BuildingLink, Basecamp, and Adobe Acrobat. Ability to streamline computerized processes.

Performance Highlights

➢ Executive Administrative Assistant skilled in implementing best practices in office management and providing administrative and clerical support for business leaders, shareholders, and sales/marketing professionals. Known for building strong business relationships across a variety of industries, taking initiative to solve problems within the realm of responsibility, and keeping the office running smoothly.

➢ Highly organized and pragmatic Office Manager who achieved significant cost savings for office supplies by negotiating with vendors and monitoring office supply budget. Skilled in the design/implementation of business process improvements. Created the company's physical filing system, organizing 10,000+ files. Coordinated the launch of the company's MDS software, created user manuals, and trained over 80% of the office staff.

Professional Experience

SEA PINES REAL ESTATE MANAGEMENT CORPORATION | HILTON HEAD, SC
Account Manager | 2014 – Present
Executive Assistant and Office Manager | 2013 – 2014
Administrative Assistant | 2011 – 2012

In business since 1985, Sea Pines Real Estate provides professional property management services for Hilton Head's most prestigious condominiums and long- and short-term rental properties.

Account Manager
- Manage the daily operations of a $135,000 portfolio consisting of 9 residential and commercial property accounts, including building staff supervision for this mid-sized property management and brokerage firm with 150 accounts. Interface with union representatives. Communicate board priorities and concerns. Provide onsite presence with residents and staff. Handle client concerns and requests on a timely basis to ensure their satisfaction with property management services.

- Ensure that the properties are maintained in compliance with city codes and state building regulations. Approve and monitor building renovations to ensure that contractors are properly licensed and insured. Schedule and file all necessary inspections of physical plant and equipment. Clear open violations, as needed. Provide computerized work order tracking.
- Cultivate business relationships with qualified, licensed service professionals. Analyze and audit all service contracts annually. Bid out all contracts for best price and coverage. Provide owners with multiple bids for large contracts.
- Work with the board of directors to create an annual operating budget to keep properties operating profitably. Prepare performance-based analyses (budgets, forecasts, revenues, operating cost analyses, and probability assessments).
- Prepare monthly financial reports, quarterly and fiscal year-end financial statements, and balance sheets with breakdown of deposits and disbursements by property. Provide accountant with all necessary financial reports for year-end reporting and tax preparation.
- Leverage extensive industry knowledge, range of professional experience, and advanced communication skills to take initiative in situations before they become problematic. Predict the needs of managers/clients prior to their requests.

Executive Assistant & Office Manager
- Provided office management. Ensured effective and efficient administrative and clerical support for 5 executives. Supported executives in the management of condos, co-ops, rentals, and commercial properties throughout 5 boroughs of NYC.
- Provided executive support to CEO and CFO. Booked meetings for CEO and CFO. Prepared reports and presentations for board meetings and took meeting minutes. Reserved conference rooms, scheduled presentations, confirmed attendance, prepared agendas, and compiled/distributed meeting minutes.
- Created condo/co-op sales package customized to each building. Reviewed each sales/leasing package to ensure accuracy and completion. Coordinated the closing process of cooperative apartments. Generated $25,000 per month in cooperative closing commissions.
- Ensured entire portfolio met city deadlines for property registration filings and biennial filings.
- Created and revised systems and procedures by analyzing operating practices, recordkeeping systems, forms control, office operations, budgetary, and staffing requirements.
- Managed computer systems/software. Created a user guide for the client management software (MDS).

Administrative Assistant
- Executed a diverse range of administrative tasks. Read, researched, composed, and routed correspondence (memos, letters, and reports), addressed internal/external communications, and brought critical issues to the attention of executive leaders. Anticipated the needs of executives and took proactive measures to keep office running smoothly.
- Created spreadsheets, charts, and financial reports for board meetings and presentations regarding the financial status of clients' accounts and properties. Processed and reconciled invoices and expense reports. Followed up on billing/collections matters relating to vendors and clients.
- Managed executives' calendars in Microsoft Outlook. Handled appointment scheduling, travel arrangements, and meeting logistics for property owners' meetings and industry conferences. Represented executives by attending meetings in their absence and serving as the executive's spokesperson.
- Devised a physical filing system integrated with the company's client management software for easier file retrieval.

Education
Bachelor of Science in Marketing and International Business, University of South Carolina, Columbia, SC 2011

Languages
English and Spanish (Written and Spoken Proficiency)

Community Involvement / Volunteer Activities
Adopt-a-Family, Bluffton, SC, 2011–Present

Scott Simon

Detroit, MI   213.234.XXXX   falseclaims@meritech.com

INSURANCE ADJUSTER/INVESTIGATOR
"Seasoned fraud squad detective is poised to join the insurance profession."

Performance Profile
Logical and analytical approach to identifying and resolving situations with high potential for conflict. Organized and creative, with solid approach to comprehensive information gathering.

Police-trained investigator, superior questioning and analytical skills, experienced in negotiations, and ability to develop trust and open communication.

Calm under pressure. Committed to applying a trained and seasoned detective's skills to the insurance profession.

Core Competencies

➢ Investigative Techniques	➢ Witness Questioning	➢ Legal Compliance
➢ Courtroom Representation	➢ Incident Documentation	➢ Negotiating
➢ Risk Assessment	➢ Report Writing	➢ Safety Principles
➢ Needs Assessment	➢ Conflict Resolution	➢ One-on-One Training

Professional Training

➢ Police Science	➢ Investigation Techniques	➢ Security
➢ Reconnaissance	➢ Surveillance	➢ Accident Investigation
➢ Photography	➢ Family Violence	➢ Child Abuse Rape
➢ Crisis Evidence	➢ Public Relations	➢ Communication Skills

Police Service

Detroit, MI	2006 – 2017
➢ **Detective Fraud Squad**	
Southfield, MI	2003 – 2006
➢ **Detective Serious Crimes**	
Ann Arbor, MI	2000 – 2003
➢ **Officer Canine Unit**	
Bad Axe, MI	1998 – 2000
➢ **Patrolman**	

Education

➢ **Master of Science, Leadership and Organizational Change**	2014
Michigan State University, E. Lansing, MI	
➢ **Bachelor of Science, Criminal Justice**	
Pfeiffer University, Charlotte, NC	2007
➢ **Information systems security coursework**	2009
Stanly Community College, Albemarle, NC	

Superior references available upon request

Mary Cassat

L.A., California 90049   (310) 555-5678   Hospitality_Edge@ameritech.com

HOSPITALITY MANAGEMENT
Operations / Sales / Marketing

Performance Profile

10+ years' progressive experience in hospitality management. A track record of delivering *measurable revenue and profit contributions.* Team building and leadership strengths with proven ability to hire, train, and motivate top- performing teams. Organized, with the ability to multitask in a fast-paced environment and respond quickly and effectively to problems, thrives on challenges. *Foreign language:* Spanish.

Core Competencies

➢ Revenue Optimization	➢ Cost Containment	➢ Recruitment & Selection
➢ Staff Development	➢ Team Building	➢ Operations Management
➢ Spanish	➢ Time Management	➢ Policy & Procedures
➢ Customer Service	➢ Productivity Growth	➢ Accounting/POS Support
➢ Brand Integrity	➢ Client Relations	➢ Inventory Control
➢ P&L	➢ Turnover Reduction	➢ Problem Solving
➢ Payroll	➢ 250 Covers Daily	➢ Liquor Inventory
➢ Scheduling	➢ 300 Pre-theatre	➢ Cash Reconciliation
➢ Food Cost Reduction	➢ Purchasing	➢ Administration
➢ Training Manuals	➢ POS Systems	➢ Marketing/Advertising

PROFESSIONAL EXPERIENCE

STAR CITY RESTAURANT, Los Angeles, CA	Present
Assistant GM. —Hollywood	2015–Present
Administrative Manager—Hollywood	2012–2015
Bartender—Santa Monica	2010–2012
Hostess—Santa Monica	2010

Assistant GM.—Hollywood   **2015– Present**

Day-to-day food and beverage operations of $5+ million fine dining establishment that averages 250 covers daily. Train, manage, and mentor cross-functional team of 60+, ensuring highest standard of customer service and brand integrity.

Supervise food & beverage inventories, manage costs and maximize profitability, monitor safe handling best practices & procedures, prepare sales and labor forecasts. P&L accountability and Payroll responsibility. Accounting & POS support.

- Orchestrated scheduling initiative that minimized overtime, captured **10% increase in productivity,** and **reduced payroll by over 10%.**
- Hired, trained, and supervised cross-functional front and back-of-house staff of 60 with minimum turnover; **achieved impact ratio over 100%.**
- Organized liquor perpetual inventory, streamlined daily procedures, **cost reduction of 2%.**

Continued

Administrative Manager—Hollywood   2012–2015

Promoted after nine months to initiate and manage administrative affairs for new location including daily cash and credit reconciliations, employee file maintenance, accounts payable, office administration, benefits administration, new hire processing, etc.

- Achieved 95% or better on all audits.
- Appointed as corporate administrative trainer; trained six managers during tenure.
- Authored Positouch Procedural Guide for use at all locations.
- Designed employee file initiative that was adopted for use company wide.
- Implemented side work, floor plan, and scheduling charts to organize restaurant opening.
- Responsibility for OSHA and Workers Comp. RESULT: perfect scores on corporate audits.

Bartender—Santa Monica   2010–2012
Hostess—Santa Monica   2010

                                                                         2006–2009

CARLA'S DINNER HOUSE, LOS ANGELES, CA

Shift Supervisor / Bartender / Server

Advanced to shift supervisor with responsibility for opening / closing, scheduling staff, maintaining inventory, purchasing, reconciling cash drawer, etc., for busy Upper East Side restaurant.

- Gained valuable experience in all aspects of restaurant operations.
- Developed "spotter" system to eliminate theft that has been implemented by other establishments throughout the area.
- Increased sales through "door to door" advertising program.

EDUCATION, CERTIFICATIONS, & AFFILIATIONS

UNIVERSITY OF CALIFORNIA, Los Angeles, CA
BA in Humanities

Professional Development / Certifications
Stellar Service Training Phoenix, AZ
Servsafe, FMP (Food Management Professionals) Certified Trainer

Professional Affiliations
Member, NAWBO (National Association of Women's Business Owners)

Computer Skills
PC and Macintosh: Word, Excel, Databases, POS Systems (Positouch, Squirrel, Micros), Restaurant Magic

Foreign Language Skills

Conversational Spanish in the workplace

Superior references available

234 Rue de Rouge
Montreal, Quebec, G1W 1K7

514-342-4334
j.saintlaurent@gmail.com

Jean Saint Laurent

Insurance Underwriter ~ Insurance Investment

Charter Insurance Professional & Investment Operations Certified

Performance Summary

Six years of experience in providing investment reporting, transaction processing, and client reporting. Contributed to continuous process improvement by streamlining the delivery of new workflow procedures. Recognized for outstanding work ethic, leadership, and financial services expertise through job promotion within the first year of employment. Maintained dealer agreements, created detailed reports, and reviewed documents during opening of new accounts. Reduced costs through analytical research of market prices.

——Professional Skills——

* Client Reporting Analysis	* Portfolio Administration	* Strategic Analysis	* Negotiations
* Renewals	* Risk Management	* Pricing Analysis	* Data Analysis
* Regulation Compliance	* Training & Mentoring	* Partnership Development	* Relationship Management
* Business Development	* Process Improvement	* Issue Resolution	* Communications
* Client Administration	* Conflict Resolution	* Report Development	* Fluent in French

——Professional Experience——

Bonhomme Investment Advisors, Montreal, Quebec
A leading investment management firm with oversight of more than $100M in assets for high net-worth clients.

Underwriter & Compliance Analyst   2010 – Present
Provided employee training with a focus on accurate and on-time reporting. Reviewed documents for opening new accounts and completion. Managed dealer agreements, memberships, and registrations. Served as a liaison between Bermuda Monetary Authority and the Bermuda Investment Advisory Services while maintaining compliance with legislation. Reviewed and updated terms of agreement attached to forms, ensuring forms reflected changes in product offerings.

- Partnered with Investment Managers to maintain up-to-date information and remain in compliance with the Monetary Authority while adhering to Know Your Client requirements.
- Researched all client files to enhance KYC requirements using industry-accepted Anti-Money Laundering (AML) database.

Investment Valuations Analyst   2008 – 2009
Provided development and analysis of investment reports, valuations, and statements, while ensuring accuracy of daily transaction imports. Performed market analysis of prices on equities, bonds, and derivatives. Created a comprehensive pricing file to maintain inventory of all holdings. Partnered with the Portfolio Management Team in report development.

- Spearheaded initiative to enhance procedures and improve operational efficiency through auditing of performance measurement calculations, client valuations, and system integrity.
- Selected to resolve complex system problems and implement new strategies and solutions, saving the company revenue lost during system outages.
- Reduced subscription cost 10% annually by negotiating prices with vendor on software.
- Key member of team that improved business processes and contributed to development of new application system.

Lacordaire Street Bank and Trust Company, Quebec City, Quebec   2004 – 2008
A provider of comprehensive financial services, investment management, research and training, and investor services with $25T assets under custody, $2T under management, $9B in revenue, and more than 20,000 employees.

Business Reporting Analyst   2006 – 2008

Reported directly to the Senior Vice President of Investor Services, providing drafting and review of business case, business requirements, and functional specifications documents. Identified and resolved a variety of issues, ensuring quick resolution of complex problems. Assisted with defining and reviewing client requirements from a fund accounting and investment operations perspective.

- Key contributor in completing a comprehensive data conversion to bring in-house recordkeeping for numerous banks within Europe. Ensured project was completed on time and in adherence to service obligations.

- Improved overall ability to design effective systems by creating business requirements and functional specifications documents.

- Identified discrepancies between legacy presentation and internal system requirements by performing Gap Analysis.

Investment Manager and Custody Associate   2004 – 2006

Selected to provide outstanding support on client settlement inquiries. Reconciled cash and stock, providing reports of assigned funds to ensure accuracy of accounting records. Communicated with internal and external clients. Provided daily servicing of multiple funds under management by investment managers and clients. Served as a liaison between clients or investment managers on management of portfolios, ensuring on-time completion of tasks. Monitored corporate actions, income and dividend receipt, and overdue payments. Worked on special projects, including international tax reclaims and user acceptance testing.

- Hand picked as a member of a newly formed team which was created to centralize tasks, including cash and stock reconciliation, account opening and closing, client billing, and reporting.

- Recognized for streamlining the completion of tasks by identifying the need and creating solution to reduce billing redundancy and completion time.

- Improved cross-functionality and enhanced staff training by creating comprehensive manual on procedures and daily tasks.

——Education & Certification——

Bachelor's Degree, Risk Management (2014)
University of Canada West, Vancouver, BC

Postgraduate Certificate-Banking and Finance
University of Canada West, Vancouver, BC

Chartered Insurance Professional
Insurance Institute of Canada, Toronto, Canada

Chartered Life Underwriter
The Risk Management Society

Investment Operations Certification
Advanced Certificate in Operational Risk
The Chartered Institute for Securities and Investment, London, England

——Affiliations——

Insurance Institute of Canada, Member
Insurance Women of Montreal, Member, Rookie of the Year 2007

54 Blue Ridge Trail
Ellijay, GA 30536

Shawn Brandon

Linked in profile
706-243-4340
shawn.brandon@gmail.com

Logistics Management

Performance Summary

Supply Chain Leader with 18 years' experience demonstrating consistent professional growth through achievement in planning and purchasing for global distribution. Demonstrated talent in leading and managing unified teams, ensuring company goals are always achieved. Technically astute, with skills in Kanban, SAP, BAAN, and Microsoft Access. Demonstrated knowledge in lean manufacturing. Experienced with development and execution of enterprise-wide redundancy elimination that increases productivity and improves quality. Strategic planner with well-honed analytic and technical proficiencies; adept in globe-spanning business initiatives and excels in the complex, time-sensitive world of logistics.

Professional Skills

Purchasing	Inventory	Strategic Planning	Worldwide Supply Chain
Lean Manufacturing	Sourcing	Turnkey Solutions	Procedure Development
Project Management	Metrics	Forecasting	Replenishment
Logistics	Life-Cycle Management	Kanban	Re-Order Points (ROP)
MRP/ERP	Negotiations	Procurement	On-Time Delivery (OTD)
SAP	BAAN	Staff Leadership	APICS Certified

"Shawn has a history of leading successful projects that have improved customer satisfaction through flawless execution." – Sharla Jones, Director of Worldwide Planning & Supply Chain

—— Performance Highlights ——

➢ Drove site availability to 98% by establishing daily meetings between Site Manufacturing Managers, Planning group, and Purchasing group.
➢ Reduced expedited expenses more than 60%.
➢ Saved $107,000 in service agreements and system cost.
➢ Key contributor of the migration of the Molecular Biology Lab, providing planning and setup of new SAP plant with a very aggressive timeline.

—— Professional Experience ——

Scientech, Alpharetta, GA   2014 to Present
Division of Applied Technologies.
Director of Worldwide Planning

Selected to oversee the entire supply chain life cycle. Hired and managed 14 staff members, providing support for Worldwide planning and procurement, instrument master scheduling, indirect procurement, DC Kanban Administration, service logistics call center, and data maintenance. Directed project initiatives for business process re-engineering and optimization. Led teams on Kaizen events.

• Reduced inventory 30%, totaling more than $9 million in one year.
• Saved $107,000 by initiating early termination of service agreement with Life Tech supply chain.
• Realized $170,000 in annual transportation savings by providing distribution planning changes.
• Increased product availability from 93% to 96%.
• Led the Supply Chain separation of ERP cloning from Applied Technologies without impact on customer service.

Applied Technologies, Alpharetta GA	1998 to 2014

Formerly Resoursystems, providing instruments and consumables for life sciences.

Senior Manager, Worldwide Planning, Alpharetta Consumables	2009 to 2014
Senior Manager, Worldwide Spares Planning and Service Logistics	2006 to 2009
Manager of Worldwide Service Logistics and Service Inventory	1998 to 2006

Senior Manager, Worldwide Planning, Alpharetta Consumables 2009 to 2014

Promoted to provide planning and Worldwide supply chain management within the Consumables Group. Analyzed and resolved complex products. Managed six staff members. Partnered with Product Management and Manufacturing on prioritizing products, providing strategic resolutions to supply issues, and reduction of losses. Utilized visual reporting tools to create reports. Provided executives with weekly summaries on concerns with the site.

- Assisted in transitioning manufacturing group to an abbreviated time schedule, an $800,000 annual savings.
- Recognized with *Platinum Award* for leading the Supply Chain for U.S. DC consolidation to Frederick, MD.
- Reduced turnaround time 50% and eliminated a $400,000 backlog.
- Cut overdue work orders 30% by establishing daily cross-functional meetings.
- Selected by the Director as a replacement before the purchase of Resoursystems.

Senior Manager, Worldwide Spares Planning and Service Logistics 2006 to 2009

Provided life-cycle management of Spares Planning. Oversaw Service Logistics throughout North America. Directed contingency strategy planning for supplier bankruptcy, which included leading organization discussions with Project Managers, Service Product Management, Finance, Senior Management, and staff to salvage product lines. Represented sites across the globe.

- Saved the company $2 million in inventory by developing alternatives to Lifetime Buys.
- Led an organization-wide program, *President's Initiative*, saving the company $1 million in revenue.

Manager of Worldwide Service Logistics and Service Inventory 1998 to 2006

Primary liaison for entire supply chain, providing process alignment across the organization and establishing territory boundaries for Europe and APAC. Streamlined process by implementing SOX-compliant Field Service cycle program, metrics, and self-help tools for Field Engineers. Served as Service Business Operations Manager, driving optimization for 28 staff members in Service Call Center, Service Administration, and Service Contract Administration functions.

- Reduced aging inventory by $750,000 and priority overnight shipments by 40%, with a total savings of $350,000 per year by designing and implementing self-help tools for Field Service Engineers.
- Served as a key speaker at a Worldwide Service Conference with more than 500 attendees.

***Previous experience as** Manager of Worldwide Logistics Service and Senior Logistics Planner at Cyber Technologies | Production Control Manger, Purchasing Supervisor, and Senior Buyer at Itek.*

"Shawn is a patient, fair, and organization team leader who brings together people of diverse skills and personalities to accomplish measurable goals." – Debbie Firestone, Founder and President of SaveAPeke

—— **Volunteer Experience**——

SaveAPeke Pekingese Dog Rescue, Blue Ridge, GA	2011 to Present

Animal rescue and adoption center
Volunteer

Provided implementation and maintenance of a Point-of-Sale Inventory Management System. Created technical documentation of the inventory management processes.

—— **Education and Professional Development** ——

Bachelor of Economics, University of Georgia, Athens, Georgia

CPIM Certification, APICS

JOSE SIERRA

6345 Painted Lady Drive, Miami, FL 33114 / 305-751-2715 / jose_sierra@gmail.com

Linked in profile

PROCUREMENT / LOGISTICS / MATERIALS MANAGEMENT

7 years of experience within a warehouse operation, as well as prior positions with the United States Marine Corps. Earned a Bachelor of Science in Business Management. Received "Business Person of the Year" award with current employer.

➢ Skilled in communicating and building relationships effectively with both vendors and partner organizations.
➢ Excellent planning, scheduling, and task management background within challenging environments.
➢ Record of success in improving team performance through training and reducing problems.

PROFESSIONAL SKILLS

❑ Logistics & Transportation	❑ Materials Requirement Planning	❑ Team Building and Leadership
❑ Inventory Management	❑ Cost Reduction and Avoidance	❑ Quality and Safety Assurance
❑ Escalated Problem Resolution	❑ Regulatory Compliance Issues	❑ Process Simplification/Redesign

PROFESSIONAL EXPERIENCE

CONGA GALERIES – Miami, FL   2010–Present
Safety & Security Officer

Ensure highest level of security, safety, and protection within a warehouse operation with over 200 employees. Communicate with internal and external customers, routing calls to the appropriate individuals. Enforce safety guidelines and regulations, documenting all pertinent events and alerting management. Identify accident trends to aid with adjustment of training methods. Report directly to the Security Supervisor.

Selected Accomplishments:

▪ **Awarded Business Person of the Year, 2017** for overall exemplary performance. Recognized for maintaining 7 years of perfect attendance.

▪ **Oversaw zero security incidents** and lost-time accident events through strict adherence to rules and procedures.

▪ **Reduced accidents within the division** by reviewing accident reports and adjusting training methods to address critical need areas.

▪ **Frequently worked alone as the lone security officer on duty,** earning highest level of trust to complete tasks with zero supervision or follow-up.

UNITED STATES MARINE CORPS – Twenty-Nine Palms, CA   2006–2009
Vehicle Director/Commander

Promoted to supervise team of 16–20 in day-to-day activities, with group including Light-Armored Vehicle Drivers and Gunners. Delivered training to Marines on safety, weapons, and tactics. Evaluated team members to determine combat readiness.

Selected Accomplishments:

▪ **Trained unit that had the highest proficiency scores** in the entire company (measured by Light-Armored Gunnery Skills Test scores), as well as ranking as the most physically fit unit company wide.

▪ **Initiated new training methods and improved existing ones** to strengthen team capabilities in core areas.

PROFESSIONAL DEVELOPMENT

B.Sc. in Business/Organizational Management, 2010: UCLA – Los Angeles, CA
Associate of Science in General Education: San Jose Community College – San Jose, CA

Military Details: Infantryman, United States Marine Corps; Last Rank: Corporal; Honorable Discharge; promoted in combat; served in Thailand, Japan, and Iraq; stationed out of Twenty-Nine Palms, CA.

Tina Turner

Middleburg, VA 20118   540-555-5470   eventwizard@comcast.net

Meeting Planner
Conferences · Events · Fundraising · Golf Tournaments

"Successful events look effortless. I take care of business with quiet efficiency."

PERFORMANCE PROFILE

14 years' experience in all aspects of event planning, development, and management. Multi-task with strong detail, problem-solving and follow-through capabilities. Demonstrated ability to manage, motivate, and build cohesive teams that achieve results.

PROFESSIONAL SKILLS

• Government	• PACs	• Associations
• Conferences & Meetings	• Special Events	• Fundraisers
• Logistics	• Meetings & Workshops	• Tours & Competitions
• Database Management	• High-Net Donors	• Vendor Management
• Team Management	• Planning/Organization	• Contracts
• Budgets	• Negotiations	• Access
• Excel	• PowerPoint	• Outlook
• MS Project	• Publisher	• MeetingTrak

PERFORMANCE HIGHLIGHTS

Planned and coordinated government, association, and private conferences, meetings, events, and fundraisers: all conference activities, workshops, meetings, tours, and special events. **Saved $72,000 on most recent meeting.**

Meeting Coordination

Negotiated hotel and vendor contracts. Prepared and administered budgets. Arranged all on-site logistics, including transportation, accommodations, meals, guest speakers, and audiovisual support.

- Coordinated 18 annual workshops for Centers for Disease Control and Prevention.
- Coordinated 2004 National Conference on Smoking and Health (2,000 participants).
- Organized 6,000-participant national annual conferences.
- Coordinated Global Scholarship Pre-Conference Training.
- Developed and supervised education sessions at CSI's 2001 National Convention.
- Directed CSI's National Seminar Series.
- Developed, promoted, and implemented CSI's National Certification Program.
- Managed logistics for a Regional Pacific Training in Guam.

Fundraising

Coordinated PAC fundraising events. Supervised high-donor club fulfillment benefits. Team player in the development and implementation of membership and retention programs for BUILD-PAC.

- Coordinated 2 PAC golf tournaments
- Spouse programs
- Parties

Continued

EVENTS MANAGEMENT HIGHLIGHTS

- Centers for Disease Control and Prevention/Office on Smoking & Health
- Tobacco Control Training & Technical Assistance Project
- Health & Human Services Department's Administration on Children, Youth and Families Grant Review Contract
- Food and Drug Administration
- Centers for Disease Control and Prevention/National Center for Health Statistics
- National Library of Medicine
- Housing & Urban Development Grant Review Contract
- CSI National Seminar Series
- CSI 1998 & 1999 National Conventions and Exhibits

PROFESSIONAL EXPERIENCE

CORPORATE SCIENCES ■ Rockville, Maryland   2013–Present
Senior Conference Specialist
ROCKVILLE CONSULTING GROUP ■ Arlington, Virginia   2008–2013
Senior Conference Coordinator
CONSTRUCTION ASSOCIATION ■ Arlington, Virginia   2003–2008
Coordinator of Education Programs
NATIONAL ASSOCIATION OF PIPE WELDERS ■ Washington, D.C.   2001–2003
Assistant Coordinator of Education Programs

EDUCATION, CERTIFICATIONS, & AFFILIATIONS

VIRGINIA POLYTECHNIC INSTITUTE ■ Blacksburg, VA
B.S., Exercise Physiology, Minor Psychology   2001

Certifications
Go Members Inc. MeetingTrak Certification ■ 2015
Certified Meeting Professional (CMP) ■ 2007

Professional Affiliations
- Meeting Professionals International – Annandale Chapter (AMPI)
- Logistical Committee
- Educational Retreat Committee
- Member Services Committee
- Community Outreach Committee
- Connected International Meeting Professionals Association (CIMPA)
- DC Special Olympics – Volunteer
- Hands On DC – Volunteer
- SPCA of Northern Virginia – Volunteer

"I take care of the details, always."

Blake Neal

Linked in profile

4256 East 53rd Street Apt 6RE
New York, NY 10028

(201) 552-8828
blake.neal@gmail.com

Assistant Apparel Merchant

PERFORMANCE PROFILE

Results-driven merchandiser with 3 years' experience in major metropolitan market, gained while working full-time to pay for college. Provides organizational support to the merchandising team and leverages organizational and analytical skills, while keeping up with current industry trends to support brands and achieve financial goals. Experienced in sales events and product placement to promote merchandise. Committed to learning and continuous development. Bachelor of Fashion Technology.

- Demonstrated communication, interpersonal, planning, problem-solving, and coordinating skills.
- Teams with internal departments to develop product lines.
- Detail-oriented, flexible, fast learner with multifunctional skills.
- Ability to work independently and within team-based environments.
- Proficient at producing weekly and monthly sales reports and formulating conclusions.
- Ability to work with the different roles of cross-functional teams and understand how they relate to the merchandising role.
- Strong financial skills and business acumen.
- Excellent verbal and writing skills, organizational skills, and the ability to multitask and prioritize multiple projects in deadline-driven environments.
- Strong PC knowledge, specifically Excel.

PROFESSIONAL SKILLS

*Merchandising & Retail	*Financial Research & Analysis	*Sample Quality Control
*Business Recommendations	*Sample Administration	*In-Store Visits
*Updates Stock & Weekly Sales Reports	*Buying Trends Analysis	*Special Projects
*Monitors Deliveries and Samples	*Coordinates Flow of Merchandise	*Database Management
*Merchandising Technical Skills	*Best Practices	*Microsoft Excel
*Purchase Orders & Reorders	*Sales, Margins, & Inventory Analysis	*Budget Management

PROFESSIONAL EXPERIENCE

Suit Specialists, New York, NY   2013– Present
Merchandiser
Suit Specialist stores have been operating in New York since 1952 and rank among the top 5 men's retail stores in the city. Selected to perform merchandising tasks including: line planning, creating and updating sales inventory reports, sales performance, margin, markdown analysis, and mannequin placement.
Managed store communications and coordinated with vendors for ITEM masters, deliveries, and samples. Responsible for setting up new items in company database.

- Managed merchandise selection and buying for the largest scarf sales event of the year in coordination with buyer, resulting in 110% of target sales for Fall 2015 promotions.

-continued-

235

(Suit Specialists, continued)

- Assisted buyer in merchandise selection, maintenance, and distribution of purchase orders, and managed OTB with planning team to ensure smooth execution of sales events.
- Conducted in-store visits to ensure the implementation and execution of seasonal plans.
- Successfully revamped scarf category in the accessory department, introduced new product sub-categories, built vendor relationships, redesigned floor plans, and increased visibility of accessory categories, resulting in a significant increase in sales.
- Worked with vendors on tight timelines, resulting in successful fill rate at new store openings.
- Revamped accessory category and introduced new products to fit customer purchasing trends, resulting in increased sales in accessory category.

Well Met Events Management, Long Island, NY   2012–2013
Event Coordinator
Well Met Events Management focuses on events, retail, grooming, and image management. Selected to manage business development of new personality development programs. Managed market research, parent interviews, and business plan preparation, resulting in management approval to launch new program.

- Developed and managed relationships with strategic business alliances including schools and retailers, and established brand leverage with marketing partners.
- Developed new cross-business products and launched service enhancements to ensure a scalable and sustainable business model.
- Created business plans and managed launch of new products by supervising a team of sales and operations executives, resulting in the highest earning potential program for Procraft within one year.
- Launched new service enhancements, providing opportunities for cross-selling and leveraging existing infrastructure, resulting in doubling of revenue earnings.
- Coordinated events to collect target data, resulting in creation of new source of data to reach targeted customer base.
- Managed BTL to ensure increased participation during children's painting exhibition event. Resulted in establishment of Well Met's credibility in creating and managing events for children.

EDUCATION

National Institute of Fashion Technology, New York, NY   2012
Bachelor of Fashion Technology
Major: Apparel Production
Awarded Best Innovative Project for 2012 Graduation Project

- Received coverage by national newspaper, the *New York Times*
- Graduation Project Details: Designed 3 season washable silk scarves for men

"Blake quickly learned the complicated systems and business processes and delivered value quickly. He was a great team player with the right attitude to gel with people from different spheres of life."

Patti Watson, Senior Manager, Well Met Events, Long Island, NY

Superior references available

Walter Stuempfig

Los Angeles, CA 90001   322. 786. 2417   multimedia_production@sbcgloabal.net

MULTIMEDIA MANAGEMENT

Multimedia Communications & Production ♦ MIS Management

"A rare combination of technology management and creative multimedia skills."

Performance Review

Uniquely qualified management professional for a digital media technical production position with a distinctive blend of hands-on technical, project management, and multimedia communications experience. Offers a skill set that spans interactive digital technologies, broadcast, radio, and print media.

Proven leader with a strength for identifying talent, building and motivating creative teams that work cooperatively to achieve goals. Highly articulate with excellent interpersonal skills and a sincere passion for blending communications with technology.

MIS Capabilities

• Systems Management	• Needs Analysis	• Strategic Planning
• Systems Configuration	• System Testing	• Systems Upgrades
• P&L	• Budgets	• Project Management
• Vendor Management	• LAN/WAN	• Telecom Integration
• Multimedia	• Network Security	• Workflow Applications
• Technology Acquisition	• System Maintenance	• Technology Integration
• Resource Planning	• Recruitment & Selection	• Performance Reviews

Multimedia Management Capabilities

• Multimedia	• Television	• Radio
• Account Management	• Client Relations	• Market Research
• Multimedia Production	• Creative Design	• Multimedia Communications
• Corp Communications	• Cross-Functional Teams	• Multimedia Presentations
• Photographers	• Videographers	• Copywriters
• Scriptwriters	• Graphic Designers	• Artists
• Musicians	• Talent	• Animators

PROFESSIONAL EXPERIENCE

LaRoche Investments, Inc., Los Angeles, CA   2004–Present
VICE PRESIDENT OF MIS   2014–Present
ASSISTANT VICE PRESIDENT OF IT/CORPORATE COMMUNICATIONS   2012–2014
CORPORATE COMMUNICATIONS OFFICER   2008–2012
ASSOCIATE   2004–2008

Advanced rapidly through series of increasingly responsible positions with U.S. division of European investment group. Initially hired to manage market research projects, advanced to plan and execute corporate communications projects, and in 2014, assumed responsibility for spearheading the introduction of emerging technologies to automate the entire company.
Current scope of responsibility is expansive and focuses on strategic planning, implementation, and administration of all information systems and technology. Lead technical staff members, manage budgets, select and oversee vendors, define business requirements, and produce deliverables through formal project plans.
Manage systems configuration and maintenance, troubleshoot problems, plan and direct upgrades, and test operations to ensure optimum systems functionality and availability.

Continued

Technical Contributions

- Pioneered the company's computerization from the ground floor; led the installation and integration of a state-of-the-art and highly secure network involving 50+ workstations running on 6 LANs interconnected by V-LAN switching technology.
- Defined requirements; planned and accelerated the implementation of advanced technology solutions, deployed on a calculated timeframe, to meet the short- and long-term needs of the organization.
- Orchestrated the introduction of sophisticated applications and multimedia technology to streamline workflow processes, expand presentation capabilities, and keep pace with the competition.
- Administered the life cycle of multiple projects from initial systems/network planning and technology acquisition through installation, training, and operation. Saved hundreds of thousands in consulting fees by managing IS and telecommunication issues in-house.

Business Contributions

- Created and produced high-impact multimedia presentations to communicate the value and benefits of individual investment projects to top-level company executives. Tailored presentations to appeal to highly sophisticated, multicultural audiences.
- Assembled and directed exceptionally well-qualified project teams from diverse creative disciplines; collaborated with and guided photographers, videographers, copywriters, scriptwriters, graphic designers, and artists to produce innovative presentations and special events.
- Performed market research and analyses to determine risks and feasibility of multiple investment projects valued at up to $150 million. Developed and recommended tactical plans to transform vision into achievement.

Schwarzer Advertising Associates, New York, NY   1996–2004

DIRECTOR OF ADVERTISING

Rainbow Advertising, Brooklyn, NY   1994–1996

ADVERTISING ACCOUNT EXECUTIVE

WFDX-TV, WFDX-FM, WKLU   1992–1994

PRODUCER

Early career involved a series of progressive creative and account management positions spanning all advertising mediums: multimedia, television, radio, and print. Worked directly with clients to assess complex and often obscure needs; conceptualized and developed advertising campaigns to communicate the desired message in an influential manner.

Achievement Highlights

- Designed, wrote, produced, and launched advertising campaigns that consistently positioned clients with a competitive distinction. Developed a reputation for ability to accurately intuit and interpret clients' desires and produce deliverables that achieved results.
- Recruited and led creative teams consisting of graphic designers, artists, musicians, talent, cartoonists, animators, videographers, photographers, and other freelancers and third-party creative services to develop and produce multimillion-dollar advertising campaigns.

EDUCATION & TRAINING

AAS, Broadcast Production, Russ Junior College, Boston, MA
Continuing education in Marketing Research and Broadcast Production
The School of Visual Arts, New York, NY

Arshile Gorky

237 Monterey • Sea Cliff, Cell: 516-000-0000 wateroperations@earthlink.net
NY 11579 Home: 516-671-5843

Operations Management Intern
Operations/ Project Management • Staff Training & Management • Safety Initiatives

Performance Profile
2 years experience in water park operations with a broad range of business, organizational, and interpersonal skills. Natural leader, able to develop strong, easy working relationships with management, staff, and the general public to ensure positive, high-quality guest experiences.

Professional Skills
- Outstanding track record of strategic contributions in visioning, planning, strategizing, and accomplishment of a range of business-related initiatives, with significant success in developing emerging concepts into full-fledged, high-performance realities.

Offer a valuable blend of leadership, creative, and analytical abilities that combine efficiency with imagination to produce bottom-line results. Proven success in planning, directing, and coordinating staff activities to maximize cost options.

Professional Experience

WALT DISNEY WORLD – LIVERPOOL, NY   Summers 2014, 2015, 2016

Professional Internship, Blizzard Beach
Recruited, following a productive four-month lifeguard internship, to contribute to the ongoing success of this popular Disney water park attraction. Performed a variety of management-level functions and team-building training for staff, and developed key organizational systems to standardize strategic functions.

- Spearheaded, developed, created, and implemented the Blizzard Beach and Typhoon Lagoon Evacuation Operations Report, coordinating all strategic safety and evacuation information.

Lifeguard Internship
Served as one of 80 lifeguards at Disney's famous Blizzard Beach water park.
Patrolled recreational areas on foot or from lifeguard stands. Rescued distressed people using rescue techniques and equipment. Contacted emergency medical personnel in case of serious injuries.
Key Contributions:

- Saved several lives in backboard and other types of rescues and resuscitations.
- Received many commendations for performance above and beyond the call of duty.

Education

B.S., Business Administration   *Anticipated Graduation, May 2017*

Marquis White

3424 Belladonna Boulevard, Orlando, FL 32802
(407) 681-0582 m.white@gmail.com

Linked in profile

Paralegal

Performance Profile

Highly organized paralegal known to uphold ethical standards of the legal profession, exercising discretion and maintaining a high level of confidentiality. Proven ability to thrive in a fast-paced environment through advanced multitasking skills. Bachelor of Arts, Paralegal Studies.

Professional Skills

✓ Self-starter with the ability to work independently in all aspects of litigation. Works well under pressure.
✓ Strong interpersonal skills with the ability to communicate effectively with all levels of employees, executives, outside counsel, and state agencies.
✓ Demonstrated success in problem-solving skills dealing with complex, ambiguous situations with diplomacy and tact.
✓ Highly organized with strong attention to detail and the ability to work effectively with tight deadlines.
✓ Outstanding research, writing, and proofreading skills.
✓ Proficient in Microsoft Office, Excel, PowerPoint, Outlook, LEXIS/NEXIS, Lender Processing Services (LPS), and Team Connect.
✓ Strong knowledge of legal terminology, legal documents, practices, and procedures.

Areas of Expertise

Research and Analytical Skills − Legal Document Preparation − Reasoning and Deductive Skills − Self-Motivated − Detail Oriented − Multitasker − Editing/Grammar − Technology Savvy − Sound Judgment and Logic − Ability to Meet Aggressive Deadlines − Accuracy − Problem-Solving Skills− Dependable − Flexible

Professional Experience

Barbara Lawson & Associates, L.P.A., Winter Haven, FL   2014–Present
Litigation Paralegal
Creditors' rights law firm with cases in all counties in Ohio and in various states for national clients. Litigation practice handling secured transactions, fraud, contract law, real estate transactions, debt collection, and commercial and residential leases. All legal work at the appellate level is handled by the litigation department. Listed as a preferred firm by Lender Processing Services and a Fannie Mae retained firm.
Selected to revitalize and reorganize the firm's litigation department.

- Promoted to assistant to the president/owner of the firm within one year and paralegal for lead litigation counsel.
- Successfully increase client satisfaction with the progress of litigation files resulting in additional referrals and new business.
- Assist with marketing and setting up new clients by drafting client bulletins and assembling materials for potential new clients.
- Manage and execute the progression of litigation casework to yield the best outcomes for clients.
- Draft and prepare legal pleadings, motions, briefs, discovery, affidavits, and settlement agreements.
- Maintain complex docket schedule. Make travel arrangements and schedules to ensure all parties are available when needed for conferences, court appearances, and depositions.
- Trial and deposition preparation including examination and preparation of evidence.
- Manage hourly billing approval, invoicing, and auditing litigation files with little attorney supervision.
- First litigation paralegal at the firm to bill time on an hourly basis, leading to increased litigation revenues.

-continued-

The Law Offices of Clayton Williams, Kissimmee, FL   2011–2014
Litigation Paralegal

Creditors' rights firm handling foreclosure/bankruptcy/loss mitigation, and eviction cases for all counties in Ohio and Kentucky for national clients. Highly ranked law firm listed as a preferred attorney by Lender Processing Services and a Fannie Mae retained firm. Listed as a "Giant of Default Law" by *HousingWire Magazine*. Member of the Mortgage Bankers Association and American Legal Financial Network. Hired as entry-level paralegal to be trained for complex litigation work for all counties in Florida.

- Sole paralegal at the firm to successfully manage large volumes of discovery work for the firm's litigation cases in Florida.
- Assigned to complex litigation sub-team (consisting of head litigation counsel and senior litigation paralegal) after only one year of employment with the firm.
- Ensured legal documents were processed in a timely manner to comply with deadlines.
- Composed and revised legal documents for attorneys including general correspondence and court filings.
- Effectively drafted and responded to interrogatories, requests for production, and requests for admissions.
- Adeptly scheduled appointments and conferences for litigation attorneys.
- Skillfully performed as a liaison between attorneys and clients to ensure timely and full communication.
- Productively drafted complaints, answers, motions, briefs, oppositions, and replies.

Education

Bachelor of Arts, Paralegal Studies, University of North Florida, FL   2010
ABA Approved Program

- **Relevant Coursework:** Legal Research and Writing, Principles and Practice of Litigation, Applied Legal Research and Litigation, Family Law, Estate Law, Tort Law, Intellectual Property Law, Civil Law and Procedure, Criminal Law, Administrative Law, and Contract Law.

Internships

Westbrook, Loomis & Parks, Orlando, FL   January-May 2009
Paralegal Intern

Leah Jones, Esq., Winter Haven, FL   June-November 2008
Paralegal Intern

University of North Florida State Paralegal Organization   2000-2008

Charity Committee

Barbara Lawson & Associates, L.P.A., Winter Haven, FL

Anneke Tso

2423 Fairfax Court
West Bloomfield, MI 48322

Cell: 248.335.2323

expertsourcer@aol.com

Director of Recruitment

"I offer process development, service delivery, and enhanced profits."

Performance Profile

Talented and forward-thinking senior recruitment leader with proven track record of success turning around company performance by distilling and managing processes, enhancing organizational structure, and developing skilled self-managed teams.

The "go-to" person for diverse organizational and process-related challenges. Confident and passionate individual with a mission to create "best in class" recruiting departments through comprehensive utilization of marketing tools and cutting-edge sales practices.

Professional Skills

Project Implementation	Strategic Planning	Onboarding/Referral Programs
Process Reengineering	Sales and Marketing	Role Competency Design
Training and Development	Recruitment Metrics	Workforce Planning
Turnaround	Financial Analysis	Strategic Planning
Disbursed Management	Sourcing Channels	Proposal Generation
CRM	Advertising	Tracking Systems
Sarbanes-Oxley	Performance Metrics	Contracts
AP	EEOC	OFCCP

Professional Experience

A & E CORPORATION, *Bloomfield, MI*   2014 to Present
Leader in Recruitment Process Outsourcing
Recruitment Manager

Sourcing strategies to support the strategic, operational, and business plan for the company. Influence senior business executives on strategy, resources, hiring forecasts, and capacity planning. Establish and oversee maintenance of effective candidate sourcing channels and both internal and external resume-tracking systems to speed the process of identifying qualified candidates and tracking effectiveness and efficiency metrics.

- Assist with proposal generation, implementation, training, and daily oversight of key account service delivery teams, overall delivery of key account results, and the management and nurturing of client relationships to deliver the highest caliber client results.
- Provide timely feedback to management and clients regarding workload and accomplishments, ensuring accuracy of data and timely, thorough completion of assignments.

SMITH & WILLIAMS CONSTRUCTION, INC., *San Francisco, CA*   2010 to 2014
Top 100 Design/Builders in the nation
Recruiting Manager

230-person corporate recruiting function. Report directly to CEO. Provided strategic direction and tactical follow-up on all levels of recruitment process re-design.

- Managed the internship program and volunteered to represent student construction organizations establishing a future flow of qualified construction management majors.
- Improved the 'candidate experience' by instituting full life-cycle recruiting to the company.
- Spearheaded company-wide skills matrix to aid in succession planning and resource management.
- Partnered with IT to create and launch career site to meet OFCCP and EEOC compliance requirements.
- Orchestrated a comprehensive multi-prong employee retention process overhaul.
- Established a 30-60-90 new employee review process, introduced buddy system, and re-engineered new hire onboarding procedures, reducing communication breakdowns and ensuring employees' complete preparedness for first day of employment.

START UP AIR, *Dulles, VA*   2002 to 2010
A low-cost airline based in DC
Recruiting Manager

Hired to develop and implement recruiting function for a start-up airline to support 2,000 hires. Assisted with the creation and management of a $1M advertising budget. Presented detailed and comprehensive reports and analyses on staffing metrics including attrition, program results, time-to-fill, and recruiter performance. Implementation of Sarbanes-Oxley narrative.

- Exceeded 2004-headcount targets by 20%, employing 2,000 external and 500 internal employees.
- C-level approval for the implementation of an applicant microsite, which significantly increased the performance of the baggage handler screening process.
- Rebuilt recruitment & selection cycle for AAP, EEOC, and OFCCP compliance. Conducted quarterly internal audits to ensure compliance.
- Created a robust Employee Referral Program (ERP) that propelled referrals to 13% of total hires resulting in lower cost-per-hire for hourly airport employees.
- Implemented legally defensible behavioral interviewing with recurrent training for hiring managers, resulting in a significant reduction in EEOC claims.

MANPOWER   1996 to 2002
Global staffing company
Technology Recruiter

"Recruitment is the lifeblood of success. I know the
challenges, the problems, and their solutions. I deliver."

Juan Hernandez

Miami, FL 33101 • 305-243-4342   juan.h@gmail.com in View my profile

Regulatory Change Management

Performance Profile

Regulatory Change Agent with seven years of experience in Line of Business Mortgage Servicing and Escrow Services at Citi's corporate headquarters, providing project management, technical writing, and escrow records management for a total portfolio valued in excess of $300 million.

Professional Skills

Diversified Financial Services	Operations Excellence	Strategic Planning & Project Mgmt.
Company & Industry Research	Lean Six Sigma (DMAIC & 5S)	Change Management
Business Analysis	Technical Writing & Communications	Stakeholder Management
Business Performance Metrics	Business Policies & Procedures	Impact Assessment
Portfolio Management	Process Design & Improvement	Problem Identification & Resolution
Escrow Services & Recordkeeping	Productivity Optimization	Exceptional Customer Service
Federal & State Mortgage Regulations	Workflow Analysis	Leadership & Team Building
Regulatory Change & Compliance	Job Roles & Organizational Structure	Training Design & Facilitation

Regulatory & Compliance Skills

Mortgage Servicing, AllRegs, COSL, OCC, OFAC, W8BEN, W8BEN-E, W8EXP, W9,
B-Notice, C-Notice, Reg D, Segregation of Duty (SOD)

Computer Skills

DAPTIV, MSP, SharePoint, Visio, Minitab, Quality Companion, Banking Mainframe, XNET,
Client Product Implementations through BPM Portal, Agiletics Escrow Software, Escrow PINNACLE web module,
People Soft Finance Work Bench, Microsoft Office: Advanced Excel, Word, PowerPoint

Performance Highlights

➢ Business Process Analyst who has led 140+ change initiatives in the past two years, which resulted in highly effective business processes/procedures and operations/technology improvements in mortgage servicing practices.

➢ Change Agent skilled in evaluating effects of federal/state banking and mortgage servicing regulations on operations performance; translating the magnitude and type of change required; and offering pragmatic, actionable recommendations to assure regulatory compliance.

➢ Group Leader who collaborates with Technical Writing Team to create project deliverables such as project descriptions, project timelines, communication plans, mitigation plans, risk assessments, post implementation support plans, etc. Able to remain calm under pressure and produce high-quality written documents/reports under extremely tight deadlines.

Professional Experience

CITIBANK–Miami, FL   2008 to Present
Mortgage Change Agent   2012 to Present

Report directly to Assistant Vice President/Team Lead of Change Management. Serve as a liaison between Compliance, Legal, and Risk to proactively manage change in the business unit. Lead projects involving investor/insurer, regulatory changes, and mortgage servicing processes.

• Review and analyze internal and external regulatory reports. Evaluate the potential impact of regulatory, compliance, and financial decisions. Make recommendations to management for planning and decision-making purposes to ensure compliance with changes to applicable regulations. Deliver the change effort; define the scope; monitor the progress; and create communications to ensure effective implementation and measure adoption.

• Coordinate and conduct annual review of policy/procedure analyses with assigned lines of business. Collaborate with department leaders to address gaps in processes and provide updates to investor/insurer and regulatory announcements.

• Provide action plan tracking and status reporting to management and Line of Business partners. Confirm that changes are communicated effectively and that employees affected by change are receiving the necessary training.

• Delegate and manage 1–5+ supporting technical writers' workloads on larger writing initiatives, which requires time management and multitasking. Review documents to ensure adherence to mortgage servicing and corporate style guides. Maintain project documents on Daptiv and SharePoint.

• Create functional requirements documents and analyze impacts for investor/insurer and regulatory changes.

Selected Accomplishments:
- Led 150+ change initiatives in the past two years.
- Authored 90+ technical documents including policies/procedures and reference guides.
- Maintain over 100 policies/procedures and reference documents for assigned lines of business on SharePoint system.

Team Lead, Escrow Services Group   2010 to 2012
- Oversaw records management for total portfolio valued at $300 million.
- Led a customer service group that provided customer support for multiple escrow products (e.g., landlords, attorneys, property owners, and pre-needs clients).
- Conducted weekly team meetings, oversaw production team and project management team. Monitored productivity, coached production team in daily work and new procedures, resolved errors and/or problems, collected and compiled data for middle and senior managers.

Selected Accomplishments:
- Lean Six Sigma Green Belt Project. Implemented DMAIC (which stands for define, measure, analyze, improve, and control) to reduce impact of Escrow Services interest check process on Escheat Department's volume by 30% and reduced Escrow process cycle time, which increased production capacity by 52%, taking it from 48% to 100%.

Customer Service Representative   2008 to 2010
- Processed clients' deposits and withdrawals. Monitored transactions for accuracy. Resolved discrepancies.
- Handled client calls and managed book of business for clients' web accounts.
- Processed client W8/W9 forms and participated in manual month-end statement preparation and mailings.
- Handled returned mail such as interest checks and statements.
- Performed research and implemented process improvement projects.

Selected Accomplishments:
- **Escrow Services Archive Project (2010)**–Implemented Lean Six Sigma 5S (which stands for sort, set in order, shine, standardize, and systematize). Decreased the number of file cabinets needed in the department from 11 to 8, streamlining recordkeeping and making it easier to access client files.
- **Escrow Services Archive Project (2008)**–Implemented Lean Six Sigma 5S to decrease the types of documents stored in file cabinets to daily work files. All other files are now stored electronically, increasing the speed in locating client files.

Education
Performance Diploma–University of Florida–Gainesville, FL, 2008

Master of Arts in Music Performance–University of Florida–Gainesville, FL, 2007
Cumulative GPA: 3.7 • Major GPA 3.8

Bachelor of Arts in Music Education–Florida State University–Tallahassee, FL, 2005
Cumulative GPA: 3.7 • Major GPA 3.6
Marching Band

Certifications / Professional Development
Mortgage Servicing Certification, PNC, 2016
Certified Lean Six Sigma Green Belt, Suntrust, 2015
Enhancing Leadership Presence, Suntrust/Strategic Communications Consulting, 2014
Efficient Business Communications, Suntrust/Strategic Communications Consulting, 2013
Leadership Communications Essentials, Suntrust/Strategic Communications Consulting, 2012
Certified Lean Six Sigma Yellow Belt, PNC, 2011

Excellent Business References Available Upon Request

SHARON WISE

Plymouth, MI 48170   444.007.1111   child_guidance@gmail.com

School Guidance Counselor

"I bring competence and team spirit, caring and a smile."

Performance Profile

Dedicated elementary, middle, and high school guidance counselor, skilled at providing positive direction for students' academic, social, and emotional well-being. Work effectively with children with ADHD and with multicultural and diverse populations.

Professional Skills

Guidance Curriculum: Classroom Guidance Lessons; Career Awareness; Conflict Resolution/Social Skills; Developmental Awareness

Individual Planning: Student Assessments; Student Placement & Scheduling; New Student Transition; Academic & Career Advisement

Responsive Services: Mental Health; Family & Teacher Consulting; Crisis Intervention & Grief Management; Psycho-Educational Support Groups

Systems Support: Program Evaluation; Program Development & Coordination; Needs Assessment

Education & Certification

MA, *School Counseling*, UNIVERSITY OF DETROIT-MERCY, Detroit, MI
MA, *Teaching*, MARYGROVE COLLEGE, Detroit, MI
BA, *Teaching - Social Studies/French*, MICHIGAN STATE UNIVERSITY, East Lansing, MI

Certified - *Counseling* - K–12 - State of Michigan
Certified - *Social Studies & French* - grades 7–12 - State of Michigan

Professional Experience

HARTLAND COMMUNITY SCHOOLS, Hartland, MI   2010– 2017
SCHOOL COUNSELOR

Provide individual and small-group counseling sessions and large-group counseling presentations within classroom and guidance office environments for a school with 800 students. Participate in parent/teacher meetings to discuss and develop emotional and behavioral strategies for students with physical, mental, and emotional challenges.

- Developed 45-minute Bully-Proofing classes and presented them to each of 30 classes in the building.
- Wrote a monthly article for the school newsletter on a topic of relevance.
- Facilitated students participating in the Midwest talent search for the Gifted & Talented program.
- Held orientation for new students and their parents, providing them with a schedule of classes and showing them around the building.
- Created 30-minute Career Awareness/Exploration sessions so students would become exposed to various career options. Organized a Career Day, arranging for 40 speakers in various fields to talk with the students about their profession.

Continued

SCHOOL COUNSELOR, continued
- Participated as a team member for the School Improvement Team (SCIT).Performed Title I coordinator duties, planning and organizing initial structure mailings, assigning students to teachers, adhering to budgets, and scheduling classes.

NOVI COMMUNITY SCHOOLS, Novi, MI   2007– 2010
GUEST TEACHER

Substituted in the middle school and high school, teaching most subjects, including special ed. Immediately tried to develop a rapport with students and engage in discussion of relevant topics. Facilitated the discussion to steer toward daily lesson plan. Discussion and debate kept students centered, entertained, and open to learning.
- Given long-term teaching assignment for students with disabilities. Taught math, science, and social studies in grades 6–8 for a full semester. There were 5–10 students in each of four classes, ages 11–13. Many students had ADHD. Wrote lesson plans, graded assignments, and consulted with parents.

DETROIT PUBLIC SCHOOLS, Detroit, MI   2003– 2007
FRENCH & SOCIAL STUDIES TEACHER

Taught five classes each day, with each class having between 30–35 students, engaging their curiosity and research abilities in structured classroom activities. Provided lectures, notes, study guides, and projects for courses in American History, Government, Economics, World Geography, Global Issues, and French.
- Devised an effective structure for parent communication.
- Gathered resources as supplemental materials to be used in conjunction with assigned texts to give students a richer experience.
- Assigned different subjects each year, showed flexibility in providing first-rate learning experience for each subject.
- Developed a system to track work and assignments while moving to different rooms for each class period.
- Provided students with practical experience, such as making menus and calendars in French.
- Member of School Improvement team and on the committee to improve student self-esteem.

Professional Commitment

Association Involvement
- American Counseling Association
- American School Counselor Association
- Michigan Counseling Association
- Michigan School Counselor Association

Recent Conference Participation
Launching Career Awareness - Oakland Education Service Agency
Legal Issues for School Counselors - Washtenaw County Counselors Association
Counseling Groups in Crisis - Michigan Association of Specialists in Group Work
A.D.H.D in the New Millennium - Oakland Schools
Bully-Proofing Your School - Oakland Schools
The Human Spirit & Technology - Michigan Counseling Association
Understanding Attachment Disorders - Medical Educational Service
Grief Counseling Skills - Cross Country University

"My work brings meaning to my life"

JAMES MARTIN

Atlanta, GA 30305

in View my profile| 678.348.2484 | james.martin@comcast.net

SENIOR REGULATORY COMPLIANCE

11+ years of compliance experience in banking capital markets, brokerage and investment firms, and insurance sector, ensuring strict adherence to legal and financial regulations to alleviate risk exposure, facilitate smooth audits, and enable company profitability. Adept at maintaining pulse on company operations to monitor, investigate, and ensure fulfillment of regulatory obligations and alignment of compliance policies. Advise key decision makers on regulatory and compliance requirements to aid in development of strategic solutions that support new programs.

Registered investment advisor whose wide-ranging expertise spans Investment Advisers Act of 1940, US Commodity Futures Trading Commission/National Futures Association (CFTC/NFA), Municipal Securities Rulemaking Board (MSRB), Financial Industry Regulatory Authority (FINRA), Dodd Frank, and Securities and Exchange Commission (SEC) laws and regulations.

PROFESSIONAL SKILLS

Regulatory Compliance	Due Diligence	Performance Management
Legal Analysis	Staff Development	Fiduciary Responsibility
Risk Assessments	Team Leadership	Anti-money Laundering (AML)
Controls	Account Surveillance	Know-Your-Customer (KYC)
Negotiations	Mediations/Arbitrations	Training & Development

PERFORMANCE HIGHLIGHTS

- Played pivotal role in alleviating AML concerns through automation of new international account forms, remediating over 500 HH in 3 months.
- Thwarted reputational and financial damage of firm by uncovering and remediating adverse practices among select financial advisors via conducting surveillance on personal trading and researching patterns.
- Increased volume of licensed support staff through implementation of Series 7 training program as well as raised number of certifications held by financial advisors by offering incentives and training program for office staff.

PROFESSIONAL EXPERIENCE

Suntrust Bank | Atlanta, GA   2007 – Present
Regulatory Compliance Manager   2012 – Present
Appointed to ensure branch adherence to internal and regulatory agency requirements as well as to provide guidance on trading strategy policies, including options, commodities, derivatives, and structured investments. Monitored office activities, from trading to complaint resolution, liaising with senior compliance executives. Guided branch to earn satisfactory FINRA and branch audit ratings.

continued

- Spearheaded smooth transition of million-dollar wealth management teams from competition to Suntrust platform.
- Bolstered office productivity by analyzing product profitability, helping financial advisors better understand products to increase their payout.
- Championed 1st successful internal audit with no significant findings, examining recordkeeping, trade tickets, correspondence, structured investments, trading activity, and client activity to ensure compliance.
- Fostered numerous strategic business relationships, forging alliance between Bank Street College of Education and branch office for summer intern program as well as proposing partnership between Carver Federal Bank and Atlanta-based African American Financial Advisors.

Financial Advisor   2007 – 2012
Managed portfolios for more than 100 clients, facilitating financial seminars and providing financial planning expertise for individual, corporate, institutional, and nonprofit clients.

EARLIER CAREER

Bank of America| **Compliance/Quality Control Associate**   2005 – 2007

EDUCATION

Bachelor of Business Administration: Georgia Southern University
Law Coursework (18 months): University of Georgia

PROFESSIONAL LICENSES

Series 3	Series 10
Series 4	Series 63
Series 7	Series 65
Series 9	Certified Financial Manager

PROFESSIONAL AFFILIATION

India Exports, Inc., Executive Assistant to Executive Director, Mentor

Superior references available upon request

ANN JOHANSEN

(912) 345-0235 • A._Johansen@att.net • 26 Angelfish Drive •St. Simons, GA 31522

CHEMICAL ENGINEER

Performance Summary

Entry-level chemical engineer seeking to combine advanced coursework and hands-on experience in wastewater treatment into a challenging career solving practical problems and contributing to useful products within the oil and gas industry. Big-picture thinker who maintains the ability to analyze and troubleshoot the smallest aspect of raw ingredients, processes, and other external forces to identify problems and improve output. Thorough understanding of laboratory operations and active contributor to improving daily operations. A determined problem solver with a strong commitment to success, an obsessive desire to produce quality work, and a need for self-improvement.

➢ Readily uses spreadsheets, industry-standard software, and other tools to identify efficient processes, optimize unit operation, and determine how changes in input will affect output.
➢ Demonstrated capability of translating theories learned in class such as troubleshooting equipment, costing personnel resources, and process design into "real world" application.
➢ Actively pursues additional knowledge of environmental field and regulations, from technical and practical perspectives.
➢ Willing to relocate—willing to travel.

PROFESSIONAL SKILLS & ABILITIES

Laboratory Operations	Process Flow Diagram	Continuous Improvement	Problem Solving
Regulatory Compliance	Automatic Process Control	Input & Product Costing	Project Management
Quantitative Analysis	Process Design & Modeling	Data Analysis	Engineering Reports

PROFESSIONAL EXPERIENCE

CITY OF BRUNSWICK• Brunswick, GA   **2015–Present**
Employed at wastewater treatment plant handling 11M gallons of wastewater daily and serving a population of 72K people.

LAB TECHNICIAN

Collect water samples from 3 wastewater treatment plants in the city and conduct tests to ensure exit streams comply with limits set by DEQ. Tests include total suspended solids (TSS), mixed liquor suspended solids (MLSS), total solids (TS), fecal coliform, ammonia nitrogen, biochemical oxygen demand (BOD), settability, carbonaceous biochemical oxygen demand (CBOD), pH, dissolved oxygen (DO), and total residual chlorine (TRC). Perform grease trap inspections at local businesses and record waste transported to disposers. Responsible for calibrating equipment in wastewater laboratory on a regular basis, primarily pH and DO meters.

- Enhanced future data access by compiling laboratory test results during several months and storing them in a shared computer.
- Added an additional level of confidence to laboratory testing by creating spreadsheets for wastewater test calculations.
- Optimized time and resource utilization by collaborating with supervisor and coworkers to prioritize and efficiently divide activities.
- Regularly conducted discharge monitoring report quality assurance (DMRQA) tests to ensure quality of laboratory testing methods.

EDUCATION & PROFESSIONAL ACTIVITIES

College Education
- **BACHELOR OF SCIENCE IN ENGINEERING (BSE), CONCENTRATION IN CHEMICAL ENGINEERING**, Clarkson University, Potsdam, NY
  Senior Project: Add pre-acidulation step to process of manufacturing tall oil soap at Union Camp Paper Mill.
  - *Team determined that adding carbon dioxide in a pre-acidulation step would lower pH of tall oil before being sent to sulfuric acid reactor and reduce amount of system sulfates.*
  - *Created Levenspiel plot to illustrate reactor size required for task and material reactor should be made of.*
  - *Utilized Stokes' Law to determine dimensions of settling tanks in the process.*

Certifications
- LAPELS Certified Engineer Intern, License #34426
- DHH Operator Certifications: Wastewater Collection I, Wastewater Treatment I & II

Technical Skills
- Windows Operating Environments, Honeywell OS, Pro II, Simulink, MATLAB, LinkoFOG, Microsoft (Word, Excel, PowerPoint)

Trevor Dixon

12239 West 48th St #132
New York, New York 10036

(917) 666-0000
trevor.designs@gmail.com

Entry-Level Fashion Design Assistant
"Breathing fashion and design since birth."

PERFORMANCE SUMMARY

Multilingual, multicultural professional with background in organizational management and design-manufacturing-to-market cycle. Excellent listening and communication skills, backed with the academic rigor of both visual arts and business degrees. Consistent track record of anticipating needs and preferences. Fluent English, French, and German and a strong desire to grow in the Fashion Industry.

- ✓ Highly organized, proactive, and detail oriented with the ability to multitask without losing focus.
- ✓ Ability to work in fast-paced, collaborative environments with critical deadlines.
- ✓ Strong interpersonal skills with the ability to work both independently and in team environments.
- ✓ Capable of thnking "on my feet" and have a strong sense of urgency.
- ✓ Excellent communication (written and verbal), interpersonal, presentational, and follow-up skills.
- ✓ Software Applications: Microsoft Suite (Excel, Word, PowerPoint, Outlook) and InDesign; Computer Savvy.

PROFESSIONAL SKILLS

Exceptional Client Satisfaction	Client Hosting	Fashion News & Trends
Administrative Skills	InDesign	Social Networking
Scheduling	Data Entry	Multilingual
Organizational Management	Visual Design	File & Record Management
Fabric Selection	Travel Arrangements & Logistics	Multicultural
Tailoring & Clothing Design	Performance Improvements	Vendor Negotiations
Project Management	Financial Planning/Budget Management	Merchandise Sourcing
Marketing Captions/Headlines	Strong Market Research Abilities	Contract Creation/Execution

PROFESSIONAL EXPERIENCE

House of Fendi, Rome, Italy   2015–Present
Designer, PR and Marketing Manager
Selected to provide initial watch design for female line; sketched and graphically designed. Direct creation of prototype including collaborating with engineers, orchestrating final product development, negotiating budgets with CEO and engineers, and serving as liaison for translations from French to German. Promoted for successful track record of positioning start-up company as an industry leader and solid investment partner.
- CEO approved designs; negotiations with materials suppliers and engineers are in process.
- Helped consolidate slogan "Accessorize Me" for a line of scarves to maintain the company as an industry leader in luxury accessories.

Custom Print, Inc., Brooklyn, NY   2013–2015
Assistant to Print Management Consultant
Local full-service printing firm, specializing in delivering high-quality printing services at wholesale prices. Volunteered for position to start a career in the USA. Responsible for computer work, updated client list, designed layouts, scheduled client appointments, vendor communications, logistics, and coordinated deliveries to clients. Met with clients to discuss marketing material design options.
- Successfully promoted full line of print management services to potential clients.

-continued-

251

(Custom Print, Inc., continued)
- Expedited order placement and product delivery to prevent downtime.
- Generated new business through networking.
- Turned a request for wedding invitation cards into a complete wedding-logo printing package, generating increased revenue for the company.

EDUCATION

Savannah College of Art & Design (SCAD), Savannah, GA   2015
MA, Fine Arts

Armstrong Atlantic State University, Savannah GA   2012
BS, Business Administration

PROFESSIONAL DEVELOPMENT

Life and Art   2012
Sponsoring Organization: SCAD Museum of Fine Arts

Marketing HNW Individuals   2010
Sponsoring Organization: College of New York

JAKE COHEN

103 East Snow ♦ Nashua, NH 03060 ♦ 603-332-0435 ♦ jake.cohen@outlook.com

ACCOUNT MANAGER
PERFORMANCE PROFILE

Entry-level, high-potential self-starter conversant with client-needs strategies and professional work experience in Sales. Collaborates effectively across all professional levels to build relationships and generate sales. Utilizes consultative solutions-selling techniques by creating value-oriented presentations based on client knowledge coupled with in-depth product understanding and natural rapport-building skills that foster enduring customer relationships. Technology adept.

PROFESSIONAL SKILLS

♦ Account Prospecting	♦ Marketing Plan Development	♦ Social Media
♦ Problem Resolution	♦ Relationship Building	♦ Product Knowledge
♦ Customer Service	♦ Presentation	♦ Goal Achievement
♦ Sales Strategy & Support	♦ Survey Analysis	♦ Negotiation
♦ Communication	♦ Market Research	♦ Leadership

EDUCATION

BA, Communication, Organizational & Marketing Communication   2016

PROFESSIONAL EXPERIENCE

The New Hampshire Insurance Group, Nashua, NH   May–August 2016
Marketing & Business Development Specialist Internship
National Interstate Insurance is a specialty property and casualty insurance holding company with a niche orientation and focus on the transportation industry.
♦ Charged with managing an agency base to grow product lines, renew existing accounts, and add new business. Proactively prospected for new accounts with agents and insureds.
♦ As collaborative partner, forged and nurtured new client relationships.

Eco Snow, Nashua, NH   January–May 2015
Sales & Marketing Internship
Garick is a leading manufacturer and distributor of sustainable natural resource products for the consumer, professional, commercial, and construction markets.
♦ Successfully managed territory of customers through daily communication and order execution.
♦ Built and maintained relationships with key accounts via interpersonal relationship selling.
♦ Made sales calls to new business prospects, which led to increased sales.

North East Pipe & Steel Inc., Lincoln, NH   May–August 2014
Sales & Marketing Internship
Midwest Pipe & Steel Inc. is a full-line $300M per year steel service center.
♦ Communicated daily with customers to generate sales and build lasting relationships.
♦ Developed and implemented sales strategies aimed at revenue growth.
♦ Processed steel orders and followed through with customer for seamless on-time delivery.
♦ Tenaciously negotiated carrier freight rates, which decreased transportation costs.

PROFESSIONAL ASSOCIATION

American Marketing Association, University of New Hampshire, Nashua, NH, AMA Online Representative

Zoe Blake

Linked in profile

4332 Judge Street
Elmhurst, NY 11373

(631) 579-5357
zoe.blake@gmail.com

Accounting / Finance

Performance Profile

Energetic and team-spirited 2016 accounting graduate seeking opportunity to contribute to an organization's goals and objectives. Accurate, precise, and ethically responsible in all work-related assignments. Quick learner with an eagerness for learning and expanding accounting capabilities. Proven ability to identify problems and implement creative solutions.

- ✓ Recent college graduate with proven analytical and critical thinking skills.
- ✓ Disciplined with a desire to succeed as evidenced by working 20 hours per week while attending college full-time.
- ✓ Exceptional skills in written documentation and verbal communication.
- ✓ Effective interpersonal and leadership skills supported by an enthusiastic, team player attitude.
- ✓ Foreign Language—proficient in Chinese.
- ✓ Technology: MS Word, Excel, PowerPoint, Access, Database, and Adobe Photoshop; Internet Savvy.

Professional Skills

- Customer Service Skills
- Accounts Payable
- Accounts Receivable
- Budget Forecasting

- GAAP
- Inventory Analysis
- Bookkeeping
- Journal Entries

- Financial Presentations
- Management Skills
- Cost Control
- Market Research

Education

Bachelor of Science in Accounting/Finance, Michigan State University, E. Lansing, MI   2016
Relevant Course Work: Intermediate Accounting I, Intermediate Accounting II, Accounting Theory, Accounting Principles, Government Accounting, Income Tax, and Auditing.

Activities

Volunteer Income Tax Assistance (V.I.T.A.)
Prepared income tax returns for low-income families and internationals.

Experience

Michigan State University, E. Lansing, MI   January 2014—Current
Students Manager, Dining Services
- Calculate weekly payroll for all employees.
- Conduct store management as well as accounting and financial presentations for daily business performance to enhance utilization of funds.
- Supervise daily sales operations and training for new hires to maintain quality and efficiency.

Student Employee   January 2012—December 2014
- Provided high-quality customer services and efficiently carried out monetary transactions.
- Assisted with opening and closing accounting procedures for Starbucks Coffee shop and campus deli store.

Student Worker, Rivers Center   January 2010—December 2012
- Arranged services to meet a large portion of the leisure, recreational, conference, and meeting needs on campus.
- Managed procedures of business conferences and banquets for campus needs.
- Successfully promoted student-faculty interaction and learning outside of the classroom environment.

JOEY HUANG, MA

Hilton Head, SC 29926   843-227-4098
huang.acupuncture@gmail.com   LinkedIn Profile

BOARD CERTIFIED ACUPUNCTURIST

* Mind, body, and spirit healing through the application of traditional acupuncture. *

Acupuncturist experienced in Classical Five-Element Acupuncture with broad background in psychotherapy and coaching. Sensitive, intuitive practitioner dedicated to restoring clients' physical, emotional, and spiritual wellness. Thoroughly evaluate clients to accurately diagnose, formulate treatment plans, and provide effective treatments while encouraging healthy lifestyles. Ethical and compassionate; natural relationship builder committed to cultivating trusting alliances with clients and colleagues. Uphold policies, procedures, and standards, including Occupational Safety & Health Administration (OSHA) regulations.

PROFESSIONAL SKILLS

History Taking/Physical Exam	Treatment Evaluation	Team Collaboration
Diagnostics	Treatment Modification	Regulatory Compliance (OSHA)
Treatment Plan Development	Documentation/Records	NADA Ear Acupuncture
Acupuncture Needling	Client Education	Clinic Management
Moxibustion	Client Counseling/Coaching	Public Speaking

TREATMENT EXPERIENCE

Arthritis	High Blood Pressure	Chronic Bladder Infection
Neuralgia	Arteriosclerosis	Infertility (Men & Women)
Sciatica	Anemia	Sexual Dysfunction
Plantar Fasciitis	Asthma	Candida
Back Pain	Irritable Bowel Syndrome (IBS)	Chronic Fatigue
Tendonitis	Constipation	Epstein-Barr Virus
Stiff Neck	Food Allergies	Multiple Sclerosis (MS)
Headaches/Migraines	Gastritis	Smoking Cessation
Sprains	Abdominal Bloating	Drugs
Muscle Spasms	Diabetes	Alcohol
Sinusitis	Dermatological Disorders	Anxiety
Sore Throat	Irregular Menstruation	Insomnia
Hay Fever	Endometriosis	Depression
Dizziness	Menopause Symptoms	Stress

Comprehensive list of treatment experience available on request

PROFESSIONAL EXPERIENCE

New York College of Traditional Medicine| New York, NY   2013 – 2016

Acupuncture Intern
Provided 900+ hours of comprehensive acupuncture treatments for this nonprofit academic institution. Conducted comprehensive intakes, including physical exams, dietary assessments, and medication/herb interaction evaluations. Formulated traditional acupuncture diagnoses, facilitated client education, and researched client medical histories. Developed treatment plans and performed acupuncture needling and moxibustion.

Acupuncture Intern, continued

Provided lifestyle coaching, maintained practitioner/client relations, and liaised with supervisors to evaluate treatment results. Assessed integrative healthcare options and provided referrals. Recorded client progress in accurate, concise manner reflecting assessments, interventions, and treatment plan modifications.

➤ Consistently received positive client evaluations and notes of appreciation; encouraged by supervisors to consider specialization based on excellence in treating complicated cases.
➤ Provided case management and collaborative healthcare for client with advanced multiple sclerosis (MS).
➤ Actively mentored incoming acupuncture intern, providing guidance on all aspects of internship.
➤ Ranked as one of clinic's Annual Gala Top Five Silent Auction Fundraisers.
➤ Improved accessibility of and interest in school library through authoring comprehensive marketing materials to promote library's collection by researching and developing 12 color posters illustrating several acupuncture collections.

Westport Veterans Clinic | Westport, CT   2012 – 2013

Acupuncturist

Provided National Acupuncture Detoxification Association (NADA) ear acupuncture treatment to regular and walk-in veterans suffering from PTSD, stress, insomnia, and other conditions. Provided client management, ensuring warm, accepting, and comfortable clinic atmosphere.

EDUCATION

Master of Arts, Acupuncture (Honors), 2014
New York College of Traditional Medicine
Accredited by Accreditation Commission for Acupuncture and Oriental Medicine (ACAOM)

Professional Internship Program
Center for Mindfulness, New Haven Medical Center

LICENSURE & CERTIFICATIONS

National Acupuncture Certification #1438984
National Certification Commission for Acupuncture and Oriental Medicine (NCCAOM)

Licensed Acupuncturist ACU.0002032, New York
Licensed Acupuncturist AC155449, Connecticut
Licensed Professional Counselor LPC.0006243, New York

PROFESSIONAL ASSOCIATIONS

American Acupuncture Council | Acupuncture Association of New York

PRIA GAPUR

7350 HOPPER PLACE | PALO ALTO, CA | 94301 | 213-321-6449 | PATTY.G@OUTLOOK.COM

ACTUARIAL ANALYST INTERN
RESEARCH & ANALYSIS • PROBLEM SOLVING • FINANCE • RISK ANALYSIS

Performance-driven analyst nearing completion of a Masters in Actuary Science, seeking the opportunity to apply finely honed analytical skills, statistical techniques, and mathematical methods to assess and minimize risk within a dynamic actuary position. Exemplary ability to research, gather, and examine data to determine risk factors to assist in decision-making efforts. Strong ability to multitask and complete multiple deliverables in a deadline-driven environment. Excellent financial modeling abilities; leverages advanced Microsoft Excel skills including pivot tables, formulas, and Vlookups to compile and organize large data sets. Solid foundation in actuarial valuations, costing, and projections. Astute problem solver with comprehensive knowledge in economic and business functions coupled with a drive to exceed expectations.

- Utilizes big-picture understanding of finance and math to assess financial cost of risk.
- Expertise performing statistical analysis within a team, developing premiums and benefits for life insurance products.
- Associate of the Society of Actuaries (ASA) designation (Feb 2016).

Professional Skills

- Planning & Analysis
- Risk Analysis/Management
- Financial Analysis
- Finance/Accounting
- Actuarial Science
- Probabilities/Statistics
- Data Research & Analysis
- Actuarial Models
- Financial Reporting

EDUCATION & PROFESSIONAL CERTIFICATIONS

Master of Science in Actuarial Science - Stanford University, New York, NY, Dec 2015
Bachelor of Science in Accounting & Management *(Minor: Finance)* - Purdue University, West Lafayette, IN, May 2014
SOA Exams Successfully Completed:

MFE/3F, Jul 2015   **FM/2**, Feb 2015   **P/1**, Nov 2014

ASA Designation Feb 2016

VEE Fulfilled: Applied Statistics, Economics, Finance

EXPERIENCE

***Analyst Intern*, Delhi Life Insurance Co., Ltd.**, New Delhi, India   May 2016 – July 2016
- Collaborated within a team of 5, contributing strong analytical skills and financial acumen to develop premiums and benefits for new insurance products.
- Utilized a range of computer applications and methodologies to conduct detailed analysis of life insurance products.
- Constructed dashboard using Excel functions such as PivotTable and VBA based on current client data.

***Financial Intern*, Bank of India**, Bangalore, India   May 2015 – Aug 2015
- Efficiently and accurately prepared financial statements by creating Excel models to analyze financial data.
- Conducted in-depth database analysis to identify trends, build reports, and present findings.
- Worked with and supported Account Managers in the analysis of client information.
- Liaised with banks on loan activities and performed international transfers.

***Mathematics Tutor*, Palo Alto University**, Palo Alto, CA   Jan 2012 – May 2012
- Delivered tutoring on Advanced Calculus and Linear Model course.
- Monitored and assessed student performance and formulated tactics to assist them in increasing their abilities.

ACTIVITIES & AFFILIATIONS

Sigma Alpha Pi
Treasurer   Fall 2013 – Fall 2014
- Played a key leadership role, managing and planning budgets, maintaining accounts, and organizing fundraising.

Stanford University CSSA
Vice President   Spring 2012
- Led recruitment strategies and initiatives, along with steering a range of cultural activities and campaigns.

COMPUTER TECHNOLOGY

Word, Excel, Access, PowerPoint, Outlook, VBA, SAS, MATLAB

JEAN MONARSKI, CPA

16 Alice Court, Murrell's Inlet, SC 29576   jean@fw.com   (843) 625-6425

Accountant

Performance Summary

New CPA with three years accounting experience. Good listening skills harnessed to an analytical mind with the business knowledge to understand what is going on behind the numbers. Analysis of sales data recently led to optimization of product availability and price, which resulted in inventory turnover increase of 11%.

Professional Skills

✓ Accounting Discrepancies	✓ Website Maintenance	✓ Consultative Selling
✓ Sales Analysis	✓ Customer Relationship	✓ Data Evaluation
✓ Accounts Receivable	✓ Journal Entries	✓ Logistics
✓ Forecast Sales & Pricing	✓ Contract Development	✓ Purchase Orders
✓ Financial Analysis	✓ Negotiation	✓ GAAP
✓ Inventory Replenishment	✓ E-commerce Technologies	✓ IFRS

Professional Experience

THE FISHERMAN'S WAREHOUSE   2014 – Present
Accountant

Imports fishing equipment directly from foreign manufacturers and distributes to individual consumers and secondary distributors.

- Negotiated contracts with a major fishing retail chain to expand market reach that resulted in strategic business alliances with retailers in Saitama, Tokyo, and Hyogo through distribution of fishing equipment imported mainly from the United States and Poland.
- Accounting journal entries and preparation of balance sheet for tax return with proper application of tax regulations.
- Launched and developed original fly fishing rods through cooperation with a manufacturer in China and negotiated contract to reduce cost down to competitive range that could compete against much larger and long-running business entities.
- Track and improve sales levels and trends and determine stock replenishments for maximization of sales and minimization of product obsolescence to protect limited working capital.
- Maintain open lines of communication between manufacturers and customers to expedite product orders and for fast problem resolution.
- Cooperation with an outsourced inventory warehouse in Mount Pleasant, SC, to automate sales order process and to facilitate inspection of defective items to protect sales opportunity.

Education

Bachelor of Arts, Economics—University of South Carolina (Academic Achievements: GPA of 3.01)   2013

References available on request

SAM RAYBURN

8391 Mecklenburg Ave
Charlotte NC 28201

704.465.8978
lawman@gmail.com

ENTRY-LEVEL CRIMINAL JUSTICE

Performance Profile

Dependable, service-focused professional with degree in Human Services and Criminal Justice complemented by work experience reflecting promotion, excellent service delivery, and meticulous attention to detail.

Able to manage multiple tasks and responsibilities in fast-paced, demanding environments; exercises calm in pressure situations. Believes in public service and ethics in criminal justice field; recognized by supervisors and coworkers as a trustworthy, reliable team member.

Core Skills

- Customer Service
- Team Leadership
- Business Ethics
- Quality Standards
- Law/Rules Enforcement
- Public Service Delivery
- Public Speaking
- Team Collaboration
- Problem Resolution
- Workplace Organization
- Multitask Management
- Presentations

Education

BSOE in Human Services, Emphasis in Criminal Justice   2016
Georgia Southern, Statesboro, GA
Worked through college, full academic schedule, and full-time & part-time jobs.

Coursework

- Police Administration
- Vice & Narcotics
- Organized Crime
- Minority Relations
- Theories of Personality
- Community Relations
- Criminal Investigations
- Social Work
- Forensic Psychology
- Urban Sociology
- Abnormal Psych
- Criminology

Professional Experience

Statesboro Blues, Statesboro, GA   2014 – Present
Team Leader, Bartender

Train all new and experienced wait staff to ensure fulfillment of all service and quality goals. In second job as Bartender, interact directly with guests and team members; handle large amounts of cash on each shift.

Contributions

❑ Contribute quality training for diverse group of bussers; demonstrate patience with new employees and provide assistance during busy periods.

❑ Ensure enforcement of TABC laws and procedures through verifying identification for all customers; maintain close observation of bar patrons to pinpoint potential problems.

❑ Place uncompromising focus on guest service delivery; commended by management team for positive attitude and attention to guests' needs.

Home Depot, Statesboro, GA   2013 – Present
Garden Shop Associate

Held responsibility for organizing garden shop, with emphasis on outside garden area; worked with team of five in arranging tables, displays, product placement, and inventory storage areas. Maintained area cleanliness and assisted customers as needed.

Contributions

❑ Earned consistently favorable performance evaluations and recommendation for promotion to Lead Associate position based on training and mentoring abilities.

❑ Maintained well organized, attractive outside garden area to secure attention of customers and influence buyer decisions for key product offerings.

Volunteer

Volunteer – University Medical Center, Statesboro, GA. Worked in outpatient pharmacy for 18-month period; assisted with verifying inventory and filling prescriptions.

MALIK DRAYTON

612- 843-0917 • m_drayton@gmail.com • 94 Lake City Drive, Minneapolis, MN 55401

ENTERPRISE SECURITY ENTRY LEVEL
IT Security & Privacy ~ Enterprise Risk ~ Information System Risk ~ Business System Analysis

PERFORMANCE SUMMARY

Innovative, approachable IT professional who draws on advanced education, hands-on experience, and a collaborative approach to bring awareness and support to an enterprise-wide approach to security and risk management. Experienced in addressing infrastructure security issues such as data integrity, authentication, and confidentiality to ensure compliance with customer expectations, industry standards, and legislative requirements. Identifies IT and operational risks, threats, and vulnerabilities by applying forensics and research, documenting business implications, and developing systems, processes, and solutions to mitigate/manage risk throughout business. Bilingual, English and Arabic; EMEA culture conversant.

➢ Uses proven methodologies and tools, proper system design, and effective processes and controls to guard against poor-quality data and security threats.
➢ Works independently or within a challenging and collaborative team environment that supports debate and discussion in a service-oriented approach to risk management.

PROFESSIONAL SKILLS & INTERESTS

Enterprise Risk Management	Network & Data Security	Security Policies & Standards	Project Management
Operating System Security	E-commerce Security	Industry Best Practices	Gathering Business Needs
Security & Risk Analysis	IT Law & Trends	Firewall Fundamentals	Client Presentations
Digital Forensics	System Development	Problem Solving	Analytical Thinking

TECHNICAL EXPERIENCE

UNIVERSITY OF MINNESOTA • Minneapolis, MN   **2013–2016**
GRADUATE TEACHING ASSISTANT – SYSTEM DEVELOPMENT & PROJECT MANAGEMENT
Supported faculty member in operations of graduate/undergraduate courses, including preparing labs and assignments, correcting labs and assignments, maintaining grade databases, and leading students in projects required for course completion. Assisted approximately 40 students per class with studies focused on technical, organization, and economic factors. Developed projects from initiation to closure to meet deliverable deadlines, despite full schedules. Created proposal reports, scope statements, team contracts, schedules, progress reports, and resource assignments. Assumed responsibility in faculty absence. **Major Projects:**

Windows Server & Linux Virtual Installation
- Provided recommendations and documented challenges regarding future requirements in complete report containing snapshots.

Virtual Networking
- Led individual/class lab projects preparing virtual environment, creating internetwork, installing 3 virtual machines, developing subnet inside internetwork that included sub-netting and routing, and implementing simple DNS infrastructure over internetwork.
- Demonstrated #2 machine could perform a "Man in the Middle Attack," such that if hosts were in switched Ethernet environment, #2 could eavesdrop on communication between #1 and #2 machines, deny service, and stop communication between 1 and 2.
- Configured routing protocols while monitoring subnets and SMTP configuration for possible issues.

Bitcoin Authentication
- Independently researched and mastered bitcoin authentication, then recommended safe environments for utilization.
- Created comprehensive term paper on bitcoin utilization, reliability, weaknesses, and possible audit transactions.

Risk Management
- Conceptualized idea for project to increase awareness of ways publicly available information can be used to formulate non- or low-tech security breach, gaining access to corporate tech that provided competitive edge.
- Directed 4-student team in creating and managing lab environment; created management-level report highlighting threats.

E-commerce Infrastructure
- Reviewed web application vulnerabilities and studied e-commerce site behavior under normal and peak conditions.

ISO 9001 Compliance Audit

- Led effort to create proposal for ISO compliance in Russian Multicultural Learning Center to prepare for bidding process on government contract for military training.
- Authored 106-page document that outlined phases of proposed project (proposal reports, scope statements, team contracts, schedules, progress reports, and resource assignments) as well as examining all aspects of ISO compliance.

MIDDLE EAST AIRLINES • Beirut, Lebanon   2010–12
IT PROJECT ANALYST TRAINING, ORACLE APPLICATIONS
Entry-level position providing exposure to a variety of functions and projects, with a focus on operating Oracle-based systems within company's IT Department. Read manuals for Oracle add-ons applications and examining features that they offer in addition to the compatibility with rules and regulations.

EDUCATION & PROFESSIONAL ACTIVITIES

COLLEGE EDUCATION
- MASTER OF SCIENCE in INFORMATION SYSTEMS SECURITY MANAGEMENT, University of Minnesota
  ~ Thesis Research & Publication: "Disaster Recovery for Mid-Sized Canadian Businesses." Provided effective and financially feasible disaster recovery/business continuity framework and implementation template where mid-sized businesses can proactively prevent disruptions and react to interruptions of vital operations.
- BACHELOR OF SCIENCE in BUSINESS, FOCUS: MANAGEMENT INFORMATION SYSTEMS, Lebanese American University

CERTIFICATIONS
- Awarded: COBIT 5 Implementation & COBIT 5 Foundation, Alberta Security Training
- In Progress: Certified Information Systems Security Professional (CISSP), Certified Information Security Manager (CISM), Project Management Professional (PMP), Informational Technology Infrastructure Library (ITIL)

PROFESSIONAL AFFILIATIONS
- Member & Edmonton Chapter Academic Director, Information Systems Audit and Control Association (ISACA)
- Member of Northern Alberta Chapter, Project Management Institute (PMI)
- Member, Institute of Electrical and Electronics Engineers

TECHNICAL SKILLS
- Operating Systems: Windows Server 2008/2012, XP, Vista; UNIX, Linux Ubuntu, Fedora, Kali, BackTrack
- Software: MS Office Suite, Visio, Microsoft Project, Single Point Sign-In, VMware
- Networking: TCP/IP, DNS, DHCP, Ethernet, SMTP
- Hardware: Servers, Hubs, Routers, Switches, PCs

Jayana Stewart

Wichita, KS 67201 | 316-459-7126 | JStewart@gmail.com

Entry-Level Mechanical Engineer

Performance Profile

High-potential recent graduate who is prepared to meet the expectations of new and challenging assignments through a strong work ethic and the motivation to do whatever it takes to get the job done. A self-starter with an established ability to balance competing demands without compromising quality or productivity.

- ◆ Bilingual communicator (English/French) with strong interpersonal skills and a strong team orientation.
- ◆ Energetic, ambitious, and well organized with solid problem-solving skills and a proven ability to focus on detail, plan, prioritize, meet deadlines, and deliver first-rate work.
- ◆ Successfully executes day-to-day initiatives requiring flexibility and think-on-your-feet abilities.
- ◆ Confidently interfaces and establishes rapport with diverse groups of people at all levels.

Professional Competencies

✓ SolidWorks	✓ Autodesk Inventor	✓ Machine Shop
✓ Bandsaw & Drill	✓ Water Jet Cutter	✓ Communication
✓ Modeling/Fabricating Robots	✓ Manufacturing	✓ 3D Printer
✓ Analytical	✓ Mill & Lathe	✓ Detail Oriented
✓ Bilingual English/French	✓ Critical Thinking	✓ Problem Resolution

Education

BS, Mechanical Engineering, University of Kansas, 2016

Mechanical Engineering Projects

Senior Design Project

- ◆ Member of six-person mechanical engineering team honored with 2nd-place award in competition against 22 other teams.
- ◆ Key role on team that designed and built autonomous vehicle that navigated through predesigned course and delivered payload from start to finish. Primary accountabilities included drawing, machining, and parts assembly.
- ◆ Delivered presentation on robot fabrication and programming process to peers and professors.

Manufacturing Processes Class Project

- ◆ Built mechanically functional handheld video game console using aluminum plates, tactile switches, 3D printer, CNC mill, and EDM.
- ◆ Utilized 3D printer to create buttons and majority of console body.
- ◆ Employed sander to create smooth finish on console's aluminum plates.

Extracurricular Activites

Design for America: KU Studio, 2015–2016

Cofounded KU Studio in 2014.

Worked collaboratively with KU Baum School of Business graduate students.

Helped spearhead project to improve student learning and teacher instruction using a nonconventional, enjoyable approach.

MATE ROV competition, 2015

Built Underwater Unmanned Vehicle (UUV) utilizing lathe, bandsaw, and drill.

Internship Experience

Intern, Northwest Industries, Saskatchewan, Canada, 2014–Present

An international manufacturer of protection tape, PVC electrical insulating tape, masking tape, OPP packing tape, PVC duct and pipe-wrapping tape.

Research & Development Department

Employed various methods, including quality-control processes, to test combinations of natural and synthetic rubber for efficacy of adhesive properties under various temperatures and conditions.

Quality Control Department

Studied and utilized various methods of quality control to ensure products met predetermined requirements; properties examined included tensile strength, shear adhesion, and electrical resistance.

Electrical & Mechanical Department

Utilized SolidWorks to model machine parts.

Computer Skills

Microsoft Word, Excel, PowerPoint; MATLAB; SolidWorks; Autodesk Inventor; LabVIEW; C++; Java

Languages

Fluent in English and French, verbal and written language.

Excellent references available on request

View my profile on **Linked in**

Kris Cohen, RN, BSN

Chattanooga, TN 37401   (423) 897-6735   ChattanoogaRN.BSN@gmail.com

Registered Nurse, BSN

Performance Summary

Reliable and team-oriented RN, experienced with post-surgical and long-term care. Demonstrates strong clinical competencies and knowledge in nursing. Motivated and thrives in a fast-paced environment; flexible with scheduling needs.

- Responsible for assessment, planning, and implementation of patient care.
- Communicates well with patients, family, and healthcare professionals.
- Able to delegate tasks to LVN and CNA while maintaining accountability.
- Applies critical thinking skills to identify, prevent, and solve patient-related problems and family concerns.

Education, Licensure, and Certifications

University of Long Island, NY
Bachelor of Science in Nursing (BSN)   2015
Tennessee Registered Nurse License #869243   2016
Basic Life Support (BLS)
Advanced Cardiac Life Support (ACLS) certifications

Professional Nursing Skills

Physical assessment	Medication administration
Urinary catheter insertion	Pain management
Intravenous (IV) therapy	Nasogastric intubation
Gastrostomy tube feeding	Diabetes management/teaching
Vacuum-assisted closure (VAC) wound care	Specimen collection
Peripherally inserted central catheter (PICC) dressing change	Colostomy/ileostomy care
Medical Surgical Nursing, 144 clinical hours	

Professional Experience

Strong Oaks Health—Chattanooga, TN   2016–Present

Staff Nurse

Provides patients with highest level of safe nursing care in a 123-bed skilled nursing facility. Receives new patients and executes body checks to assess physical condition upon admission. Initiates IV start and IV therapy and administers medication as ordered by physicians. Communicates the patient's change of condition to physician in SBAR format. Diverse responsibilities include:

- Maintaining narcotic control, including correctly signing, counting, and cosigning wastage.
- Supervising certified nursing assistants for patient care assignments.
- Providing treatment of surgical wounds and setting up wounds (VAC) for wound care.
- Preparing discharge documentation and reconciled medication list to patient upon discharge.

Linked in profile

Regina G. Livingston

Linked in profile

234 Ivy Crescent, Branford, CT 06405 ♦ 203-265-3505 ♦ rgivingston@gmail.com

Entry-Level Sales Associate

Performance Summary

High-potential business professional with a solid track record of delivering sales and customer service excellence to expand customer base and grow bottom-line performance. Finely honed ability to engage customers and build strong relationships. A self-starter with well-developed initiative and the ability to balance competing demands without compromising quality or productivity.

- Enthusiastic, optimistic, and personable with a genuine desire to provide outstanding service.
- An eager learner who quickly integrates new knowledge and skills into job performance to contribute, grow, and excel.
- Model professionalism, loyalty, and teamwork with a high standard of ethics; subscribes to a straightforward, hands-on style in getting the job done.
- Works productively and independently in varied environments with minimal direction and supervision.

Education

BA, Political Science, honors, UConn
Dec 2016

Professional Competencies

- Retail Sales
- Adaptable & Flexible
- Well Prepared & Organized
- Customer Service
- Communication
- Time Management
- Problem Resolution
- Critical Thinking
- Disciplined Work Ethic

Professional Experience

JC Penney, Meriden, CT
Summer 2016
JC Penney is a chain of 1,060 mid-range department stores in 49 states.
Sales Associate

Charged with greeting and delivering first-class assistance to customers, asking questions and listening to shoppers' needs, then providing options and advice on meeting those needs.
- Performed sales functions and operated electronic cash registers.
- Maintained selling-floor presentations and restocking as needed.
- Ensured fitting rooms were ready for customers by promptly clearing merchandise and returning it to selling floor. Maintained neat and well-organized work area.
- Conducted loss prevention, inventory control, and compliance procedures.

Bob's Burger Joint, Branford, CT
Summer 2014 & 2015
Bob's Burger Joint topped the list of the five fastest-growing restaurant chains in the U.S.
Cashier

- Assisted in opening and closing store to ensure restaurant was welcoming, well organized, and prepared for service in morning and clean and secure in evening.
- Handled cash transactions and trained new cashiers on electronic cash register system.
- Managed customer complaints, resolving issues to ensure happy customers and repeat business.

University of Connecticut Extracurricular Activities

♦ Women's basketball team
♦ Regular volunteer at North Branford Food Bank
♦ Student Mentoring Programs

Honors & Awards

♦ Grasso Scholar
♦ Dean's List
♦ Graduated High School with Associate of Science degree from Eastfield College
♦ Won upselling competitions at Bob's Burger Joint
♦ Recognized for customer service excellence at JC Penney

Technical Skills

Microsoft Excel, PowerPoint, Word, Access, and Publisher

Languages

Spanish

Community Service

♦ North Branford Food Bank
♦ Branford Community Garden
♦ Toys for Tots
♦ CERT Training
♦ Timberland Project

Regina G. Livingston

Branford, CT 06405　　　rgivingston@gmail.com　　　972-922-4505

Performance Summary

Entry-Level Sales Associate

High-potential business professional with a solid record of delivering sales and customer service excellence to expand customer base and grow bottom-line performance. Finely honed ability to engage customers and build strong relationships. A self-starter with well-developed initiative and the ability to balance multiple competing demands without compromising quality or productivity.

♦ Enthusiastic, optimistic, and personable with a genuine desire to provide outstanding service.
♦ An eager learner who quickly integrates new knowledge and skills into job performance to contribute, grow, and excel.
♦ Model professionalism, loyalty, and teamwork with a high standard of ethics; subscribes to a straightforward, hands-on style in getting the job done.
♦ Works productively and independently in varied environments with minimal direction and supervision.

Education

BA, Political Science, Graduated with Honors, University of Connecticut, Dec 2016

Professional Competencies

♦ Retail Sales
♦ Adaptable & Flexible
♦ Well Prepared & Organized
♦ Customer Service
♦ Communication
♦ Time Management
♦ Problem Resolution
♦ Communication
♦ Disciplined Work Ethic

Professional Experience

JC Penney, Meriden, CT　　　Summer 2016
JC Penney is a chain of 1,060 mid-range department stores in 49 states.

Sales Associate
Charged with greeting and delivering first class assistance to customers, asking questions and listening to shoppers' needs, then providing options and advice on meeting those needs.
♦ Performed sales functions and operated electronic cash registers.
♦ Maintained selling floor presentations and restocking as needed.
♦ Ensured fitting rooms were ready for customers by promptly clearing merchandise and returning it to selling floor. Maintained neat and well-organized work area.
♦ Conducted loss prevention, inventory control, and compliance procedures.

Bob's Burger Joint, Branford, CT　　　Summer 2014 & 2015
Bob's Burger Joint topped the list of the five fastest-growing restaurant chains in the U.S.

Cashier
♦ Assisted in opening and closing store to ensure restaurant was welcoming, well organized, and prepared for service in morning and clean and secure in evening.
♦ Handled cash transactions and trained new cashiers on electronic cash register system.
♦ Managed customer complaints, resolving issues to ensure happy customers and repeat business.
♦ Cleaned lobby and bathrooms, meeting restaurant's high standards. Restocked supplies.

Brian Cooper

11A Central Park St., Sea Cliff, New York 11579

516.669.2579   Conservation11579@gmail.com

Geographic Information Systems (GIS)

Performance Profile

Entry-level **Geographic Information Systems** professional with multiple certifications covering GIS, **environmental safety**, and **rescue** measures. Self-motivated, disciplined with a desire to succeed as evidenced by attending college full-time while working full-time. **Advanced problem-solving** and **multitasking** skills for fast-paced environments. Experience coordinating city planning departments, and subcontractors during planning and building phases of projects.

- ✓ Accurate **field notes** using **multiple software** applications.
- ✓ Solid **cost assessment** analysis skills.
- ✓ Advanced analytical and **problem-solving skills.**
- ✓ Proven background in leading **GIS** teams.

Professional Skills

- Project management
- Research analysis and reporting
- P&L management
- Disaster preparation and recovery
- Word, Excel, PowerPoint
- Windows XP, MAC OS
- Arc GIS, Arc INFO, Arc Catalog

- GIS Map interpretation and analysis
- Environmental resource management
- Team-building and leadership skills
- Land use planning
- Excellent time management skills
- Plan and develop business proposals
- Business development

Professional Highlights

- **The Urban Scene:** Analysis of urban lifestyles, **land use** and design, population trends, and utilization of urban life spaces.
- **Map Interpretation and Analysis:** Interpretation of maps with emphasis on critical analysis, scale, and projection.
- **Geographical Analysis: Advanced quantitative techniques** used by geographer in analysis of spatial phenomena. Emphasis on **multivariate statistical methods** for geographical analysis using statistical software.
- **Land Use Planning:** Issues and responses concerning **land use, coastal zones, environmental resource management**, planning parameters for residences, industrial areas, and urban and regional revitalization.
- **Hazards and Risk Management:** Broad overview of hazards and disasters (natural or technological), emphasizing the physical and social dynamics that interact to produce hazard, the spatial and temporal distribution of various hazards, disaster preparation, and loss reduction.

Education & Training

Bachelor of Arts, Geography, California State University, Long Beach, California   2014
Areas of emphasis: GIS, natural resource management

Intermediate GIS, GIS cartography and base map development, GIS in environment technology.
Rio Hondo Community College, Whittier, California
GIS Certification   Completion date: 2013

Professional Organizations/Licenses

American First Responder CPR Certification   2005
DRE License, California Department of Real Estate   2005
PADI Rescue   2004

Excellent references available

KENNETH DERBY

Portland, Oregon   541-543-4243   ken.derby@live.com

Linked in profile

ANALYTICS PRODUCT MANAGER

"I leverage big data to drive strategic business decisions that amplify profitability and growth."

PERFORMANCE PROFILE

Nineteen years' combined product management and data analytics expertise with recent success in mobile/web applications for Microsoft. Possess broad understanding of data analytics specialty area, remaining abreast of market trends and requirements while ensuring cutting-edge use of big data to deliver measurable business value for customers. Conceptualize and realize best-in-class customer experiences by scrutinizing user analytics and data to steer decision making.

Build and direct collaborative cross-functional teams known for successfully launching products, despite involvement of complex hardware, software, and back-end components. Design targeted product stories, fine-tuning concepts for technical and non-technical audiences. Collate and prioritize stakeholder requirements, ensuring clarity during product development.

PROFESSIONAL SKILLS

Product Management	Analytics Solution Design	Business Requirements Gathering
Enterprise Network Security	Cross-functional Team Leadership	Communication and Collaboration
Online Media and Publication	Software and Hardware Design	Mobile Devices and Applications
Technical Marketing	Product Marketing	Partner/Stakeholder Management
Cloud Computing	SCRUM Methodology	B2C and B2B Social Networking
Project and Program Management	Media Advertising	Database Design

TECHNICAL SKILLS

Google Analytics	Adobe Analytics Suite	comScore
Localytics	Websense	Visual Revenue
Tableau	Oracle	Microsoft Access/Excel
SQL	Weka	Orange
JMP Pro	Microsoft Business Intelligence	SharePoint

PERFORMANCE HIGHLIGHTS

⬦ **Product Management** – Supported delivery of over $1B in annual revenue through analysis and interpretation of big data to enact forward-looking business decisions for Microsoft Business Intelligence solutions.

⬦ **Data Analytics** – Transformed data-driven strategic planning and development across Microsoft applications and content properties by implementing Adobe Analytics tool.

⬦ **Technology Savvy** – Developed and produced cloud-based, AI-recommended technology that was presented by Bill Gates and Steve Ballmer at global technology conferences in 2006 and 2007.

⬦ **Product Management** – Yielded $150M+ in annual revenue and captured 13% market share in security appliance segment via strategic positioning of Samsung/Check Point software security solutions based on industry trends and customer needs.

PROFESSIONAL EXPERIENCE

Microsoft – MSN Portal	2005 – Present
Technology company.	
Senior Product Manager/Planner, Analytics	2012 – Present
Senior Program Manager, MSN Entertainment Video and Sports	2008 – 2012
Senior Product Planner, MSN/Windows Live	2005 – 2008

Senior Product Manager/Planner, Analytics   2012 – Present

Promoted to oversee cross-organizational product management of Microsoft Business Intelligence solutions. Drive strategic direction of MSN portal and optimization of content experience to boost user engagement by delivering real-time analytics. Facilitate monthly business reviews for MSN portal. Discover revenue-generating opportunities by executing data analysis to align advertisers and user base with MSN. Envision and implement market share maximization strategies to strengthen MSN portal's Internet property ranking. Supervise 2 contract employees.

- ✦ Contributed to $1B+ in annual revenue by leveraging big data to make strategic business decisions for MSN portal.
- ✦ Embedded positive change to data-driven strategic planning and development spanning Microsoft applications and content properties through introduction of global Adobe Analytics solution.
- ✦ Enabled forecasting of impact of future product releases, mitigating negative performance effects, by coordinating forward-looking planning process.
- ✦ Set foundation for $36M in projected advertising revenue through formulation of 3-year search strategy.
- ✦ Yielded $10M in annual revenue through conceptualization and implementation of customer-targeting strategies.
- ✦ Elevated global audience 20% within 30 days of designing and launching process to track Facebook engagement, establishing Facebook as high-growth source of traffic.
- ✦ Defined requirements and shepherded project to deliver global analytics solutions to align with One Microsoft business strategy, lower costs, and unify reporting.
- ✦ Shrank engineering expenses 20% via creation of predictive models to determine business impact of design modifications.
- ✦ Enabled settlement of $500K from $14M in music industry payment litigation after defining legal cost mitigation solution for Microsoft LCA.

Senior Program Manager, MSN Entertainment Video and Sports   2008 – 2012

Appointed to optimize user experience, boost search transfers, and fuel competitive market growth by delivering in-depth product and user insights. Drove vision and strategy to amplify revenue, market share, and customer satisfaction. Discovered opportunities for and built business plans to capture cost savings, leveraging outsourcing as appropriate.

- ✦ Laid groundwork for MSN Entertainment's new Wonderwall property through in-depth examination of market data; since its launch, Wonderwall has delivered over $250M.
- ✦ Captured $500K cost savings by envisioning revenue growth strategy and business plan for Entertainment vertical to outsource content development to Berman Braun.
- ✦ Spearheaded interdisciplinary team that delivered inaugural social integration with Digg and Facebook on MSN portal; today, Facebook fuels 3% of MSN's worldwide audience.
- ✦ Earned 3 performance awards for strategy and insight, prolific output, and cross-company collaboration.

Senior Product Planner, MSN/Windows Live   2005 – 2008

Brought onboard to oversee long-term strategy and vision, value proposition, and customer advocacy. Determined market and product requirements for 5 distinct product and service offerings.

- ✦ Delivered new cloud-based, AI-recommended technology, as illustration of Microsoft's initial online device and service strategy, that was chosen and presented by Bill Gates at 2006 CES Keynote and Steve Ballmer at 2007 GSM World Conference Keynote.
- ✦ Originated several million dollars in global revenue through delivery and management of 4 advanced recommendation services for Messenger.
- ✦ Actualized and directed MSN Entertainment's RSS integration with Windows Live Spaces.
- ✦ Conveyed strategic recommendations for 3 confidential M&A initiatives after conducting extensive due diligence.

Samsung Enterprise Solutions	Mountain View, California	2002 – 2005

Multinational communications and technology.

R&D Product Manager

Challenged to oversee product life cycle for integrated partner product line, from development strategy to sales support and customer satisfaction. Drove analysis of new customer market opportunities to expand existing business and security product line into enterprise mobile solutions. Elicited future product requirements from customers and remained abreast of industry trends. Monitored weekly P&L and channel inventory for all regions to maximize marketing programs. Assessed M&A targets to optimize ROI and secure strategic intellectual property.

- Contributed to $150M+ in annual revenue, coupled with 13% market share in security appliance segment, through strategic management of Samsung/Check Point software security solutions product line.
- Played influential role in closing premier reseller partners, such as Siemens HiPath product group in Germany, by designing product solution compatibility.
- Minimized customer attrition and maximized contract renewal through creation of feature prioritization tool.
- Advocated and launched 2 new IDS/IPS product lines leveraging $3M development budget.
- Piloted development of security products VoIP strategy inclusive of new positioning for Check Point's firewall as Session Border Gateway.
- Facilitated effective negotiation of OEM deals through establishment of margin/forecasting tool.

Bell Laboratories, Computer Division | Sunnyvale, California	1999 – 2002

Communications & technology.

Senior Technical Marketing Manager
Designated to establish and lead Cuptertino competitive benchmark testing lab and 3-member team. Conducted sales engineering team training (in U.S. and abroad) on new products, competitive positioning, and customer deployment procedures. Crafted clear, concise customer sizing guides for enterprise products.

- Augmented sales 5% by envisioning and introducing technical marketing program based on competitive landscape.
- Substantially elevated product sales via conducting and documenting highly detailed competitive analysis.
- Selected for Value Champion award subsequent to delivering best-in-show security demo at Demo World 2004.

EARLIER CAREER

Mutiny, Inc., Houston, Texas – **Technical Designer/Product Manager**   1997 – 1999

EDUCATION

Master of Predictive Analytics (in progress), Santa Clara University, Santa Clara, California
Bachelor of Science in Information Systems Management, University of Houston, College of Technology, Houston, Texas

PROFESSIONAL ACCREDITATIONS

Check Point Certified Security Administrator (CCSA) and Check Point Certified Security Expert (CCSE)

ONGOING PROFESSIONAL EDUCATION

- Executive and Media Communication Training, Microsoft and Samsung
- VoIP Mobility Training
- Six Sigma Training

Superior references from world-class companies available

Jen Ellis

Branson, MO 65615   417-234-3640   BankMgr65615@gmail.com

Linked **in** profile

Branch Manager

Performance Profile

Branch Manager & Loan Officer with 12 years of experience managing branch banking and lending activities, improving business processes, and leading a team of financial services professionals who generate approximately $9 million in loans each year.

Professional Skills

Asset Preservation & Loss Prevention	State & Federal Regulatory Compliance	Verbal & Written Communications
Loan Applications & Processing	Requirements Elicitation	Lead Generation / Prospecting
Credit Administration / Credit Analysis	Financial Statements & Financial Audits	Customer Accounts Setup
Credit Quality / FICO Credit Scores	Data Entry & Database Management	Customer Relationship Management
Banking Products & Financial Services	Strategic Business Planning	New Business Development
Mortgage Lending & Underwriting	Economics, Accounting, & Finance	Staff Training & Supervision
Asset Management / Portfolio Valuation	Statistical Analysis & Market Trends	Teamwork & Collaboration
Loan Reviews, Approvals, & Closings	Spreadsheets, Flat Files, & Databases	Exceptional Customer Service
Documentation for Funding	General Ledger Accounting	Cross-Selling Opportunities

Performance Highlights

- Strategic Business Leader who leverages financial data and market trends analysis to drive business decisions.
- Credit Administrator proficient in interviewing clients, gathering financial information, processing loan applications, analyzing and interpreting credit quality for loan approval or denial, and closing asset-based loans.
- Compliance Resource for fair lending and responsible banking laws. Solid understanding of Community Reinvestment Act (CRA), Interagency Fair Lending Examination Procedures (IFLEP), and CRA Examination Procedures (CRAEP).
- Loan Manager with knowledge and experience in asset management/valuation, working with distressed properties and reviewing collateral reporting packages comprised of accounts receivable aging, inventory reports, sales journals, cash receipts registers, accounts payable listings, and other financial reports.

Professional Experience

WELLS FARGO, Branson, MO   2010 to Present
Branch Manager / Assistant Branch Manager

Promoted from Assistant Branch Manager to Branch Manager in July of 2012. Serve in a business development and sales role. Offer personal and real estate loans as well as credit insurance. Generate $9 million in loans each year, provide exceptional customer service, and build strong customer relationships.

- Recruit, hire, train, supervise, and evaluate performance of branch employees working in lending and loan collection.
- Monitor and direct loan activities. Analyze and deter risks associated with personal and real estate loans. Perform due diligence and conduct thorough credit risk assessments to provide an accurate risk profile and portfolio analysis pertinent to sustaining portfolio value and branch growth.
- Meet with clients to determine loan needs and discuss rates, terms, and underwriting requirements. Assist clients in loan application process. Analyze loan applicants' financial data to determine credit worthiness, including income, property valuations, credit report, credit history, etc.
- Oversee customer service activities, loan presentations, collection of outstanding loan payments, and provide troubleshooting for a high-volume call center.

Branson, MO 65615   417-234-3640   BankMgr65615@gmail.com

Branson, MO 65615   417-234-3640   BankMgr65615@gmail.com

Notable Achievements:
- Awarded "Branch of the Month" for July 2010 and September 2011.
- Personally received "Branch Manager of the Month" on numerous occasions in past 7 years.
- Increased employee productivity and cultivated a positive workplace environment by facilitating onboarding, employee training, and job shadowing for new bank employees and bank managers. Trained new hires and coached staff to optimal performance.
- Increased lending activities by 10% across loan staff by auditing staff performance against job requirements and instituting structured collection and solicitation procedures, which increased sales and reduced losses.
- Branch was recognized in top 20% for deterrence of losses, through the introduction of delinquency controls.

SMITH & ASSOCIATES, INC., Columbus, OH   2004 to 2010
Investigative Supervisor

Built a successful, full-service investigative firm that offered consulting services to insurance companies, large corporations, attorneys, and private citizens. Directed a team of investigators handling concurrent caseloads of fraud, security, and other criminal cases, including homicides. Conducted formal and ad hoc meetings with team members to gather information and maintain positive investigative outcomes.

- Conducted initial client needs assessments to properly analyze clients' situations and recommend solutions.
- Performed case reviews and managed ongoing investigative activities such as surveillance, interview, data collection, etc.
- Advised clients on asset security, workplace violence, fraud awareness, and theft prevention. Also investigated and reported on workers' compensation and insurance fraud cases for clients.
- Performed background checks for clients vetting new hires. Researched candidates' criminal and credit/financial histories. Verified accuracy of gaps in employment. Verified identity of candidates in certain instances. Provided business clients with the necessary information to develop a safe and reputable work environment.
- Conducted facility security audits, discussed security measures with security guards and other onsite staff. Audited each building structure and access points to identify weaknesses and security risks. Reviewed and advised on evacuation plans/procedures and other emergency response preparedness measures.
- Established internal business operating procedures and company policies.
- Oversaw budget administration, new business development, team management, and administration of case reports. Established new client accounts and negotiated service contracts.
- Oversaw accounting and finances. Managed accounts receivable, accounts payable, and payroll. Led the collection of contract payments. Maintained billing records and statement balances. Monitored expense records to ensure case budgetary restraints were met. Collaborated with an outside accounting firm to file business and personal taxes.
- Worked closely with claims examiners, customer service reps, outsourced suppliers, and other third parties involved in the data verification process.

Education

Bachelor of Arts in Criminal Justice – College of the Ozarks, Point Lookout, MO

Professional Development Courses

Coaching for Results | Advanced Selling | Real Estate Sales | Sales Management
Leadership, Exercising Influence in the Workplace | Branch Management, Analytics, and Profitability

Raffaela Zanotti, CPA

34 Stonewall Trail
Rye, NY 10580

914.243.4240
r.zanotti.cpa@att.net

Client Services Manager

PERFORMANCE SUMMARY

Twelve years' experience with a global management consulting firm delivering value through improving business processes, reducing costs, and increasing profitability for a wide range of Fortune 500 clients across diverse industries including pharmaceutical, manufacturing, retail, technology, healthcare, life sciences, and telecom companies. Leader with a proven track record of managing all phases of client service, including sales, proposal development, project delivery, team management, and executive relationship management.

- ✓ Strong GAAP, SOX, and financial statement presentation skills.
- ✓ Manage client service teams, plan and execute business process reviews, and manage budgets.
- ✓ Active client communications to manage expectations, meet deadlines, and lead change efforts.
- ✓ Act as a primary contact for C-level executives during projects.
- ✓ Manage multiple concurrent engagements to ensure direction and address issues.

PROFESSIONAL SKILLS

SOX & SEC Regulatory Compliance	COSO & Internal Controls	Sales & Proposal Development
Financial Statement Analysis	Business Review & Assessment	GAAP
Risk Assessment	Strategic Development & Training	Capital Budgeting
Business Process Improvement	Engagement Team Management	Planning, Budgeting, & Forecasting
Plan & Execute Client Engagements	Metrics & KPI Development	Executive Client Relationships
Process & Policies Development	Staff Planning	Organization Design

PROFESSIONAL EXPERIENCE

Balanciaga Consulting Group, Manhattan, NY — 2005–Present
Manager — 2010–Present
Senior Consultant — 2007–2010
Consultant — 2005–2007
Manager — 2010–Present

Global management consulting firm focused on clients with a variety of business problems, including establishing strategy, organization design, and change management, and improving operations to grow business, increase efficiency, and manage risk. Manage day-to-day project activities for multiple client engagements for Fortune 500 clients.

- Designed and executed process improvements for annual and long-range strategic and planning processes aligning financial planning with operational forecasts; reduced planning cycle by two months.
- Improved management reporting by eliminating unnecessary reports and creating consistent information across reports. Established new metrics and KPIs focused on key decision-making results.
- Developed agendas for three new CFOs to help with prioritizing initiatives and evaluating direct reports, and created plans to help guide their first 180 days in office.
- Relocated an underperforming national accounts support center from NY to NJ. Staffing realignments, training, and process improvements resulted in increased customer satisfaction and $1M annual savings.

-continued-

274

(Professional Experience, continued)

Senior Consultant   2007–2010

Responsible for leading individual pieces of larger/complicated client engagements. Worked with clients and subject matter experts to identify areas for improvement and created recommendations. Developed material and assisted in conducting client meetings and workshops.

- Assessed client's current process to close, consolidate, and report financial results, and created a new process that reduced the amount of analysis at month's end, resulting in a timesaver of four days.
- Made improvements to the Accounts Payable (AP) process through technology enhancements and updated employee training, resulting in a 30% reduction in backlog of invoices, and a reduction in staffing.
- Redesigned global chart of accounts across business units and geographies, reducing number of accounts from 5000+ to 2000. Eliminated reporting redundancy, and created consistent analysis and reporting.
- Developed strategy for CFO and finance department to reduce costs and improve efficiency through a shared service center, improved treasury operations, and timely and accurate reporting to management.
- Performed market sizing and assessment study for client looking to grow customer base across the United States. Study focused on researching market size and trends, resulting in a successful strategy to grow sales.

Consultant   2005–2007

Served in a variety of engagements to collect data and information to perform current state assessments and trend analysis for clients. Reviewed industry standards and developed new processes, structures, and created client deliverables.

- Implemented a financial review program for 60 facilities to collect month-end data, review performance trends, and monitor internal controls.
- Established a shared service center by relocating accounting process from individual locations, resulting in reduced costs, increased efficiency, and scalability to accommodate projected business growth.
- Assisted client struggling with Sarbanes-Oxley demands. Implemented internal controls and compliance programs focused on PCAOB and SEC compliance, preventing client's stock from being delisted.
- Developed a training program to accompany new budgeting and planning system and process. Delivered live training to 40+ global users who executed a successful planning cycle on the new system.
- Assisted company implementing new SAP (ERP) by adjusting current AP, AR, and General Accounting practices for the new system. New processes resulted in standardization and improved efficiency.

EDUCATION & PROFESSIONAL LICENSES

University of Pennsylvania, Philadelphia, PA   2003
Master of Accounting

University of Pennsylvania, Philadelphia, PA   2002
BBA, Accounting and Finance

Certified Public Accountant (New York)   Active

PROFESSIONAL ORGANIZATIONS

American Institute of Certified Public Accountants
New York Society of Certified Public Accountants

Elise Petit

24 Newfoundland Place

Toronto, Ontario MB4 1B5

Linked in profile

647.243.4342

e.g.petit@gmail.com
Controller

PERFORMANCE PROFILE

Certified Management Accountant (CMA) with 18+ years of progressive full-cycle accounting and managerial experience. Results-driven leader with a proven track record that reflects strong business acumen, financial development skills, strategic planning, financial reporting skills, and a demonstrated commitment to organizational growth. Skilled in analyzing existing operations and implementing cost-effective systems, strategies, and processes to improve organizational performance and profitability.

- Extensive knowledge of accounting, budgeting, and cost-control principles.
- In-depth knowledge of preparation of financial reports and analysis of financial data.
- Streamlines financial operations to maximize performance and profitability.
- Strategic business planning and analysis, including identification of operational business issues, risks, and opportunities.
- Solid interpersonal skills and cross-functional team interactions combined with leadership abilities.
- Comprehensive knowledge of accounting reporting and automated financial systems.
- Strong organizational and project management skills; ability to manage multiple projects, set priorities, and meet deadlines.

PROFESSIONAL SKILLS

*Forecasting & Budget Planning	*Project Management	*Internal Controls
*Full-Cycle Accounting	*GAAP	*CMA
*Leadership & Mentoring Skills	*Financial Planning & Analysis	*Variance Analysis
*Audits & Taxation	*Policies & Procedures	*ERP Systems
*Cost Controls	*General Ledger	*Inventory Control Programs
*Balance Sheet & Income Statement	*Bank Reconciliations	*Journal Entries
*Systems Administration	*Foreign Exchange Transactions	*Capital Leasing
*Daily Operating System Updates	*Client Collection Schedules	*ACCPAC
*Accounts Receivable (A/R)	*Accounts Payable (A/P)	*Sales Commissions
*Great Plains Dynamics	*Sage MAS (ERP system)	*Excel

PROFESSIONAL EXPERIENCE

Canada Conveyor Corporation, Toronto, Ontario   2002–Present
Senior Accountant
Industry leader in Eastern Canada with annual revenue of $80M. Company installs and maintains industrial conveyor belt systems. Responsible for final adjusting journal entries, financials, financial statement analysis, and GL account reconciliations. Managed payroll for the entire company that has grown from 100 employees to over 250 employees in the past decade. Prepares year-end working papers and communicates with external auditors for annual audits.

- Streamlined payroll reporting for improvement of tracking working hours of hourly staff.
- Delivered semi-monthly payroll on time for 12 years, meeting all deadlines.
- Accomplished a proven track record of delivering timely financial statements, consistently meeting corporate deadlines.
- Assisted in the transition from UNIX-based system to ERP operating system.

-continued-

(Professional Experience, continued)

Margaux Manufacturing, Inc., Toronto, Ontario   1999–2002
Inventory/Purchasing Supervisor and Project Manager
International company with 75+ employees with locations in Canada, the United States, and Australia. Produces vehicle engine additives and costume jewelry. Designed inventory control program to track production and control inventory levels.

- Negotiated with suppliers to locate optimum suppliers based on cost, customer service, and delivery times, resulting in cost savings.
- Effectively communicated with other departments to ensure proper inventory level control procedures were established and regulated, saving the company money in excess inventory.
- Conducted daily operating systems updates and weekly bonus procedures for sales representatives.

Mississauga Indemnification Services, Inc., Mississauga, Ontario   1998–1999
Accountant and Accounts Receivable Administrator
National company with revenues in excess of $12M specializing in replacing goods for insurance claims. Effectively administered payroll for company with 60+ employees. Prepared monthly financial statements through trial balance using ACCPAC.

- Developed a series of spreadsheets for easier reporting and tracking of company information, resulting in better analysis of financial information.
- Effectively administered payroll for 55 non-executive employees.
- Collected accounts receivables with a monthly average of $1M and approximately 40% of payables up to $500K monthly.

EDUCATION

University of Ottawa, Ottawa, Ontario   1998
Bachelor of Commerce
Major: Accounting

PROFESSIONAL DEVELOPMENT & CERTIFICATIONS

Level 1 – Payroll Administrator Certification   1997

CMA Designation   2003

Superior references available

Teresa Mamalakis

5 Snowdrop Lane

Asheville, NC 28805

Linked in profile

(732) 441-7004

t.mamalakis@gmail.com

Director of Financial Planning & Analysis

"I streamline processes to reduce expenses, increase sales, and provide necessary metrics for strategic decision making."

PERFORMANCE PROFILE

15+ years' experience with financial planning and analysis, ranging from financial services, manufacturing, and retail distribution, to global corporate reporting; backed by a proven track record in high-growth, multinational companies. Exceptional knowledge of accounting concepts, standards and practices, and fiscal planning. Strong financial acumen and extensive understanding of business drivers. Exhibits professional standards of integrity and ethics in all transactions. Solid academic background in finance.

- Demonstrates extensive knowledge of financial assessments and identifies key metrics critical to business performance.
- Excellent analytical, critical thinking, innovative, problem-solving, and organizational skills with strong attention to detail.
- Excellent interpersonal and communication skills with the ability to work with cross-functional teams.
- Effectively interfaces with all levels of financial and IT management teams.
- Strong leadership skills with an emphasis on teamwork, innovation, and integrity.
- Exceptional communication and presentation skills with the ability to deliver strategic messages to senior leadership.
- Works with complex concepts, analyzes data, and makes recommendations for increased productivity.
- Solid judgment skills, with the ability to work in fast-paced and challenging environments and consistently meet deadlines.

FINANCIAL PLANNING SKILLS

*Data Analytics & Profitability Analysis	*Reporting Skills	*Strategic Planning
*Identifies Opportunities & Risks	*Financial Acumen	*System Process Improvements
*Fiscal Planning	*Negotiation Skills	*Latest Estimates
*Presentation Skills	*Rolling Forecast	*Profit & Loss Statements
*Accounting Concepts, Standards, & Practices	*Forecasting & Budgeting	*Financial Modeling
*Expense Control	*Balance Sheet	*Cash Flow
*Best Practices	*Management Consulting	*Project Management Skills
*Inventory Control: FIFO & LIFO	*Capital Budgeting	*Depreciation
*Activity-Based Costing	*Cost of Sales	*Product Cost Control
*Assisted in Sales Presentations	*Project Costing	*Net Income

TECHNOLOGY SKILLS

*MS Word, Excel, Access, Outlook, & PowerPoint	*SAP	*Oracle Essbase
*Hyperion Planning	*FI/CO	*Business Warehouse (BW)
*Strategic Enterprise Management (SEM)	*Microsoft Project	*AS400
*Business Planning & Consolidation (BPC)	*VAI-S2K	*Quick View
*Advanced Business Application Programming (ABAP)	*Apple OSX	*VBA

-continued-

PROFESSIONAL EXPERIENCE

Underwood & Associates, Charlotte, NC　　　　　　　　　　2015–Present
Senior Manager of Financial Planning
$250M domestic leader in sales of retail and wholesale tobacco products. Selected to manage $60M of stock inventory throughout company. Charged with revamping receiving process for warehouse and retail locations. Prepares annual business plans for retail, wholesale, and Internet businesses. Prepares annual sales and expense budgets with quarterly latest estimate updates. Interacts with management team on strategy and forward-looking business plans.

- Conducts annual physical inventory, routine cash, and payroll audits throughout company.
- Decreased inventory by $10M to reach optimum inventory levels.
- Realigned assortment with sales patterns, resulting in a savings of approximately $400K annually.
- Reduced aging inventory by 50% +, down from $750K to less than $350K, reaching acceptable levels.
- Partnered with IT to develop in-house aging report; monitoring of inventory was elevated from annual to monthly review.
- Re-engineered budget process by engaging stakeholders to participate in process, resulting in improved accuracy and obtainable long-range plans.
- Developed bottom-up approach to planning sales, budgeting expenses, and exposing critical risks. Reduced expense budget by $3M (10%).
- Reduced time, expense, and labor while improving accuracy of physical inventory by partnering with IT to enhance inventory control system and implement the use of barcoding and scanners. Reduced staff needed for physical inventory count, from 20 to 6 employees.
- Reduced shrinkage, theft, and shortages at store locations by partnering with internal security manager to increase the number of security cameras. Reduced shrinkage by more than $100K annually.

Carolina Consulting – Client: Best Pharmaceuticals, Winston-Salem, NC　　　　2012–2015
Consultant / Business Analyst
Business process improvement services; ranked in the top 10 of Enterprise Performance Management space (EPM); $2M in sales. Hired to develop and implement finance models to integrate with Hyperion planning software. Created functional specifications, according to the needs of local Regeneron finance team. Participated in sales presentations with potential clients to assist in new business development efforts.

- Financial process liaison between technical team and client requirements.
- Developed month- and quarter-end financial reports for board of directors.
- Created rolling forecast and 5-year strategic planning initiatives.
- Integrated complex client planning model templates to work in new environment, resulting in accelerating the migration period from 9 to under 6 months.
- Developed bottom-up approach for budgeting and planning to identify opportunities and risks; engaged managers and cross-functional channels for accountability for budgets and sales targets.
- Discovered significant risk in payroll expense by implementing a time-management tool, which tracks by projects, resulting in a reduction in payroll costs by $1.2M over a 12-month period.

Luxeco (Coach Leathergoods), Charlotte, NC　　　　　　　　2004–2012
Manager – Strategic Planning and Analysis　　　　　　　　　　2006–2012
Senior Retail Accountant, New York, NY　　　　　　　　　　　2004–2006

Manager – Strategic Planning and Analysis　　　　　　　　2006–2012
Hired to power the company budgeting and planning effort, including wholesale, retail, Internet, and mail order. Forecasted sales, cost of sales, stock assortments, and budgeting expenses. Produced monthly P&L statement, cash

-continued-

flow statements, and balance sheet. Reported financial results and recommendations for improvements to senior management.

- Responsible for preparation of consolidated business plans and forecasts for North America, including retail and wholesale divisions and 40 retail boutiques.
- Built consolidation reports for upper management, saving the company $29K in consulting fees.
- Reduced maintenance costs by creating national accounts with suppliers for lighting costs for retail boutiques. Replaced local suppliers with variable costs, saving the company $500K.
- Reduced rent expense by $2.4 million in 24 months by implementing a comprehensive review of leases, exposing overpayments, late fees, and percent of rent being erroneously paid to landlords.

Senior Retail Accountant, New York, NY   2004–2006
Hired to oversee and manage financial operations for 40 retail boutiques, including expenses, budgets, and variance to plan analysis. Produced monthly P&L and cash flow statements, and balance sheet. Reported financial results to senior management with recommendations for improving results.
- Conducted physical inventory for retail boutiques with an inventory value of $1M per store and warehouse inventory of $20M.
- Implemented internal physical inventory program using in-house-developed software rather than outside vendors, resulting in savings of $80K per year.
- Coordinated with IT department to develop POS software to reduce credit card chargebacks, resulting in a savings of $100K in lost sales per year.
- Reduced expenses by 17% for retail boutiques by developing a second version of P&L highlighting managers' controllable expenses and tying incentive bonuses to net income. Resulted in a $3.4 million reduction in controllable expenses over a three-year period.

Princess House, Bronx, NY   2000–2004
Senior Business Manager
Tabletop products company. Hired for budgeting and financial planning department. Responsible for tracking sales and expense performance of 260 boutiques. Created pro forma models to analyze potential new store locations and acquisitions.
- Streamlined planning process by implementing strategy to allocate resources strategically rather than functionally, tying performance to budget targets, and reduced expenses by approximately $3M over 12 months.
- Reduced payroll expense by $2.1M over 12 months across 260 store locations by tying payroll hours to sales and empowering managers to meet corporate defined goals.

Dunhill Companies Business Consultant   1998–2000
Business consultant servicing NASE Insurance, POT, and Bailey, Banks & Biddle Jewelers

NASE Insurance, Plainfield, NJ   2000
Financial Analyst
$84B international financial services and insurance products firm. Hired to perform financial reporting, month-end close, and overall expense variance analysis. Managed forecasting and budgeting efforts for NASE Mortgage Capital Company (NMCC).
- Reported financial results to SEC in preparation for IPO.
- Developed access database to track performance of mortgage-backed securities for proposed marketing.
- Effectively managed P&L reporting for all domestic profit centers.

-continued-

280

POT (Subsidiary of Venus Global Management), Parsippany, NJ   1999–2000
Senior Financial Analyst
Global alternative asset management firm; $2.8B in sales. Responsible for P&L reporting on Northeast and Southeast regional profit centers.
- Instrumental in merger and acquisition support as a member of due diligence team with primary responsibility for acquisition models.
- Analyzed takeover targets, created pro forma statement and models, and performed analysis.

Bailey, Banks & Biddle Jewelers, Parsippany, NJ   1998–1999
Planning Analyst
International producer and seller of fine jewelry and luxury goods. Hired to prepare business plans for all domestic retail locations totaling $3.8B in sales. Charged with analyzing and reporting key indicators, including sales, expenses, and profit margins. Responsible for identifying areas within retail chain for reduction of expenses.
- Reduced payroll expense by $1.1M across 65% of boutiques.
- Re-engineered budget and planning efforts by including stakeholders for responsibility of stores' success, resulting in increased probability by +5.5% over the following six months.

Bank US NA, New York, NY   1993–1998
Manager
Global diversified financial services and products firm; $68B in sales. Hired to contribute to month-end close process, supporting three business offices in San Francisco, Los Angeles, and Miami. Created expense variance reporting for monitoring expenses, planning sales, and managing general accounting support. Produced long-range forecasts with monthly update for three business offices.
- Revamped intercompany reporting for three business offices, resulting in elimination of duplicate entries, reducing the time to close.
- Reduced expenses by $120K for three major sales offices by implementing new expense controls.
- Assisted in increasing annual sales at the Miami office by creating a monthly query identifying high net worth individuals (HNWI). Monthly report was utilized to target and cross-sell existing as well as other products.

EDUCATION & CERTIFICATIONS

Clarkson University, Potsdam, NY   1990
Bachelor of Arts in International Finance
Minor: Political Science

SAP Certification; Cost Management and Controlling Certification; Certified Microsoft Office Professional

Superior references available

Kathy Miller Ed.D., MSM

341B Haines Place
Bakersfield, CA 93311

(661) 543-3243
k.miller@verizon.net

Director National & Global Accounts

PERFORMANCE PROFILE

Exceptional pharmaceutical sales record, backed by rigorous academic training and including 10 years in National & Global Accounts. Experienced as National Account Analyst in the venture capital industry and National Account Consulting, providing a unique background and analytical skills necessary to consistently outperform sales quotas, develop new business, build strong customer relationships, and effectively manage sales teams. Exceptional skills in all stages of the sales cycle and strategic planning.

- ✓ Builds and nurtures long-term customer relationships with executive-level decision makers; easily develops rapport with C-level management, physician opinion leaders, and clinical staff.
- ✓ Knowledgeable in healthcare marketplace, including competition, industry regulations, trends, customer needs, and pricing.
- ✓ Strong contract development, negotiating, and implementation (pull-through) skills.
- ✓ Leads the planning process for new product launches for managed care and commercial payers.
- ✓ Excellent written and oral communication skills; delivers high-impact presentations.
- ✓ Multitasker with the ability to manage multiple projects simultaneously in fast-paced environments with changing requirements and priorities.
- ✓ Manages strategic planning process, prepares forecasts, and develops growth strategies.
- ✓ Cross-functional team leadership skills with CAMs, RAMs, marketing, field sales, and customers.

BUSINESS DEVELOPMENT SKILLS

*Develops Strategic Business Plans	*Excellent Analytical Skills	*Profit Margin Enhancement
*Fiscal Responsibilities	*Efficient Resource Allocation	*Forecasting & Budgeting
*Ensures End-User & Patient Access	*Negotiations & Contracting Skills	*Executes Pull-Through
*Ensures Physician Reimbursement	*Identifies Industry Trends	*Managed Care
*Long-Term Customer Relationships	*Healthcare Provider Relations	*Identifies Customer Needs
*Customer Advocate	*Product Launch Strategies	*Business Acumen
*Policies & Procedures	*CRM Applications	*Performance Metric Reporting

SALES MANAGEMENT SKILLS

*Sales Management	*Leadership & Mentoring Skills	*Budget Accountability
*Hires & Trains Managers	*Sales Training & Development	*Reporting Procedures
*Contract Pull-Through Procedures	*Establishes Best Practices	*Assist Field Sales
*Quota & Incentive Plan Development	*Identifies Policies & Procedures	*Compensation Plans
*Industry Guidelines	*Regulatory Compliance	*Customer Relations

PROFESSIONAL EXPERIENCE

NanoTech, Inc., Bakersfield, CA   2014–Present
Director National Accounts
Hired to develop contracting strategies supporting the launch of a new product and build relationships with decision makers at Medicare intermediaries (MACs), commercial payers, Group Purchasing Organizations (GPOs), and disease state opinion leaders in oncology marketplace.

- Researches and analyzes competitive information regarding the oncology marketplace to assist in reaching company's goals and objectives.
- Collaborates with scientific and marketing team members, including external advertising and consulting agencies to create customer-oriented messaging.
- Developing early-stage contract template designed to optimize product uptake, providing end-users with product access for appropriate patients by partnering with payers and GPOs.

California Venture Capital, Palo Alto, CA   2010–2014
Biopharmaceutical National Account Analyst and Consultant
Venture capital and consulting service for organizations with novel human therapeutics and medical devices. Hired to consult start-up organizations regarding the establishment or improvement of national account departments. Provided strategic analysis and guidance for selling into disease-specific marketplaces. Guided organizations to incorporate policies and procedures, enabling start-up companies to maximize profit margins while complying with industry guidelines and government regulations.

- Successfully assisted in the establishment of national account departments at four start-up organizations.
- Instrumental in the establishment of a national accounts department for a major pharmaceutical organization to support the launch of a surgical device.
- Researched and analyzed market conditions for pharmaceuticals and medical devices designed to treat numerous disease states and facilitated successful product launches.

PharmaBrands, Inc., Seattle, WA   2006–2010
Senior Clinical Specialist
Hired to increase sales volume, market share, and profitability of a mature drug. Analyzed the marketplace and collaborated with key U.S. opinion leaders as well as innovative overseas healthcare providers to formulate a strategic plan to increase product uptake. Collaborated across multiple organizations to gain commitment and resources to increase sales and medication-related patient outcomes. Participated in the administration of phase IV research.

- Influenced positive changes to reimbursement policies (step edits) at commercial payers.
- Established relationships with global disease state opinion leaders, marketing personnel, a nationwide patient advocacy group, and select local chapters to research and perform strategic marketplace analysis.
- Instrumental in building pilot program for the introduction of continuous quality improvement (CQI) tactics into pulmonary disease management, including a patient/family educational component focused on benefits of compliance.
- Advanced pilot program into a national initiative resulting in increased sales. Turned around 80% of territories performing below quota, resulting in 90% of territories reaching quota within six months of implementation.
- Pilot program increased medication-related patient outcomes by 14%.

Quota Achievements
2007—110%; 2008—114.7%; 2009—111.54%; 2010—108.93%

Biogen, Austin, TX   2000–2006
Corporate Account Manager
World's largest biotech organization providing drugs for unmet medical needs. Hired to build relationships with executive-level decision makers to assist in managing $225M in product sales at 14 corporate accounts and 3 national accounts. Led contract negotiations, monitored compliance, and conducted internal/external business reviews quarterly. Identified growth obstacles, created solutions, and motivated product stakeholders to participate in co-branded initiatives developed to aid each party in achieving its goals.

- Provided internal contract pull-through efforts by collaborating with marketing personnel, regional managers, district managers, and sales representatives.

-continued-

- Influenced external contract pull-through efforts by building strong relationships with senior management and key opinion leaders at accounts.
- Signed 100% of annual customer contracts prior to due date.
- Exceeded expected profit margins annually by negotiating contracts utilizing the aspiration price model.
- Developed program increasing from 56% to 77% the national number of patients who experienced therapeutic results targeted by Medicare, payer intermediaries, and quality assurance agencies.
- Selected as national account/corporate account trainer.

Biogen Corporate Account Quota Achievements
2004—107.6%; 2003—105.4%; 2002—108.3%; 2001—105.1%; 2000—105.2%

Regional Accounts Manager   1998–2000
Promoted from previous position as district sales manager (1996–1998) within two years. Supported the national "Plan of Action" by collaborating with national account managers and coordinating the pull-through process for joint initiatives. Negotiated contracts, monitored contract compliance, and led the pull-through efforts for co-branded product initiatives at several large corporate healthcare providers located in 11 states. Conducted regular internal and external business reviews each quarter; managed $180M in sales.

- Converted $2.3M account from competitor's product to Amgen product.
- Created pilot program for sales initiative to increase appropriate product use and medication-related patient outcomes, resulting in increased number of patients in Medicare target range for outcomes and reimbursement from 59% to 78%.
- Successfully completed contracting process on time annually, resulting in uninterrupted sales.
- Exceeded required profit margins at contracted accounts and exceeded sales quota annually.
- Acted as a resource to payer representatives by calling on local MACs and small commercial payers.

Biogen Regional Account Sales to Quota
2000—108.7%; 1999—111.3%; 1998—107%

District Sales Manager, Indianapolis, IN   1996–1998
Responsibilities included supervising eight representatives and one clinical nurse specialist marketing biotechnology to key executives, physicians, local payers, distributors, and Medicare regulatory agencies. Hired and trained new staff while developing existing personnel to improve business acumen. Managed $36M in annual sales.

- Exceeded sales quota and objective each year.
- Oversaw contracting efforts with 194 healthcare providers, ensuring uninterrupted business.
- Instrumental in successfully reopening contract efforts with the CMMA group purchasing organization.
- Committee member of Payer Advisory Board focused on strategies to provide end-user and patient access.

Biogen District Sales Manager Sales to Quota
1998—104.7%; 1997—107.2%; 1996—106.6%

Professional Sales Representative, Chicago, IL   1991–1996
Provided pull-through for mandated contract sales and marketing initiatives. Marketed cutting-edge recombinant DNA human therapeutics to subspecialty physician practices.

- Developed the American Stores Retail Option Program allowing patients to use their commercial insurance plan at any of the 87 Osco drug store locations.
- Led the district in sales 3 of 5 years, including the results generated by academic sales territories.
- Negotiated contracts and oversaw implementation at 36 oncology and dialysis clinics.

-continued-

EDUCATION

University of Colorado Skaggs School of Pharmacy, Aurora, CO   2015
Doctorate
Major: Pharmacy
Focus: Pharmaceutical Biotechnology
GPA 3.89

University of Colorado Skaggs School of Pharmacy, Aurora, CO   2010
Master of Science
Major: Pharmacy
GPA 3.89

University of Colorado, Denver, CO   2002
Master of Science
Major: Management
GPA 4.0

University of Colorado, Leeds School of Business, Boulder, CO   1990
Bachelor of Science
Major: Management and Marketing
GPA 4.66

PROFESSIONAL DEVELOPMENT

Cultural Intelligence: Facilitator Training, 2013
Understanding Changes in Healthcare Reform, 2013
Biopharmaceutical Sales and Marketing in Today's Multicultural Environment, 2012
Healthcare Reform and Its Effects on Providers, 2011
Emotional Intelligence: Motivating Customers and Coworkers, 2011
Transformational Leadership in the Medical Setting, 2010
Large Account Management: Collaborating Within and Across Organizations, 2010
New Frontiers in Healthcare: Rare Disease Management, 2009

PROFESSIONAL CERTIFICATIONS

Certified Medical Representative

Nationally Certified Paramedic

Specialty Training Received:
- Advanced Cardiac Life Support
- Pre-Hospital Trauma Life Support
- Pediatric Advanced Life Support
- Neonatal Transport Specialist

PROFESSIONAL ORGANIZATION/AFFILIATIONS

International Women in Leadership Association
United States Department of State: Global Leadership Program
National Association of Reimbursement Professionals
University of Colorado Alumni Association

-continued-

285

PUBLICATIONS

Miller, K. (n.d.). Cultural Intelligence and Leadership: A Study of Pharmaceutical Leaders in India. *International Journal of Marketing Management* 2015.

GLOBAL EXPERIENCE AND CULTURAL DIVERSITY AWARENESS

Performed consulting and research at Indian nanotechnology pharmaceutical organization (Delhi, Agra, Una, India).

International liaison for key opinion leaders: Essen, Germany; Rotterdam, Netherlands; Istanbul, Turkey; Turin, Italy; Toronto, Canada; London, England.

International Business Conduct Training: Germany, India, and China.

United States Department of State: Global Leadership Program.

International Center of Indiana: International Leadership Event Host.

Extensive travel and business experience in Europe and Asia.

CORPORATE AWARDS

PharmaBrands

Leadership Honors Award, 2012; Outstanding Contribution Award, 2008, 2009; Spot Stock Option Award, 2008, 2009

Recognition of Excellence: Customer Satisfaction Award, 2008; Collaboration Award, 2007

Essence of Pulmozyme Award, 2006, 2007; Orphan Product Advocate of the Year, 2007; Citation for Advancing Patient Care, 2006; Pulmozyme Sales Excellence Award, 2006, 2007, 2008; Outstanding Sales Achievement Award, 2009; Program Pull-Through Award, 2007

Biogen Corporate Account Manager/Training Manager

President's Club Award, 2001, 2002; Spot Stock Option Award, 2000, 2002, 2003; Innovations in Patient Care Award, 2001, 2002, 2003; Leadership Resource Award, 2000

Biogen Regional Account Manager

Innovations in Patient Care Award, 2000; All Star Award, 1998, 2000; President's Club Award, 1998, 1999

Biogen District Sales Manager

All Star Award, 1996 (x 2), 1998; President's Club Award, 1996, 1997, 1998; Regional Sales Leader, 1997

Biogen Professional Sales Representative

President's Club Award, 1992, 1994, 1994, 1996; All Star Award, 1994 (x2), 1995 (x3), 1996 (x2); District Sales Leader, 1992, 1993, 1994; Corporate Accounts Retail Partnership Award, 1993

COMMUNITY/VOLUNTEER ACTIVITIES

International Center of Indiana: International Leadership Volunteer Event Host (4 years)

United States Department of State: Global Leadership Program

CAROLINE MULFORD

(860) 243-4345 › c.mulford@att.net › Greenwich, Connecticut

DIRECTOR OF OPERATIONS
Healthcare Management

PERFORMANCE PROFILE

Accomplished, results-driven healthcare leader with 20+ years' experience in healthcare service operations management, improvement, and redesign. Focused on optimizing healthcare operations through continuous quality improvement, lean methodologies, systems thinking, and reengineering to increase efficiency, productivity, quality, and patient satisfaction.

Effective coach and mentor with proven success in building and managing high-performing teams as evidenced by low turnover, high satisfaction, and excellent customer service. Led numerous interdisciplinary healthcare teams in system-wide projects that substantially increased revenue, decreased costs, and improved patient satisfaction. Skilled communicator capable of interacting with all organizational levels including C-suite, physicians, other staff.

LEADERSHIP COMPETENCIES

- *In/Outpatient Consulting*
- *Strategic Planning*
- *Lean Healthcare*
- *Operations Management*
- *Healthcare Consulting*

- *Process & Access Improvement*
- *Revenue Cycle Management*
- *Manager & Team Development*
- *Physician Practice Management*
- *Call Center Management*

- *Policy Creation & Implementation*
- *Efficiency & Productivity Improvement*
- *Labor Utilization*
- *Project Management*
- *Metric Development & Measurement*

PROFESSIONAL EXPERIENCE

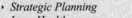

HEALTHCARE OPTIMIZATION CONSULTANTS, RYE, NY   2014-Present
Offer consulting services to physicians and healthcare systems to facilitate and improve operational processes.

Healthcare Operations Consultant

Partner with physicians and healthcare systems to design and implement an integrated healthcare service model that delivers value to the market. Manage mergers, affiliations, and operations within the physicians' practice or health system. Provide analysis, improvement, standardization, and implementation of optimized operational processes. Develop and implement performance metrics.

- Currently working with a 4-physician specialty group to manage a merger with other specialty practices.

- Providing consulting expertise on pre-planning, compatibility/feasibility studies, operational improvement analysis, governance, capital requirement, practice management system evaluation, compensation, benefits, payer and vendor negotiations, locations, and implementation.

HOWARD BAKER MEDICAL CENTER, NORWALK, CT   2002-2014
Nationally recognized academic medical center and *U.S. News & World Report* Top 100 Hospital with 1.9M outpatient visits, 54,000 hospital discharges, 12,000 employees, and $1B in revenue.
Director, Vanderbilt Medical Group Operations   2005-2014
Administrator, Howard Baker Medical Group Network Practices   2002-2004

Director, Vanderbilt Medical Group (VMG) Operations   2005-2014

Designed, implemented, and managed centralized outpatient registration and scheduling operations to ensure accurate, timely, and efficient access while promoting a patient- and customer-focused environment. Led all aspects of call center operations including establishment of design parameters, performance standards, customer satisfaction, cost containment, compliance measurement, and reporting.

- Implemented and managed centralized patient registration for the entire physician group comprised of over 80 clinics and 700 physicians.

- Conceived and implemented process and technology improvements that led to 270% productivity increase, annual cost avoidance of $5M, a 300% reduction in registration denials, and a <1% call abandonment rate for 300,000 annual calls.

- Earned several promotions and assumed new responsibilities including managing Guest Services, Central Appointment Call Center, Operator Services, Nurse Triage, and Space & Facilities.

- Led large system-wide projects such as revenue cycle initiatives (point of service collections), centralized access for referring physician appointments, hospital discharge appointments, automated appointment reminders, and outpatient referral assistance, all on time, within budget, and with positive ROI.

- Developed and maintained a culture in departments and call centers that resulted in an employee satisfaction in the 95th percentile and low turnover rate of 5%.

Administrator, Howard Baker Medical Group Network Practices   2002-2004

Oversaw administration of 8 multi-specialty physician-based satellite clinics including Primary Care, General Pediatrics, Dermatology, Neurology, Gastroenterology, and Sports Medicine. Led planning, implementation, coordination, and evaluation of practice activities. Developed, implemented, and administered 2 new practice startups. Managed physician contracts, practice budget, new workflow improvements, policies, and procedures.

- Identified and implemented operational improvements in a pediatric group practice that resulted in a positive net contribution of $120,000 in the first 10 months.

- Implemented policies and procedures in a dermatology practice that improved collection rate from 50% to 64% in 6 months.

- Led successful implementation of 2 new outpatient clinics on time and on budget.

JAKE RYAN GROUP, LTD., NEW HAVEN, CT   1997-2002
Premier, Inc. drives the transformation to high-quality, cost-effective healthcare through a collaborative alliance of hospital systems. Premier collects data on 2.5M real-time clinical transactions daily and approximately $40B in annual purchasing data.

Senior Consultant

Provided operational improvement consulting services to hospitals and multi-specialty clinics. Participated in all aspects of the consulting engagements including project management, staff supervision, client interaction and relationships, advanced data research, presentation of results to senior executives, and assisted clients with development of work plans. Served as subject matter expert on projects and drove all aspects of an engagement from problem identification to strategic implementation.

- Provided labor and workforce management consulting using proprietary software (Operations Outlook). Identified savings of over $400,000 in labor costs for 2 hospitals.

- Completed an operational assessment of a 5-physician primary care group. Identified over $250,000 in savings. The practice realized a $10,000 monthly revenue increase after only 3 months.

- Led Occupational Health strategy project for a hospital system that resulted in $277,000 net contribution margin in 3 years compared to a historical loss of $50,000 annually.

TED BRYCE CLINIC FOUNDATION, NEW HAVEN, CT   1992-1996
A 400-physician academic multi-specialty clinic and national leader in medical research with over 6,000 employees and 600,000 outpatient visits. Ranked first in quality care of Gulf Coast region.

Administrative Director, Plastic & Reconstructive Surgery   1994-1996

Performed administrative management of the Plastic & Reconstructive Surgery departments, including planning, staffing, staff development, budgeting, marketing, production, and distribution.

- Developed and implemented a business development campaign that targeted high-end spas for potential cosmetic surgery cases. Resulted in a 10% increase in cases in one year.

EDUCATION

Vanderbilt University, Owen Graduate School of Management, Nashville, TN
Healthcare Management, Advanced Certificate   2012

Columbia Business School, New York, NY
MBA, Business Administration   1998

State University of New York, Cortland, NY
BS, Industrial and Systems Engineering   1994

PROFESSIONAL MEMBERSHIPS & VOLUNTEER EXPERIENCE

Medical Group Management Association (MGMA), Member
Big Sisters Organization, Mentor

DARCY BINGLEY

Marblehead, Massachusetts 01945 | 339.243.4345 | d.bingley@gmail.com

Linked **in** profile

DIRECTOR OF STRATEGIC ALLIANCES & BUSINESS DEVELOPMENT | ACCOUNT EXECUTIVE | SENIOR MANAGER

Driving innovation, fueling growth, and eliminating waste while introducing energy-saving and sustainability solutions for multinational and government clients.

Energy consulting executive who positions organizations for success via long-term sustainability plans, state-of-the-art solutions/products, and streamlined business processes. Natural relationship builder adept at cultivating and maintaining mutually beneficial partnerships with high-tech, manufacturing, and government clients. Evaluate client needs to formulate strategic energy-saving and sustainability plans, leveraging industrial process and industry expertise to navigate and influence energy policy decisions, curb energy consumption, and reduce energy costs.

Solutions-focused innovator known for pioneering design and launch of groundbreaking software products that provide clients with transparent energy consumption data and support continuous process improvement across quality, throughput, waste, costs, and sustainability. Skillfully identify, secure, and execute complex, multimillion-dollar initiatives, ensuring completion within strict time, budget, and quality requirements. Passionate about protecting environment for public enjoyment. Hold HSPD-12 Clearance from Department of Homeland Security.

PROFESSIONAL SKILLS

Business Development	Business Partnering	Cost Control
Account Management	Lean Manufacturing	Operations Management
Client Relationship Development	Budget Management ($25M)	Team Building & Leadership
Strategic Business Planning	Needs Assessment	Proposal Development
Product Development & Launch	Investment Analysis	Negotiations
Project Management	Business & Financial Analysis	Renewable Energy
Process Re-engineering	Forecasting & Modeling	Regulatory Compliance

PERFORMANCE HIGHLIGHTS

➤ Drove new and existing business for Enovity via developing and promoting enterprise software package/maintenance module for smart buildings that was deployed across 73 facilities; energy dashboard module is forecasted to launch across 34 additional facilities in Q12015, generating energy-saving opportunities for clients.

➤ Identified more than $6M in utility/gas savings for clients while generating equal amount of revenue for Enovity through management of program focused on identifying natural gas energy savings for industrial clients.

➤ Increased facility runtimes 25% and reduced waste 15% for Discovery Foods' California-based manufacturing plant via optimizing process improvements, earning recognition as Process Engineering Expert.

➤ Currently in strategic partnership with federal government to achieve 30% energy consumption reduction by FY2015.

PROFESSIONAL EXPERIENCE

Wickham Tech Systems, Inc. | Boston, MA   2008 – Present
$32M+ consulting firm specializing in commissioning and energy efficiency. Entered into strategic partnership with Orix (Japan) in 2013, providing sustainability and energy efficiency consulting for multinational companies.

DIRECTOR – TECHNICAL SERVICES
Advanced to oversee vertical line of business focused on building systems integration while managing firm's largest account (General Services Administration). Monitor market and identify trends to propose new product/technical solutions, attract new clients, and secure new accounts, managing all aspects of project life cycle for long-term, high-caliber initiatives. Lead 10-member team in ensuring customer satisfaction and retention.

DIRECTOR – TECHNICAL SERVICES, continued

Formulate business/corporate strategies for key accounts. Collaborate with senior staff to cross-sell products, driving overall company growth. Deliver presentations on integrated building systems at industry conferences.

➢ Consistently maintained between $3M and $5M in profits of existing accounts (25% of company revenue), delivering average 12% EBITDA, through cultivating solid, mutually beneficial alliances with federal sector clients.
➢ Personally generated 10% of all company-wide sales and played pivotal role in delivering 20% revenue growth within new and existing accounts.
➢ Established company standard for number of energy site audits executed within 60 days after spearheading on-time, on-budget delivery of $800K government project with 50 site locations in 60-day timeframe.
➢ Secured $500K+ in sales from enterprise software solution tool for energy and facility management.
➢ Developed and implemented key performance metrics for multimillion-dollar projects, tracking profit margins, budgets, and forecasted revenue for initiatives.

Bennet Foods Corporation | Plains, NJ   2007 – 2008
Middle-market food manufacturing company under private equity ownership. Sold to Windsor Quality Food Company in 2010.

PROJECT & PROCESS ENGINEERING MANAGER – PRODUCT DEVELOPMENT & ENGINEERING
Personally tapped to streamline and optimize existing processes in order to drive profitability and growth. Proposed solutions to key decision makers (private equity partners), developing and presenting financial models to gain authorization on required capital funds. Designed solutions based on statistical process control models. Controlled project budgets of up to $5M. Participated in board meetings and weekly meetings with CFO.

➢ Played integral role in transforming highly manual, limited Texas processing plant into automated, efficient facility, increasing yield 50%, cutting costs 50%, reducing waste 10%, and enabling plant to meet 6-month product launch deadline and high customer demands.
➢ Enhanced product quality while driving development of new products and managing capital projects valued at up to $5M.
➢ Contributed to developing sustainable packaging practices and processes to meet client's (Walmart) sustainability goals through partnership with supply chain staff to inspect packaging materials.

Catherine De Bourg Wineries | Washingtonville, NY   2004 – 2007
Largest exporter of New York wines.

SENIOR PROCESS ENGINEER – CORPORATE ENGINEERING
Brought onboard as trusted advisor, incorporating Lean Six Sigma principles to spearhead capital projects and process improvement initiatives at satellite wineries in Orange and Niagara counties. Liaised between operations, satellite wineries, and corporate engineering in development of projects, formulation of project budgets (up to $25M), and proposal of forecasted results. Served as active participant on Gallo Committee, bringing sustainable practices to wineries. Supervised 2 control technicians in delivery of various projects.

➢ Optimized critical wine-making processes, achieving 25% throughput increase, accelerating processing time, and enhancing product quality through institution of rigorous statistical process control and Six Sigma–based principles.
➢ Strengthened communication between corporate engineering and satellite wineries by engaging company owners, corporate, and local winery teams, introducing company-wide operations consistency.

Collins Logistics, Inc. | Pittsburgh, PA   2000 – 2004

Specialty electronic-grade chemical manufacturing firm serving multinational clients, such as Intel.

PROCESS & RELIABILITY ENGINEERING MANAGER
Hired as staff engineer and earned promotion to manager within 2 years after applying analytical approach to process design and developing processes to meet demanding customer requirements. Directed day-to-day operations for 24-hour chemical processing facility, ensuring that operations were maintained, yielded necessary throughput and quality, and met strict customer standards. Supervised up to 8 plant staff and indirectly managed 70+ employees across shifts. Ensured safe operations, mitigating risk exposure to plant personnel and nearby community.

➤ Enhanced processing efficiency while sustaining product quality by spearheading process engineering efforts.
➤ Realized 25% reduction in unplanned maintenance downtime and improved product quality by as much as 1,000% through coordination of processing plant transformations and capital projects.
➤ Formulated hundreds of SOPs to address stringent quality and compliance standards within 6-month period while managing plant's largest division.

EARLIER CAREER

Austen Oil Group | RESERVOIR ENGINEER – OPERATIONS & ENGINEERING | 1998 – 2000

EDUCATION

Master of Business Administration, Business Administration & Entrepreneurship
Boston University
Master of Business Administration, Business Administration & Finance (Honors)
Brown University
Master of Science, Chemical Engineering
Clarkson University
Bachelor of Science, Chemical Engineering (cum laude)
State University of New York

EXTRACURRICULAR ACTIVITIES

➤ Member of the New England Ballroom Dance association & Dance USA
➤ Competitive ballroom dancer, regional champion, social dances, and current MA state champion, Foxtrot

References available upon request

Patrice Evans MBA

Anaheim, CA 92812
657.436.6668 patrice.evans@att.net

DISASTER RECOVERY & BUSINESS CONTINUITY PLANNING • INTERNAL CONTROLS

Linked in.

Disaster Recovery and Business Continuity Planning Coordinator

Professional Profile

➢ Business Continuity and Internal Controls professional with strong accounting experience across diverse industries, including mass media, manufacturing, software development, and financial services.

➢ Director of Policies and Controls skilled in developing and implementing enterprise-wide business continuity and disaster recovery strategies and solutions. Expertise in business continuity planning, analysis, implementation, training, exercises, and continuous process improvements to ensure the safety of employees and the protection of intellectual property and essential resources, functions, and business services.

Professional Skills

Business Continuity Management (BCM)	Financial Accounting	Leadership & Teambuilding
Business Continuity Planning (BCP)	Financial Analysis & Reporting	C-Level Communications & Presentations
Business Impact Assessments (BIA)	Risk Mitigation Strategies	Incident / Crisis Communication Program
Internal Controls Management	Project Management	BCM Awareness & Training
Business Process Mapping (BPM)	Resource Allocation	Vendor Relationship Management
Crisis Management / Disaster Recovery (DR)	Process Improvements	Analytical & Problem-Solving Skills
Policies, Procedures, & Systems Development	Productivity Optimization	Creativity, Integrity, Initiative, & Drive

Computer Skills

Proficient Microsoft Office Suite: Word, Excel, PowerPoint, Access, and Outlook, Microsoft Office 365, Visio, and Project. PeopleSoft Financials, SharePoint, and Essbase.

Performance Highlights

- Director of Policies and Controls at Condé Nast who championed and influenced the inclusion of business continuity and disaster recovery protocols into functional strategies for this global media company with $1 billion in annual revenues.
  - Collaborated with technology team to develop a business continuity wiki application on the CN corporate intranet. Managed essential informatics for senior management and response team during a crisis or incident.
  - Led the development and implementation of a new Vendor Portal application, which led to a reduction of 3 FTEs from a staff of 6, yielded $142,000 in annual savings, and reduced the average cycle time from 2.5 weeks to 4 days.
- Plant Controller at Repauno Products, LLC, who joined this startup company and established the company's initial accounting system and internal controls. Directed and coached staff members in setting up accounts payable, order entry, customer services, purchasing, and payroll functions. Successfully led migration from ISO 9002:1994 to ISO 9001:2000, resulting in the company being the first producer of sodium nitrite in the USA to attain this quality certification.

Professional Experience

C LIFESTYLES MAGAZINE GROUP, Anaheim, CA	2003 – 2016

Privately held global mass media company with portfolio of industry-leading print, video, and digital brands includes *Coastal Living, C-Magazine, California Home Style, and CA Weekender* among others.

Director, Policies & Controls	2011 – 2016
Senior Manager, Policies & Controls	2008 – 2011
Manager, Accounting	2003 – 2008

continued

Director, Policies & Controls
2011 – 2016

Reported to Senior VP – Corporate Controller. Managed business continuity, ensuring that all departments within Accounting Services maintained processes and procedures that were cost effective, efficient, and deterred fraud.

- Collaborated with IT and senior business leaders to create the Initial Business Continuity Plan for C Lifestyles Magazine Group.
- Created a checklist that helped guide the response team, created testing protocols, and established a steering committee and core team.
- Led and facilitated corporate response efforts for designated incidents/crisis situations. Monitored and evaluated BCP tests and reported findings to management.
- Chosen to lead newly formed Vendor Controls group that provided oversight of all vendors, onboarded new vendors, monitored changes to existing vendor information, and prevented fraud in a vendor master file containing almost 200,000 vendors. Managed the business/technology team charged with developing and implementing the ~$70,000 vendor portal application, which came in on time and 7% under budget, which saved ~$5,000.

Senior Manager, Policies & Controls
2008 – 2011

Selected to lead newly created Policies & Controls group that ensured all accounting services departments had adequate policies and internal controls in place for all critical business processes.
- Coordinated all business continuity planning (BCP) efforts company wide.
- Collaborated with auditors on Internal Controls audit report and contributed accounting expertise to special projects in conjunction with the brands and corporate groups.
- Created and developed "The Business Director Policies & Controls Guidelines" Document. With the Corporate Controller, coauthored and co-presented "The Business of Content" presentation series, which was delivered to over 250 employees.
- Saved the company $120,000 by reducing headcount by 2 FTEs.

Manager, Accounting
2003 – 2008

Led accounting team that captured and reported financial information for the company's California Home Style, digital, and intercompany operations.
- Integrated California Home Style's company's accounting into C Lifestyles. Learned all of California Home Style's accounting practices and integrated them into CL's, performing monthly accounting close and related balance sheet analysis.
- Performed account analysis, reviewed staff work (journal entries and account analysis), and handled ad hoc requests.
- Trained and mentored 6 staff accountants.

SUNSHINE PRODUCTS, Los Angeles, CA
1999 – 2003

Specialty chemical manufacturer and distributor of sodium nitrite, a chemical used by diverse industries such as automotive (OEM) parts and food processors. Sunshine Products, formerly a division of US Salt, was purchased by General Chemical Corporation in 2006. At the time, the company had ~$10 million in annual revenue and 23 employees.

Plant Controller / ISO Management Representative

Reported to the General Manager. Managed all aspects of accounting, finance, and logistics, as well as quality and support services, including purchasing, production planning, quality assurance, and human resources.
- Served as a liaison to corporate holding company for all information services and accounting/finance needs.
- Led successful migration from ISO 9002:1994 standard to the new ISO 9001:2000 standard. The company was the first producer of sodium nitrite to attain this quality certification.

HOUSE OF TEXTILES, INC., Los Angeles, CA
1993 – 1999

Manufacturer of fabrics, wall coverings, and decorative home furnishings with ~$45 million in annual revenue and 225 employees.

Manager, Accounting	1997 – 1999
Senior Cost Analyst	1995 – 1997
Manager, Financial Projects	1993 – 1995

House of Textiles, continued

As Accounting Manager, reported to VP – Corporate Controller. Managed all accounting functions, including issuance of financial statements and coordinating cross-functional initiatives through 5 division presidents.

- Determined criteria for new automated general ledger system. Evaluated several systems and determined the best option. Presented findings for executive approval and installed new system in record time, resulting in improving monthly closing cycle by 3 business days, providing better information, and reducing user complaints of inaccuracies by 65%.
- Realized $250,000 in productivity gains by evaluating, selecting, and installing an activity-based costing system that provided fast, accurate cost-per-data for tracking overhead expense, which improved processing time by 50% and transmission time by 75%.
- Coached, mentored, and rebuilt a cohesive and effective 6-person team of accounting professionals, effectively reversing a trend toward a competitive collection of individuals pulling in different directions. Fostered a collaborative and productive workplace environment and built solid business relationships.
- Major areas of work performed included monthly, quarterly, and year-end financial statements, monthly close process, special projects, and review of staff work (journal entries and account reconciliations).

Education

Master of Business Administration (MBA), Colorado State University
Bachelor of Business Administration (BBA), Fort Lewis College

Professional Certifications

Certified Business Manager (CBM)   2003
Certified Lead Auditor – ISO 9001:2000 Quality Systems
Certified Internal Auditor – ISO 9000:1994 Quality Systems

Hobbies & Interests

Golf and International Travel

Superior references available on request

Charles Chalmers

Linked in profile

Manhattan, NY 11658   GalleryDirector@earthlink.net   (212) 555-1432

Gallery Director/Curator

Performance Summary

My professional life is focused on art in all it embraces: drawing, painting, sculpture, photography, cinema, video, audio, performance and digital art, art history, and criticism.

My personal life is similarly committed. Recently relocated from Manhattan, I intend to make a contribution to the *** Arts community commensurate with my knowledge, enthusiasm, and sensibilities.

Professional Competencies

✓ Art History	✓ Installation of Art	✓ Recruitment & Selection
✓ Art Theory	✓ Space Fluidity	✓ Private Collectors
✓ Art Research	✓ Hang/Light/Label	✓ Catering
✓ Art Communities	✓ Themed/Sequenced	✓ Graphics
✓ Alumni Networks	✓ Space Reconfiguration	✓ Photoshop
✓ Artist Networks	✓ Dynamic Dialogue	✓ PR
✓ Art Handlers	✓ Social Networking	✓ Intercultural Exchanges

Professional Highlights

Art History
Thorough knowledge of art history from caves of Lascaux through current artists such as Bruce Nauman, Jessica Stockholder, and Luc Tuymans. Film history from Lumiere Brothers to Almodovar. Current with key critical art and film theory. Ongoing workshops and lectures with the likes of Matthew Barney, Louise Bourgeois, and Andy Goldsworthy.

Research New Artists
Connected to cutting-edge art and artists through involvement with the art communities and galleries of New York and Boston and the faculty, student, and alumni networks of RISD, Columbia, Boston Museum School, New England School of Art & Design, and now Mass Art. Twenty years of Manhattan gallery openings and networking with artists at MOMA, PS1, Guggenheim, Whitney, Metropolitan, and Film Forum. Attend International Center for Photography workshops and lectures.

PR Materials
Energizing invitations, comprehensive press kits, illustrated press releases, and artist binder materials. Sensitive to placing art in historical/cultural context. Photoshop.

Management
Fourteen years' art staff management experience, including curriculum development. Responsible for art instructors, art handlers, and maintenance crews, as well as working with printers, catering, and graphic arts staff.

continued

296

Professional Experience

1994-2005 Chair of Visual Arts, The Green Briar School
Curriculum development, portfolio preparation, internal and external monthly shows, theater sets, monthly video news show. Taught art history and all the studio arts, managed staff of three.

1989-2004 President, Art Workshops
Private art studio and art history curriculum, staff of four. Private groups to Manhattan museums and gallery tours.

1989-Present Freelance artist, photographer, and editor
Highlights from the *sublime* to the *ridiculous* include: Taught photography at Trinity School, Manhattan; photographer for the Ramones; editor of *Pioneer*, insurance industry trade magazine; assistant to Claudia Weill, documentary filmmaker, director of *Girlfriends*.

Education

MFA. Magna cum laude. Columbia University, 1988
Awards: Forman Prize for film criticism
Taught undergraduate Intro to Film, under Milos Forman and Andre Bazin.

Subscriptions
Art in America, Art News, Artforum, New York Times, Parkett, Sight & Sound, Film Comment, Modern Painters.

Memberships
MOMA/PS1, Whitney Museum of American Art, Guggenheim, Metropolitan Museum of Art, DIA.

Superior references available

Rem Koolhaus

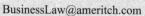

Sunnyvale, CA   408.555.5555   BusinessLaw@ameritch.com

GENERAL COUNSEL
Technology Industries – Global M&A Expertise
"A rare combination of legal and business acumen, intellectual agility, and focus"

Performance Summary

Twenty-five-year track record of success in delivering legal, strategic, and business results for companies in technology industries. Encyclopedic knowledge of the international business and legal landscape. Corporate strategy & transactions expert with extensive global experience in M&A, JV, licensing, vendor agreements, public/private placements, divestitures, and other initiatives.

Counsel and business advisor to C-suite, owners, and Board members. Strong general management and operational skills. Financially disciplined and focused on the company and stakeholders. Seasoned dealmaker and formidable negotiator — expert in handling complex financial, business, and cultural matters, including sixty M&A and divestures.

Core Skills

- IPO
- Patents
- Joint Ventures
- Licensing
- Shareholder Value
- Risk Management
- Divestitures
- JV

- M&A
- Litigation, Initiation
- Regulatory Compliance
- IP Management
- Operational
- Labor Law
- Board Advisory
- Investor Relations

- Growth and Exit Strategy
- Public & Private/Debt & Equity
- Startup Strategy & Capital
- Placements
- Pre/Post M&A
- Outside Counsel Management
- Executive Decision Support
- Sarbanes-Oxley

Technologies

- Global Telecoms
- Connectivity
- Managed Networks
- Security

- IT
- Hosting
- Software Licenses
- Global Joint Ventures

- Internet
- Technology Transfers
- Network/Voice-based apps
- Technology Licensing

CORPORATE EXPERIENCE

Silicon Associates, Mountain View, CA   2008 to Present
Specialists in Corporate Strategy and Development, Capital Raising, Corporate Governance, Growth Management, Transactions
MANAGING DIRECTOR

Executive in charge of all aspects of business operations – business development, P&L, contract negotiation, client deliverables, and engagement management. Competitively differentiated by early and continued collaboration with C-suite client executives in overall enterprise strategy to support legal structures for client growth initiatives.

Growth and Exit Strategies

- Partnered with executive team of $15 million software services company to deliver exit strategy and clear path toward strategic value enhancements.

- Advised a $35 million business services firm on growth strategies and exit options.
- **Capital Raising** – Advised and participated in private equity fundraising for an early-stage Brazilian agro venture.
- **Startup Strategy & Capital Raising** – Delivered in-depth legal, growth, business, and corporate development support to start up "green" state-of-the-art European data center provider, leading negotiations with private equity participants and advising on acquisition strategy.

SpeedNet, INC., Reston, Portland, WA, London, Chenmai, Beijing   1998 to 2008
VC-Backed Startup – Internet Business Communications Provider in Connectivity,
Hosting, Security, Managed Networks, and Related Professional Services
SVP & GENERAL COUNSEL – CORPORATE SECRETARY   2002 to 2008
VP & GENERAL COUNSEL – CORPORATE SECRETARY   1998 to 2002

Fifth employee hired and key member of the senior executive team – recruited to contribute business acumen, commercial insights, and general counsel services related to startup operations, growth transactions, and exit strategy. Involved with all enterprise-level vision, strategy decisions.
Managed department of 6 legal professionals supporting cross-functional business operations, corporate governance, legal affairs, transactions, SEC reporting, and regulatory compliance in the US and 15 countries. IP portfolio, deal sourcing/corporate transactions, contracts/agreements, risk management, regulatory compliance.

Legal Services & Corporate Development Management – Strategies, Transactions, & Results
- **Capital Raising & IPO** – Directed Series C–round private placement of $130 million equity investment. Principal in structure and execution of IPO – diligence, preparation of filings, road show, dual listing on Nasdaq National Market and Amsterdam stock exchanges – resulting in $330+ million in net proceeds to the company.
- **Corporate Governance** – Developed and rolled out corporate governance policies and annual compliance program to business operations spanning 15 countries. Implemented Sarbanes-Oxley policies throughout organization.
- **M&A, Divestiture, & Post M&A Transition/Integration** – Led due diligence, negotiations, and closing of 35 corporate acquisitions – Internet services providers and hosting companies – in 15 countries. Directed key aspects of post-close integration and transition, including realization of synergies, governance, brand, and culture. Managed bidding process, negotiations, and divestiture of non-value-added operations in 6 countries, enabling company to reduce quarterly cash burn by 80% and focus on core markets.
- **Investor Relations Strategy** – Achieved strategic turnaround and growth strategy (2002 through 2004) while protecting investor confidence with a proactive outreach program. Addressed potential de-listing by developing and presenting recuperative strategy first to Board, then to Nasdaq.
- **Exit Strategy Planning & Execution** – Called by Board to address liquidity crisis. Teamed with the COO to formulate the exit strategy. Negotiated several auxiliary deals – including sale of non-core operating unit within 8 days – to produce operating revenues. Led ultimate auction process to optimize capital return to shareholders.

Distinctions
- Drove growth through international market penetration and strategic acquisitions to exceed objectives of $0 to $86 million in 24 months. Reduced cash burn rate by 80%, from $25+ million to less than $5 million per quarter. Decreased D&O/E&O premiums by $900,000 *p.a.*
- Served as the company's second-ranking officer in global business and legal matters 2003 to 2008.
- Assumed direct accountability for investor relations and corporate development functions.

Sprint, Washington, D.C.   1994 to 1998
Global pioneer in Telecommunications Solutions, Equipment, and Services
DIRECTOR – VENTURES & ALLIANCES – Sprint Corporate   1996 to 1998
SENIOR COUNSEL – LAW & PUBLIC POLICY   1996
SENIOR ATTORNEY – LAW & PUBLIC POLICY   1994 to 1995

Sprint Mass Markets Group – Legal
Provided legal counsel and business support to key areas of operations – IT systems/product development, marketing strategy, sales tools, software licensing, contracts – and advised senior-level management on transactional, IP, and regulatory matters.

- **M&A** – Managed project to identify and track synergy opportunities – valued at $1+ billion per year.
- **Global Joint Venture** – Managed Sprint's interest in CCI ($1.2 billion global telecom joint venture) with British Telecom. Team lead in negotiations to unwind complex alliance structure.
- **Intellectual Property** – Led legal team in analysis and resolution of key IP ownership issues between three global Telecom companies.
- **Technology Licensing** – Secured substantial reduction in desktop licensing fees through new $23 million multi-year agreement with Microsoft.
- **Pre-/Post-Merger Business Transition & Integration** – Member of merger, transition, and implementation team dealing with organizational, financial, commercial, and regulatory issues. Collaborated in formulating post-merger internal trading program and commercial model.

Distinctions
- Recruited by the VP Ventures & Alliances to serve at Sprint headquarters.
- Promoted from Senior Attorney to Senior Counsel within one year of hire.
- Two-time winner of the Sprint Circle of Excellence Award for contributions to Sprint Mass Markets.
- Contributed critical legal counsel and commercial support to new product launches – Sprint Paging/Internet/1-800-Music– representing millions in annual sales revenue.
- Led Sprint policy formulation in addressing online copyright issues, software piracy, online hosting of pornography.
- Structured and negotiated long-term exclusive affiliation agreements with third parties.

LAW FIRM EXPERIENCE

SUE, GRABBIT & RUNNE, Washington, D.C.   1988 to 1994
International Law Firm – Specialization in Corporate Transactions for Public &
Private Companies
SENIOR ASSOCIATE
Corporate transactional practice, including financing, acquisitions, dispositions, and mergers for private and publicly listed clients. Originally recruited by Rogovin Huge & Schiller, the New York– based international law firm that merged with Sue Runne in 1990.

SLAUGHTER & REDINGER, P.C., Charlottesville, VA   1985 to 1988
International Law Firm – Specialization European and South American Inbound
Investments and Domestic Legal Issues
SENIOR ASSOCIATE
Provided commercial real estate, corporate and partnership, tax, litigation, immigration, and securities law advice, and M&A and private placement services. Early achievements include pursuing litigation appeal and arguing before 4th Circuit Federal Court of Appeals, handling solo a jury trial, and negotiating major commercial real estate project agreements.

EDUCATION

J.D. and M.A. – Foreign Affairs   1985
Elected, Order of the Coif – Member, Editorial Board, Virginia Journal of
International Law
UNIVERSITY OF VIRGINIA – School of Law and Graduate School of Arts &
Sciences, Charlottesville, VA

B.A. with honors – Philosophy   1981
Magna cum laude – Elected, Phi Beta Kappa Andrew Mutch Scholar to Aberdeen
University, Aberdeen, Scotland – Awarded St. Andrew's Society Scholarship
BUCKNELL UNIVERSITY, Lewisburg, PA

PROFESSIONAL & BOARD AFFILIATIONS

Association for Corporate Growth (ACG)
Association of Corporate Counsel (ACC)
Member of California, D.C. Bars, Massachusetts Bar (pending)

Superior references

Steven Christopher, PHR

Newark, DE 19702
302.234.2434 |steve.christopher@att.net

Linked in profile

HUMAN RESOURCES MANAGEMENT • TALENT ACQUISITION
SUCCESSION PLANNING • CHANGE MANAGEMENT

Professional Profile

Senior Human Resources Manager and Certified Professional in Human Resources (PHR) with 13+ years in the hospitality industry. Proven ability to structure HR strategy that aligns with corporate goals/objectives and provides tactical direction for the achievement of key initiatives to recruit, select, train, retain, and motivate top talent through the development of premier compensation programs, improved onboarding, and employee training, coaching, and succession planning.

Professional Skills

Multisite Human Resources Management	Employment Law (EEO, ADA, FMLA, WOTC)	Communications / Presentations
Strategic Planning & Budgeting	State & Federal Regulatory Compliance	Managerial Training on HR Matters
HR Policies, Procedures, & Programs	Workforce Planning / Restructuring	Staff Training & Development
Organizational Development	HR Audits / Succession Planning	Employee Engagement & Motivation
Talent Acquisition & Retention	Online Recruiting / Social Media Recruiting	Employee Performance Evaluation
Compensation & Benefits Administration	Pre-Employment Screenings	Critical Thinking & Problem Solving
Employee Relationship Management	Employee Onboarding & Employee Retention	Conflict Resolution & Teambuilding
Automated HR Records Management	Employee Separations & Reductions	Special Events Coordination

Computer Skills

Applicant Tracking Systems | Talent Management Systems | Microsoft Office Suite: Word, Excel, PowerPoint, and Outlook
Google+, Google Hangouts, Skype, GoToMeeting, Facebook, and LinkedIn

Performance Highlights

➢ **Trusted Advisor to Executive Leadership** with experience counseling/coaching business leaders and operations managers regarding employee relations issues. Demonstrated record of reducing labor costs while keeping non-union shops' HR functions running smoothly while complying with local, state, and federal employment laws and regulations.

➢ **Senior HR Manager** with demonstrated success designing/implementing employee orientation programs and employee engagement survey processes (reporting results and developing action plans for improving employee engagement and productivity).

➢ **Corporate HR Program Manager** who leads with purpose, genuinely cares about people, holds employees to high standards of performance, and influences positive outcomes for the company's success.

Professional Experience

CHRISTOPHER CAPITAL
Human Resources Manager

New Castle, DE
2012 – Present

Owner/Operator of 120 Dairy Queen franchises in Delaware, Maryland, and New Jersey, serving all of the I-95 corridor exits, employing 4,900 people in 4 states with annual revenue of $75 million.

- Advise executive leaders, senior managers, and general managers in the areas of employment laws, regulatory compliance, employee relations, workforce development, and succession planning.
- Manage human resources activities for 62 restaurants and 1,200 employees. Manage HR programs, including compensation, benefits, and staffing. Supervise 2 HR specialists/generalists and 1 administrative assistant.
- Partner with operations managers to recruit, train, and develop exempt-level workforce. Guide and improve the employee performance management process, including job specs/requirements, employee appraisal process, staff ranking, individual development plans, compensation, promotions, and recognitions.
- Develop and guide the HR team to ensure overall effectiveness and achievement of departmental and company goals.
- Provide ongoing investigation of various HR issues throughout the multi-unit corporation to create a positive workplace environment. Administer compensation for exempt and non-exempt employees.

Notable Achievements:
- Reduced hourly employee turnover by 25% by developing/implementing best practices in managerial coaching and employee relationship management.

302

continued

- Saved the company an estimated $577,000 by aggressively fighting unemployment compensation claims.
- Avoided fines during Immigration and Customs Enforcement audit of I-9s, as well as U.S. Department of Labor Wage and Hour audit through proactive compliance training.
- Redesigned and implemented interviewing process for non-exempt employees, resulting in onboarding of productive and loyal employees.
- Developed and implemented anti-harassment training program to exempt-level employees.
- Rewrote all job descriptions.
- Conducted wage and salary survey for both exempt and non-exempt employees.

EMERALD PRINCESS RIVERBOAT CASINO
Ocean City, MD
2007 – 2012
Human Resources Supervisor

Emerald Princess is a riverboat-style casino and hotel with 500 slot machines, 10 tables/games, and 200 hotel rooms.

- Facilitated employee relations programs for all 600 employees, including mediating conversations between management and employees, investigating incidents, facilitating the peer review program, overseeing the proper termination of employees, and scrutinizing all corrective disciplinary measures.
- Managed the Human Resources Training Department to ensure that new hires received federally mandated training.
- Developed and implemented HR policies throughout the corporation. Designed and implemented the peer review board.
- Served as the Director on Duty in the absence of the Human Resources Director.
- Planned, organized, and budgeted for employee-related events such as holiday parties and recognition ceremonies.
- Conducted wage and salary survey for exempt and non-exempt employees.

Notable Achievements:
- Saved the company over $300,000 by successfully defending all Title VII charges.
- Attained 95% win rate with unemployment compensation claims.
- Kept the corporation union-free. Provided positive ongoing employee relationship management, resulting in zero labor organizing attempts.
- Reduced employee turnover by 50% over 4 years through various employee relations and employee engagement programs, such as designing and implementing an employee relations focus group for the General Manager.

DYNAMIC GROUP, INC.
Newark, NJ
2003 – 2007
Project Manager

A market research corporation with clients such as Ford, Venus Swimwear, and Dunkin Donuts.

- Oversaw daily management of 15+ separate marketing research projects and provided ongoing customer service for clients during market research studies.
- Managed a production staff creating questionnaires, reports, and various materials needed during the research study timeline.
- Designed employee and customer satisfaction questionnaires for fielding. Checked CATI programs for fielding accuracy and monitored the daily progress of each study in the fielding process.
- Oversaw creation and launch of a website for client usage during a national automotive employee satisfaction survey.

SEARS & ROEBUCK, INC.
Plains, NJ
1997 – 2003
Visual/Advertising Associate

Clothing retailer.

- Implemented corporate advertising, marketing promotions, and season set-sell planners for all departments.
- Created an atmosphere conducive to shoppers. Organized all staff and customer VIP events.
- Created the dorm-mate program. Set up showrooms in a male and female dorm room at Rutgers University.
- Audited prices on a weekly basis to ensure correct sale pricing in the point-of-sale registers. Corrected any pricing errors.

Education
Bachelor of Business Administration (BBA), Rutgers University, Camden, NY, 1997 | Major: Marketing

Certification & Professional Development
PHR, Professional in Human Resources Certification
ServSafe Certification | CARE Certified Trainer | Positive Employee Relations

Professional Affiliations
Member of the Wilmington DE Chapter of Society for Human Resources Management (SHRM)

Bonnie Cameron

Linked in profile

34 Arrowhead Court

505-340-2434 Pueblo, NM 87024

Purchasing Manager

PERFORMANCE SUMMARY

Twenty-five years' experience in business administration, marketing, and retail store operations with a history of professional growth and consistent achievement. Excellent management abilities, merchandising, inventory control, and purchasing skills. Demonstrates strong commitment to maintaining high levels of customer service while driving revenue growth through marketing and promotional strategies. Strong academic background with a B.A. in Business Administration and Accounting.

- ✓ Expertise in purchasing, inventory control, merchandising strategy, and customer service.
- ✓ Accurate in monitoring large inventory levels to maintain proper levels of inventory, establish reorder points, minimize lead times, set delivery dates, reduce stock-outs, and expedite the supply of critical items.
- ✓ Manages budgets and performs purchase planning/forecasting by analyzing sales data and market trends.
- ✓ Effectively communicates with all levels of the organization, vendors, and customers.
- ✓ Outstanding project planning and project management skills while meeting tight deadlines.
- ✓ Ability to adapt within fast-paced environments, learn new systems, and respond to shifting business strategies.
- ✓ Analytical with excellent decision-making, team-building, and leadership qualities.
- ✓ Technology: Excel, Microsoft Word, Management Outlook, Lotus Webmail, EDI, and JDA systems.

PROFESSIONAL COMPETENCIES

Purchasing Procedures & Techniques	Project Management	Electronic Data Interchange (EDI)
Inventory Control	Strategic Planning	Reduced Stock-outs & Inventory Turns
Establish Reorder Points	Purchase Orders	Invoice Payment & Processing
Vendor Relationship Management	Customer Service	Staff Leadership & Development
Forecasting	Business Strategies	Loss & Damage Claims
Delivery Schedules / Lead Time	Sales Reports	Merchandising Strategies
Budget and Profit/Loss Management	Sales/Profitability	Policies and Procedures
Analyze Sales Data and Market Trends	Negotiation Skills	Loss Prevention

PROFESSIONAL EXPERIENCE

Home Goods, Pueblo, NM   1999–Present
Store Manager   2002–Present
Multimillion-dollar retail operation selling domestic merchandise and home furnishings. Tailors merchandise promotions and presentations for local market. Responsible for various tasks in the overall operation of the store, including measuring business trends, maximizing sales/profitability, expenses, payroll, shortages, customer service, loss prevention, safety, receiving, and all aspects of merchandising and inventory control. Supervised up to 40 employees. Progressed rapidly and promoted to positions with increasing responsibilities.

- Manages and purchases merchandise for annual inventory level of $3M+.
- Managed store inventory levels in 2010 and 2011 with an invisible waste of .38% of total store sales; store was chosen as best in the district.
- Increased sales by 12% in 2011 over companywide store sales of 5.9%.
- Coordinated and completed 2011 store remodeling project under budget.
- Monitors sales performance and merchandising strategy through the analysis of sales reports and comparison-shopping.
- Establish pricing on all custom orders for profit margin enhancement.

Home Goods, continued

Assistant Store Manager   2000–2001

Oversaw staff of sales associates, maintained schedules, conducted performance evaluations, and performed training sessions for employees. Merchandised store and developed unique presentations.

Department Manager   1999–2000

Responsible for customer service, displays, and marketing.

Wal-Mart Corporation, Santa Fe, NM   1985–1999
Store Manager   1997–1999

Responsible for management, supervision, and all store operations for a $12M Kmart Department store. Progressed rapidly and promoted in positions with increasing responsibilities. Supervised up to 118 employees.

- Successfully directed and supervised store-remodeling project remaining under budget. Included adding the new "Pantry" section.
- Handled and resolved all escalated customer issues.
- Provided education and guidance to operations personnel for increased efficiency.
- Analyzed and developed long-range merchandise and operational strategies; store P&L responsibilities.
- Provided strong leadership skills to store employees faced with new competition in the area resulting in location remaining competitive.

Store Manager, Las Cruces, NM   1995–1997

Developed and supervised store personnel and organization with a range of 65 to 115 employees. Responsible for sales and profitability of multimillion-dollar operation. Analyzed and developed long-range merchandise and operations strategies.

Closing Store Manager, Roswell, NM   1995

Directed and supervised store operations. Responsible for sales and expense controls in closing the store operation.

EDUCATION & PROFESSIONAL DEVELOPMENT

New Mexico State University, Las Cruces, NM
Bachelor of Arts in Business Administration and Accounting

Supervising People and Leading a Team
Sponsoring Organization: The Denman Group

Superior references available

2434B Jones Street
Savannah, GA 31401

Jon Garibaldi

912.342.4345
Jon.Garibaldi@gmail.com
Linked **in** profile

Sales Manager

Performance Summary

High-impact Sales Manager with more than 12 years of extensive experience in Marketing, Procurement, Sales, and Customer Relations. Deep knowledge across all sales and marketing disciplines, including project management, product launch, sales growth, business/product development, competitive research, and client communications.

Maintains a consistent focus on the bottom line; driving revenue growth, maximizing profitability, and capitalizing on all viable expansion opportunities. Creative, innovative, and forward thinking; adept at handling complex challenges with thoughtful, clearly-defined strategies that drive double-digit revenue growth.

Professional Skills

Outside Sales	Account Management	Territory Development	Strategic Planning
Customer Relationships	Proposal Development	Needs Identification	Product Management
Market Planning	Commodity Management	Vendor Management	Staff Training
Contract Negotiations	Sales Growth	Proposal Letters	Metrics Management
Financial Planning	Product Releases	Procurement	International Experience

——Professional Experience——

Georgia Power Group, Savannah, GA   2011 to Present
Gas turbines, steam turbines, and generators for power plants with $215.2M in revenue.
Marketing Specialist

Communicate with engineering to create comprehensive marketing plans and sales forecasts, build proposals, and negotiate contracts. Provide training to customers on GBP products catalog. Develop proposal letters for engineered parts for gas, steam, and generators. Collaborate with engineers on providing technical information to obtain quotes from supply management and to provide technical scope for customer proposals.

- Met and surpassed all financial goals and objectives, with $210 million in sales in one year.
- Established new marketing plans for product bulletins with $6 million target.
- Recognized with "getting things done" award for reducing quote response time from previously recorded metrics.
- Generated $5.3 million in sales by quoting customers on upcoming outages with appropriate project scope.
- Contributed to securing $75 million in new sales in one year by creating new customer proposals.

Altamaha Power, Inc., Townsend, GA   2010 to 2011
Manufacturer of generators for power plants.
Sales and Marketing Specialist

Selected to drive revenue growth through establishment of long-term customer relationships. Reduced cost by domestically procuring parts previously manufactured in Japan. Created spare parts list for new equipment and maintained inventory for generator fleet.

- Exceeded sales targets by $1 million and increased margins by 5% in sales of generator spare parts.
- Increased spare parts margin 20% by sourcing domestically.
- Decreased customer response time by improving communication and streamlining the quoting process with Tokyo headquarters.
- Promoted Voltage Regulator service by creating new marketing materials.
- Generated 20% increase of marketing materials in promotion of Voltage Regulator service.

Georgia Power Group, Savannah, GA   2001 to 2010

Provider of gas turbines, steam turbines, and generators for power plants with $97M in revenue.

Sales Support Specialist   2008 – 2010

Established and cultivated strong customer relationships with new and potential customers. Reviewed customer data and trends for sales planning. Revitalized current customer relationships. Provided support and oversight of all customer orders, including order entry, delivery, quality, and invoicing. Drove improvements in customer relationships. Created customer quotes for outage planning.

- Surpassed all sales targets by up to $750,000 in one year.
- Significantly reduced lead to proposal times for O&M and capital equipment.
- Reduced quote response lead time by focusing and prioritizing customer requests.

Procurement Specialist   2001 – 2003 & 2006 – 2008

Managed a $10 million inventory of raw material. Served as a liaison between Supply Management and Gas Turbine product line. Coordinated with Inventory Control group to reduce lot sizes and optimize stock purchases. Provided subject matter expertise on Six Sigma Project within the Inventory Department. Forecasted and procured raw materials for service spare part business.

- Spearheaded the automation of more than 1,000 items to supply base, saving company 10% in cost.
- Led the development of new strategic plans, successfully reducing raw materials inventory by $500,000.
- Recognized with "Spot Award" in 2003 for outstanding customer service.
- Reduced cost $150,000 in fiber optic cables.
- Saved 20% in cost by sourcing and qualifying new source for gaskets.

Marketing Specialist   2003 – 2005

Provided commercialization of product modifications for the Gas Turbine product line. Implemented business strategies for increasing sales of product modifications for Gas Turbine product line.

- Created new strategic business plans to enhance overall effectiveness of sales of services and product enhancements.
- Identified improvements to 12 product modifications to improve lead time from technical service communication.
- Drafted Product Bulletins to expedite the process of sending the communication to the customer.

—— **Education** ——

BBA, Georgia Tech, Scheller College of Business, Atlanta GA   2003

307

Jake Bohannon

24 Franconia Trail
Lincoln, NH 03251

in View my profile

(603) 526-9036
jake@bohannonconstruction.com

Start-Up Construction Manager

PERFORMANCE PROFILE

Twenty years in construction management, with proven record of success in overseeing all phases of construction, infrastructure, and environmental projects. Experience includes full onsite construction management, estimating, budgeting, contracting, purchasing, scheduling, monitoring, and inspection of all work from start to finish. Responsible for HAZWOPER initiatives and a diverse set of other construction projects. Backed by a solid reputation in the industry, solid credentials, and a proven history of on-time and on-budget quality projects.

- Builds and nurtures relationships with clients, staff, vendors, and construction inspectors.
- Promotes the successful execution of projects for owners.
- Project setup, subcontracting and staffing strategies, client relations, and contract changes.
- Delivers high-quality finished projects on time and within budget.
- Directs daily operations and problems that develop during projects.
- Assures all projects are built to specification.
- Optimum flexibility in contracting and procurement.
- Strong interpersonal skills, communication skills, and attention to detail.

PROFESSIONAL SKILLS

*Start-Up Specialist	*Safety and Regulatory Compliance	*Project Plan Execution
*Scheduling	*Contractor Coordination	*Bidding & Estimating
*Budgets and P&L	*Vendor & Client Negotiations	*HAZWOPER
*Customer Relationships	*Manage, Train, and Mentor Employees	*Environmental Stewardship
*Certified Welding Inspector (CWI)	*Subcontractor Relations	*Fiscal Responsibility
*Equipment Installations	*Mechanical Inspector	*Fabrication
*Construction Management	*Residential & Commercial	*General Contractor
*Site Safety	*OSHA	*Cost Containment
*Crew & Subcontractor Supervision	*Project Management	*Sales
*Profit Margin Enhancement	*Construction Inspector Relationships	*Procurement

PROFESSIONAL EXPERIENCE

Beckman Construction Services, Inc., Lincoln, NH   2005–Present
Construction Manager
General contractor specializing in construction management, including remodeling, installing, and start-up of mechanical equipment for residential, commercial, and industrial customers. Ensures profitability by accurate bidding, and by avoiding project delays, disputes, waste, accurate bidding, and customer overruns. Ensures workers have a productive and safe environment. Manages sales, contracts, production, finances, scheduling, subcontractors, talents, resources, and customer relations. Supervises 15+ employees and subcontractors.

- Consistently sustains the company's profitability by effectively managing money and assets.

-continued-

(Beckman Construction Services, Inc., continued)
- Manages the company's profitability by implementing a cost control system to track expenses, supplier negotiations, on-time scheduling, reduced waste, and accurate bidding.
- Builds loyal clientele, as demonstrated by a 90% rate of current customers and up to 10% of new customers from referrals.
- Provides advice to the client on technical and construction concerns.
- Perfect safety record.
- Builds and nurtures loyal and productive relationships with subcontractors.

Bohannon and Sons Construction Services LLP, Lincoln, NH   1996–2005
Owner/ Construction Manager
General contractor working with the state, cities, counties, and the New Hampshire Water Resource Board. Specialties include remodeling commercial and residential properties, structural steel and concrete work, building relocations, snagging and clearing waterways, custom signs, and wrought iron ornamentation. Forecasted and created budgets, and built up loyal clientele.
- Negotiated contract with the IBEW to gut and remodel newly purchased office building.
- Achieved "high-quality firm" reputation due to innovative thinking and, effectively completing the job, resulting in an overflow of business proposals.
- Promoted a safe and productive working environment 24/7; perfect safety record with no lost time.
- Sustained the company's profitability by effectively managing money and assets.
- Managed sales, contracts, production, finances, scheduling, subcontractors, and customer relations.

PROFESSIONAL LICENSES

TWIC Card (Transportation Worker Identification Credential), NH   2016
Homeland Security USA Government

New Hampshire Residential Building Contractor License (#BC553343), MN   2016

Vermont Building Contractor License (#268449), ND   2015

Domestic Limited Liability Partnership (Bohannon and Sons' Construction Services, LLP), NH   2014
Federal ID # 55-06692573

Domestic Limited Liability Company (Bohannon Holdings, LLC), NH   2014
Federal ID #21-38179548

PROFESSIONAL DEVELOPMENT & CERTIFICATES

Certified Welding Inspector (CWI #12879392), Troy, OH   2012
University of Hobart Institute of Welding Technology

Arc Welding Inspection and Quality Control Certificate, Troy, OH   2012
University of Hobart Institute of Welding Technology

Certified Pipeline Welding Inspector (CPWWI#63793695), Burton, TX   2012
National Pipeline Welding Inspector School

Preparation for AWS CWI Certified Welding Inspector Examination, Troy, OH   2012
Hobart Institute of Welding Technology

Arc Welding Inspection & Quality Control Certificate, Troy, OH   2012
Hobart Institute of Welding Technology

Certified Pipeline Welding Inspector (CWI #13268845), Troy, OH   2012
National Welding Inspection School

ANDREA MONARSKI MD, MBA

Cheshire, CT   203.526.9036

Linked in profile

a.monarski@gmail.com

Senior Operations, Business Development, Strategy Officer

"Impeccable medical, healthcare, and business leadership credentials, focused on bettering under-served communities."

Performance Profile

An MD with a Stanford MBA, enriched with 20 years' Medical, Healthcare, Operations Management, Business Development, Fundraising, and Diplomatic experience with blue-chip global organizations.

- A Doctor who has been in the trenches with patients and families facing life-or-death decisions.
- An Operations Management leader able to design and implement scalable health programs.
- A business leader possessing the finesse to lead international negotiations with corporate and nonprofit Boards, CFOs, General Counsel, and international Private Equity groups.
- The diplomatic skills to instigate and pursue healthcare initiatives with Ministers of Health, Embassy, and Government officials of foreign nations: Europe, India, Middle East, and China.

"The only person I know who came to Yale to take a pay cut."

– Milton Hale, Vice Dean of Yale School of Management, Yale University

Management Skills

Vision, Strategy, & Leadership	Operations Management	P&L | Financial Management
Budget Plan, Analysis, & Control	Program & Project Management	Consensus Building
Training & Development	Metric-Driven Results	Communications & PR
Coalition Building	Mentoring & Teaching	Regulatory Compliance

Medical Skills

Emerging Markets Healthcare	Cardiac Management	Hospital and Clinic Management
Physician Management	Clinical Research	Bio-Medical Devices
Community Advocacy	H.C. Economics	Preventive Health Care
Regulatory Affairs EMEA	Supply Chain	Contract Negotiations
Care Team Management	Patient Psychology	Biotech Product Development

Performance Highlights

- Strong success metrics piloting organizations with complex business challenges.
- Proven business acumen and history of inspiring team members to achieve lofty goals.
- Adept communication of complex concepts to diverse stakeholder audiences and achievement of consensus in ever-changing team environments.
- Skillful communicator with diverse international cultures and socio-economic backgrounds.
- Business development tactician with expertise in plan strategy, development, and execution.

Professional Experience

Yale-New Haven Hospital – New Haven, CT   2009 – 2016
Head of International Healthcare Strategy and Business Development

Developed and executed strategic assessment and design of the International Healthcare Business Plan for attracting international patients. Established consensus among diverse Yale-New Haven stakeholders, resulting in 35% increase in annual revenues.

continued

Andrea Monarski   203.526.9036   **a.monarski@gmail.com**

- Shaped and advised the Yale School of Medicine Strategic Planning Committee on current state of affairs, competitive analysis, and opportunities for "Yale School of Medicine's Role in the World and the Community."
- Brought members of the university and community to consensus on Yale-New Haven Medicine's strengths, weaknesses, and opportunities.
- Adept at consensus building between the C-suite execs, academic professors, and doctors, along with general staff at all levels.
- Directed multiparty international negotiations and implemented international joint ventures.

> *"Understanding of emerging healthcare markets uncovered new and unique revenue streams.*
> *The impact was a 35% yearly increase in revenue."*
> – Ana Verner, Associate Vice President, Network and Program Development, Yale-New Haven Hospital

Meriden-Wallingford Hospital – Meriden, CT	2000 – 2009
CEO, Managing Partner	2007 – 2009
CFO, Board of Directors	2001 – 2007
Partner, Board of Directors	2007 – 2009
Clinical Associate of Medicine	2000 – 2009

Directed all strategic and operational activities for 25 cardiologists and 150+ staff. Prepared financial models, performed negotiations, set and monitored outcome and quality standards, and integrated new businesses. Grew corporation from an $8 million to $25 million business.

- Consolidated physical plant and operational systems to reduce costs by 20% while increasing revenue 20%.
- Performed clinical activities as a physician in invasive and noninvasive electrophysiology; coordinated a large patient care team, including technologists, nurses, and administrative staff.
- Founded and directed the Department of Electrophysiology, St. Mary Medical Center, 1998 – 2010. Developed operative throughput times, decreased implant costs by 25%, and exceeded national benchmarks for safety and outcomes.
- Founded and led the Sudden Death Survivor support group.
- Founded and managed The Arrhythmia Institute™, a freestanding single-specialty heart rhythm center providing comprehensive patient services, community education, and publications.

St. Mary Medical Center, Nonprofit Foundation – Langhorne, PA	1998 – 2000
Board of Directors	

Developed new relationships and funding sources. Motivated potential donors to become active donors through community education and sharing of personal experiences. Recruited board members with diverse backgrounds and talents.

Yale-New Haven Hospital – New Haven, CT	1994 – 1998
Fellow in Cardiology and Clinical Electrophysiology	
American Board of Internal Medicine: Electrophysiology, Cardiology, and Internal Medicine	

Meriden-Wallingford Hospital – Wallingford, CT	1991 – 1994
Medical Resident and Intern	

Concurrent Consulting Engagements 2000 – 2015

PharmaTeach, Inc.
- Served as Medical Director for regulatory issues and scientific education.

continued

WorldBanc. International Exchange, Levi Shehrer Group
- Served as clinical expert on biotechnology trends affecting physician usage/device preference.
- Presented to clients on trends and updates in field of electrophysiology cardiac devices.

Global Healthcare Management, Inc. Symposium
- Provided medical insight into current treatment and therapeutic trends.

Guardian Scientific
- Influenced the Cardiac Lead Design and Development Team and the Business Advisory Strategic Board.
- Advised and participated in the development of novel new pacing lead technologies from bench to bedside. Analyzed and recommended R&D resource allocation, industry trends, and marketing effectiveness.

Megamed, Inc.
- Shaped the Product Development Board's focus and future product lines.

Biosystems, Inc.
- Advised the regulatory analysis and clinical research teams.
- Evaluated design elements.
- Created surgical techniques for new implantable bio-monitoring devices.

Education

Yale School of Business, Yale University – New Haven, CT   2009 – 2011
MBA, graduated with Honors

- Planned and executed Global Consulting Project for development of advanced cancer therapy.
- Developed business plan for mobile children's health clinics in Jackson County School District, Mississippi.
- Participated in the Global Strategic Management International Seminar, Shanghai, China.
- Voted best negotiator in graduating class.

Yale School of Medicine, Yale University – New Haven, CT   1987 – 1991
Doctor of Medicine

- Awarded The Henry Keller Mohler Memorial Prize in Therapeutics and The Annie Simpson General Medical Award, 1991.
- Accepted into The Hobart Amory Hare Honor Medical Society, 1991.

Boston University – Boston, MA   1983 – 1987
Bachelor of Arts, Psychology

- Graduated with general and departmental honors, 1987.
- Semifinalist in The General Electric National Science Competition, 1983.

A lifetime of commitment

Superior medical, educational, business, and diplomatic references available

GENERAL INDEX

Index of Resumes by Industry and Job Title